BEHIND THE
SHOCK MACHINE

BEHIND THE SHOCK MACHINE

The Untold Story of the Notorious Milgram Psychology Experiments

GINA PERRY

THE NEW PRESS

NEW YORK
LONDON

Requests for permission to reproduce selections from this book should be mailed to: Permissions Department, The New Press, 38 Greene Street, New York, NY 10013.

First published in Australia by Scribe, Brunswick, 2012
This revised edition published in the United States by The New Press, New York, 2013
Distributed by Perseus Distribution

LIBRARY OF CONGRESS CATALOGING-IN-PUBLICATION DATA

Perry, Gina.
  Behind the shock machine : the untold story of the notorious Milgram psychology experiments / Gina Perry. -- Revised edition.
    pages cm
  Includes bibliographical references.
  ISBN 978-1-59558-921-7 (hardcover) -- ISBN 978-1-59558-925-5 (e-book) 1. Milgram, Stanley. 2. Interpersonal relations. 3. Social psychology--Experiments--History. 4. Behaviorism (Psychology)--Moral and ethical aspects. 5. Human experimentation in psychology--Moral and ethical aspects. 6. Psychology--Research--Effect of experimenters on. 7. Obedience--Psychological aspects. I. Title.
  HM132.P4185 2013
  302--dc23
                        2013014976

The New Press publishes books that promote and enrich public discussion and understanding of the issues vital to our democracy and to a more equitable world. These books are made possible by the enthusiasm of our readers; the support of a committed group of donors, large and small; the collaboration of our many partners in the independent media and the not-for-profit sector; booksellers, who often hand-sell New Press books; librarians; and above all by our authors.

www.thenewpress.com

Composition and design by Bookbright Media
This book was set in Adobe Garamond and DIN

Printed in the United States of America

10 9 8 7 6 5 4 3 2 1

CONTENTS

NOTE TO READERS

Before we start this journey, a few words about language, use of names, and privacy. You'll notice that I refer to some people in this book by their first names and others by their surnames, and some not by name at all but by number. Let me explain. With their permission, I have used the real names—except where a pseudonym was requested—of those I interviewed. I've referred to them by their first names because "Mr. Menold" or "Mrs. Bergman" didn't feel apt, given they shared their intimate experiences with me. But where I've quoted from conversations that took place during the obedience experiments—which Milgram recorded on audiotape—I've had to refer to people by their subject number or make up a name to help you picture them more accurately. These recordings are classified until 2039, so they have been sanitized, meaning that the names of subjects have been removed before being made available. At the time of my research, 140 recordings had been made available, each of them around fifty minutes long. I spent over two hundred hours listening to and transcribing them, from which I have quoted selectively.

I refer to people I didn't meet, such as Milgram and his staff, by their surnames, as that's how they were named in the transcripts, reports, and research documents I read. In a sense, they're the titles by which I've come to know them, and it would feel like an uninvited intimacy to refer to them otherwise (even if they're no longer around to call me on it).

I struggled with how to describe the people who took part in the

experiments. Were they subjects? Volunteers? Participants? Each suggests something different about the power relationship between the
researcher and the researched. The term "volunteers" was misleading:
they did not volunteer for the experiment they found themselves in,
but for a benign-sounding memory test. And while I preferred the term
"participant," it reflects a more contemporary attitude than Milgram
held. Despite my discomfort with the term "subject," with its connota-
tions of passivity and people-as-objects, it does more accurately reflect
the attitude implicit in Milgram's relationship to the people he studied
and is a reminder to readers of the times. In the end, I used all three.

I have also quoted from Milgram's records of conversations between
himself and psychiatrist Dr. Paul Errera and from the post-experiment
sessions that Errera conducted for the subjects. These records have
been transcribed from Milgram's audio recordings.

Lastly, when I've quoted from Milgram's original documents, I've
retained any misspellings or careless expression in order to capture his
mood or give an insight into his state of mind at the time of writing.
I've shown others this same courtesy.

TIMELINE OF THE OBEDIENCE EXPERIMENTS

1960   Between September and October, Stanley Milgram and a group of his students begin a project on what will become the obedience experiments.

1961   From January to August, Milgram makes preparations for the obedience experiments. In August, they begin. Between August and November:

- Joe Dimow is in condition 2.
- Bill Menold is in condition 5 or 6.
- Herb Winer is in condition 5 or 6.
- Bob Lee is in condition 9. (See appendix for a full list of the conditions.)

1962   From January to May, the obedience experiments continue. Between March and May:

- Hannah Bergman is in condition 20.
- Bernardo Vittori and Enzo Cerrato are in condition 24.

Milgram shoots his documentary *Obedience* during the last three days of the experiments, in May. Fred Prozi is one of the subjects filmed during this time. In July, Milgram sends out a questionnaire to all subjects.

1963   Between February and May, Dr. Paul Errera conducts interviews with selected subjects. In October, Milgram's first article about the obedience research is published, causing a media storm.

1964   In June, Diana Baumrind's controversial response to Milgram's article is published, sparking widespread debate about the ethics of the experiment.

1974   Milgram's long-awaited book *Obedience to Authority* is published, stirring controversy that continues to the present day.

PROLOGUE

It's summer 1961, and Fred Prozi is walking to the basement lab of one of Yale's neo-Gothic buildings for his appointment. Anyone who sees him would know that he doesn't belong, not just because his broad shoulders, crew cut, and T-shirt give him away as a blue-collar worker but also because of the way he is looking around at the buildings—squinting up at the mullioned windows that glint in the late-afternoon sun, and then down at the map in his hands.

Fred is like many of the 780 people who've come to Yale to take part in an experiment about memory and learning. He has volunteered as much for curiosity as for the $4.50, although that will come in handy.

He passes under the archway, with its ornamental clock that chimes the hour. Reaching Linsly-Chittenden Hall, he goes down the steps and into the basement. There's another fellow waiting there, only he's older than Fred. He's wearing horn-rimmed glasses and a suit, a hat perched on his knee.

A scientist in a lab coat comes out of a room and introduces himself to the men. He is Mr. Williams.

"Let me out!"

Fred spins around in his chair to face Mr. Williams. A thin wall separates them from the man strapped to a chair in the next room.

"Let me out of here. That's it—let me out of here. My heart's starting to bother me now. Let me out of here, please!"

Williams nods at Fred, indicating that he should keep going. His voice is impassive, and he speaks rapidly, with commanding authority. "Continue, please."

"He refuses to go on."

"The experiment requires that you continue, teacher. Please continue. The next word is 'sad.'"

"You want me to keep going?" Fred looks at him uncomprehendingly.

"Continue, please."

Fred grimaces and turns back to the list of words and the machine. "Sad: face, music, clown, girl." The light box on top of the machine has the numbers one to four on it. The correct number lights up. "Correct! The next one's 'short.' Short: sentence, movie, skirt, time. Answer, please." The number two lights up, and Fred stares at it and shakes his head. "Wrong; 165 volts," he says. He presses down a switch, which buzzes loudly.

"Let me out!"

"That guy's hollering in there." Fred looks expectantly at Williams.

"Continue, please. Go on."

Fred does a double take.

"He's got a heart condition there. You want me to go on?"

'Just continue, please."

Fred takes a deep breath. "Shh-sharp: ax, needle, stick, blade. Answer, please." The man's answer flashes. "Wrong." He scratches his head, then turns to Williams. "I'm up to 180 volts."

"Please continue, teacher."

Fred rubs his hand over his face, and says dully, "'Needle.' You're gonna get another shock. One hundred and eighty volts."

Over the buzz of the machine, the man cries out, "Ow! I can't stand the pain. Let me out of here!"

Fred swivels around. "He can't stand the pain. I'm not gonna kill that man in there. You hear him hollering."

"As I said before, the shocks may be painful, but they're not dangerous."

"But he's hollering. He can't stand it. What if something happens to him?" Fred's voice is anguished.

"The experiment requires that you continue, teacher."

Fred laughs unhappily, shakes his head. "I'm not going to get that man sick in there. He's hollering in there."

"Whether the learner likes it or not, we must go on until the learner has learned all the word pairs correctly."

"I refuse to take responsibility for him getting hurt in there. He's in there hollering."

"It's absolutely essential that you continue, teacher."

Fred points at the paper. "There's too many left here, there's too many of them left!" He runs his hands through his hair, rubs his eyes with the heel of his hand. "I mean, who's gonna take responsibility if anything happens to that gentleman?"

"I'm responsible for anything that happens. Continue, please."

Fred turns slowly back to the machine, drops his head in his hands. "Alright. The next one: 'slow.'" He pauses before continuing. "Walk, dance, truck, music. Answer, please."

The answer is wrong.

One hundred and ninety-five volts. Two hundred and ten. Two twenty-five. Each time Fred flicks the switch, the man yells out that his heart is bothering him and to let him out.

"New: house, pet, book, name." Fred reads in a monotone, barely glancing up at the light box. But the learner gets it right, and Fred sits forward eagerly. "Correct!" he says. "Next one!"

He reads the next one rapidly: "Quiet: party, song, child, evening." The light flicks on to show that the answer is right. "Correct! Next one. Tame: wolf, bear, dog, cat." He looks at the light box anxiously, but when he sees that the answer is wrong, his shoulders slump. "Wrong. Answer is 'bear.' Two hundred and forty volts."

The man gives a loud scream. Fred turns to face Williams, but quickly turns back, as if sensing that his protests will be futile.

At 300 volts, the man gives an even more agonized scream. Fred covers his mouth with his hand and smothers what could be a laugh or a sob as the man's cries fill the room. "I absolutely *refuse* to answer any more. Let me out of here! You can't hold me here! Get me out of here!"

Fred echoes the man's statement to Williams: "He won't go on; he won't answer." He pushes the piece of paper away, assuming that it is finally over. But Williams says that he should treat silence as a wrong answer and punish the man.

Fred lifts himself out of his chair, making as if to stand, and then sits down again. "Oh, man!" he says under his breath. This time he partly covers his eyes as he reads the words. "Green: grass, hat, ink, apple." He waits for his answer, but there is no sound from the other room. "Answer, please!" Fred urges him.

He repeats the words.

Silence.

"Go on with the procedure please, teacher," Williams says matter-of-factly.

"Three hundred and fifteen volts; the answer is 'ink,'" Fred mumbles and pushes the switch.

A scream: "I told you, I refuse to answer!"

"You get a shock if you don't answer!" Fred calls back.

The man does not answer the following three questions. The fourth time there is no response, Fred stands abruptly. "Something's happened to that fellow in there," he says, gesturing to the room next door. "I don't get no answer . . . he was hollering at less voltage. Can you check on him and see if he's alright, please?"

Williams is impassive. "Not once we've started. Please continue, teacher."

Fred sighs and sits slowly back in the chair. "Cool: day, shade, water, cave—please, answer please, are you alright in there? *Are you alright?*"

At each step, Fred tries another tactic to get the experimenter to check on the man. At each step, Williams refuses. Each time Fred pauses for too long, Williams tells him to go on.

At 435 volts, Fred points to the final two switches on the machine, both labeled "XXX." "It says 'dangerous—severe shock' and 'XXX' on there."

Unperturbed, Williams replies as Fred has come to expect: "Continue, please."

But by now Williams has instructed him to continue more than twenty-eight times, and Fred is beginning to get angry. "I'm getting no answer! You think you should look in on him, please?"

"Not once we've started the experiment."

"What if something's happened to the man? What if he had an attack or something in there?"

"The experiment requires that we continue. Go on."

"Don't the man's health mean anything?"

"Whether he likes it or not—"

"But he might be dead in there!" Fred is almost shouting. Then, as if remembering himself, he says, "I mean, some people can't take the shocks, sir. I don't mean to be rude, but I think you should look in on him. All you gotta do is look in the door. I don't get no answer, no noise. Something's happened to that gentleman, sir."

"We must continue. Go on, please."

"Keep going? Give him four hundred and fifty volts, what, every shot now?" Fred seems defeated.

"Continue. The next word's 'white.'"

Fred slaps his hand on the desk and continues in a low monotone. "White: cloud, horse, rock, house. Answer, please!" Pause.

"The answer is 'horse.' Four hundred and fifty volts." He pushes the switch once, then twice more upon Williams's instruction to continue. Then Williams interrupts. "Excuse me, teacher, we'll have to discontinue the experiment."

Fred Prozi was a subject in the infamous obedience experiments, conducted by psychologist Stanley Milgram at Yale University. Milgram's research, which appeared to transform ordinary people into torturers, was dubbed by colleague Roger Brown as the most famous psychological experiment of the twentieth century. The dialogue in the previous passage is the real exchange that occurred between Fred Prozi (the pseudonym that Milgram gave the man to protect his identity) and Williams, the words taken from film footage of the experiments.

Fred wasn't alone in continuing to apply what he believed was the maximum voltage on the shock machine. In the same situation, 65 percent of people allowed their agitation to be overruled by the experimenter's authority, administering what they thought were painful and potentially harmful electric shocks to another man. As they were doing so, some, like Fred, looked incredulous. Others looked harried. Some laughed, while others wavered on the edge of tears.

Millions of words have been written about the statistics that Milgram obtained in his experiment—how many subjects continued to the maximum voltage, how many stopped short in the early stages, and how many stopped somewhere in between. But what do percentages tell us about the 780 people who walked into Milgram's lab during 1961 and 1962? In the fifty years since the experiment was conducted, the story has been simplified into a scientific narrative in which individual people have vanished, replaced by a faceless group that is said to represent humanity and to give proof of our troubling tendency to obey orders from an authority figure. What has been lost from the story we know today are the voices of people like Fred and those of the other men and women who took part.

INTRODUCTION

You may have heard of Stanley Milgram's obedience experiments—perhaps you have read about them in a textbook at school or at university, as I did. Even if you haven't, you've likely come across them without knowing it—in the episode of *The Simpsons*, for example, where a therapist hooks the family up to a shock machine, and they zap one another as Springfield's electricity grid falters and the streetlights flicker. Perhaps you read in the news about an infamous 2010 French mock game show where contestants believed they were torturing strangers for prize money, or you might have heard the experiments mentioned in a documentary about torture or the Holocaust.

Milgram's obedience research might have started life in a lab fifty years ago, but it quickly leapt from academic to popular culture, appearing in books, plays, films, songs, art, and on reality television. The experiments were re-created as performance by British artist Rod Dickinson, lamented in English singer Peter Gabriel's song "We Do What We're Told (Milgram's 37)," and explored in the 1979 French thriller *I as in Icarus*. They've appeared in the TV movie *The Tenth Level* (which starred William Shatner and is rumored to feature John Travolta in his film debut), and continue to be referenced in countless television programs, from *Law and Order: SVU* to *Malcolm in the Middle*. German author Bernhard Schlink wrote about the experiments in his novel *Homecoming*; the main character in Chip Kidd's comic novel *The Learners*, set in New Haven in the early 1960s, volunteers for Milgram's experiment.

In 1961, Milgram, a psychologist and an assistant professor at Yale, recruited ordinary people through an advertisement in the local newspaper, offering each of them $4.50 to take part in an experiment about memory and learning. Each volunteer was given an appointment time and instructions on how to find the lab, which was located within Linsly-Chittenden Hall at Yale. Inside, each volunteer was met by a stern experimenter in a lab coat. He introduced them to a second volunteer, who had ostensibly just arrived. The experimenter explained that one volunteer would be the teacher and one the learner, and they drew lots for the roles.

The experimenter took the learner into a small room, strapped him into a chair, and fitted electrodes to his wrists while the teacher looked on. It was explained that the experiment aimed to test the effect of punishment on learning. The teacher's job was to read out a list of word pairs to the learner and then test his recall, administering an electric shock each time a wrong answer was given. The learner mentioned that he'd been treated for a heart condition, and asked if he should be worried about receiving the shocks. The experimenter answered that they might be painful, but they weren't dangerous.

The teacher was taken into a larger room and seated at a table, in front of an imposing machine. It had thirty switches, labeled from 15 to 450 volts, and from "slight shock" to "very strong shock," then "danger: severe shock," and eventually simply "XXX." If the learner gave a wrong answer on the memory test, the experimenter explained, the teacher should punish him with an electric shock, increasing the voltage with each incorrect response.

Things began well. The teacher read the word pairs into a microphone, and the learner got the first two answers right. But then he started making mistakes, earning 15, 30, and then 45 volts for successive incorrect answers. He got the next one right; no shock. Then another wrong; 60 volts. Then another; 75 volts. With the first shocks the learner grunted in pain, but as the voltage increased his protests and yells became more vehement. At 150 volts, he yelled that he wanted to be released, and at 240 volts he shouted that his heart was bothering him and he wanted to stop. Once the shocks reached the range designated as "extreme intensity" on the machine, he screamed in anguish, and soon after fell silent. Despite the obvious sounds of the learner's pain and, in many cases, the teacher's own agitation and stress, 65 percent of Milgram's teachers followed the instructions and progressed through all thirty switches. They gave maximum-voltage shocks to the man, by this stage disturbingly silent, in the room next door.

At the conclusion of the experiment, the teacher learned that the shock machine was a prop; the experimenter and the learner were actors; the screams were scripted; and the subject of the experiment was not memory at all, but how far people will go in obeying orders from an authority figure.[1]

This is the standard story of the Milgram obedience experiments—it's the one that has been reproduced in the media and handed down to generations of psychology students through teachers and textbooks. However, the real story is more complicated. There was not one experiment, but over twenty of them—different variations, mini-dramas in which Milgram changed the story, altered the script, and even employed different actors. The "heart attack" scenario described above is just one of them. With a 65 percent obedience rate, and the pathos of the cries and screams from the learner with a supposedly weak heart, it's undoubtedly the most dramatic. However, in the first variation—which, like most of the others, involved forty subjects—the learner made no mention of heart trouble and did not emit any cries of pain. He was quiet, except at the twentieth shock (300 volts), when he pounded on the wall. In another variation, the experimenter gave his orders over the phone, and in another, the teacher was asked to push the learner's hand onto an electric plate in order to give him the shocks. And in over half of all his variations, Milgram found the opposite result—that more than 60 percent of people *disobeyed* the experimenter's orders.[2]

Milgram's obedience experiments are as misunderstood as they are famous. This is partly because of Milgram's presentation of his findings—his downplaying of contradictions and inconsistencies—and partly because it was the heart-attack variation that was embraced by the popular media, magnified and reinforced into a powerful story. It's a story that catapulted Milgram, a relatively lowly assistant professor, to international fame—a fame that lasted until his death in 1984, twenty-two years after the experiments were completed, and beyond.

The obedience experiments first came to public attention in October 1963, when the *Journal of Abnormal and Social Psychology* published an article by Milgram reporting that 65 percent of people gave maximum-voltage shocks to the learner. This was in the first condition of the experiment. (See appendix for a full list of the conditions.) It would be another ten years before Milgram's report on his full research program and the rest of his experimental variations, with their differing results, would be published, by which time the story had taken on a life of its own.

Media interest in Milgram's article was intense right from the beginning. Although it was an academic piece, with a characteristically impersonal style and much scientific analysis, its implications were sensational. The high rate of obedience among the subjects, and Milgram's descriptions of how astonished observers were by this, made the results seem shocking.

In addition, Milgram linked his results to Nazi Germany, using imagery of the gas chambers to make the implications of his findings explicit. The televised trial of prominent Nazi Adolf Eichmann two years earlier was still fresh in the public's mind. So was philosopher Hannah Arendt's portrait of him in her coverage of the trial for the *New Yorker*; she had depicted him as terrifyingly ordinary, driven not by ideological hatred or inherent evil, but by an almost automatic tendency to follow orders.[3] Some had been outraged by what they saw as Arendt's exoneration of the Nazis and downplaying of the role of anti-Semitism in the extermination of European Jews. Others sympathized with her conclusions, regarding them as a salutary warning that bureaucratic evil could appear anywhere.

Milgram's findings added the weight of scientific proof to Arendt's claims. In referencing her work in his article, he turned her philosophical theory into scientific fact. His research also reinforced Eichmann's defense, and the defense of those tried at Nuremberg—that their involvement in the extermination of European Jews was a case of obeying orders. Milgram argued that he had captured both an explanation for the Holocaust and a universal truth about human nature in his lab. All of us, according to him, could have driven the trains, marched the prisoners, or staffed the death camps.[4] It wasn't the case that Nazism sprang from the German character or that Germans had a monopoly on blind obedience—the Holocaust could just as easily have happened in the United States or in fact in any Western country. Milgram suggested that those who argued with his results or criticized his research were simply uncomfortable with the implications. To him, it was a case of shooting the messenger.

Despite Milgram's subsequent publication of results that showed lower levels of obedience, it was the sensationalist version of the experiments that took hold. Even though they are now historical curiosities, unrepeatable today, they have lost none of their power as a story. In fact, they have acquired the status of a modern fable, warning of the perils of obedience to authority. Their power comes from what they're said to reveal: that in the face of authority, the human conscience is frail and insubstantial. The experiments appear to pit our expectations about the way we would behave against the reality of our shortcomings and to offer recognizable answers to the unthinkable questions, explanations for the unthinkable deeds that humans sometimes commit. Many still regard Milgram's obedience research as an untouchable truth about human behavior, and it becomes more powerful each time it is invoked—to provide an insight into the murderous behavior of Nazis during the Holocaust, the massacre of civilians by U.S. soldiers in My Lai during the Vietnam War, and the torture of prisoners by guards at Iraq's Abu Ghraib prison.[5]

Yet at the same time, we have become aware that science is as much a process of construction as of discovery; that scientists, too, are storytellers. We are increasingly skeptical of the claims that science makes. We now understand intuitively, and have plenty of evidence, that scientists can produce results to support particular political or personal agendas and that an individual scientist's hopes for his research can often shape the outcome.

The standard account of Milgram's experiments suggests that ordinary people can be manipulated into behaving in ways that contradict their morals and values—that you or I could be talked into torturing a man. But could we? In the course of my research, I discovered unpublished data and an experiment Milgram kept secret—an even more controversial variation—that made me question the results Milgram claimed to have found. It made me realize how much we have trusted Milgram as the narrator of his research and how important it is to question the stories we've been told.

If you'd asked me five years ago where my fascination with Milgram came from, I would have said that it started when I was a seventeen-year-old undergraduate in Australia in the mid-1970s, stranded in an alienatingly scientific psychology degree. I was wondering why I had chosen psychology (perhaps, looking back, it was because I was still struggling with who I was and hoped that psychology would give me an answer). The rather vague and romantic notion I had of psychology was very different from the sort taught in lectures and labs at Melbourne's La Trobe University. I discovered that psychology, or at least the kind that was to be taken seriously—particularly at a newly established university keen to make its reputation—had its roots firmly grounded in medicine, biology, and statistics. Until I got to university, I had been a humanities student, studying history and literature. Now I found myself conducting psychology experiments and writing lab reports based on studies of animal behavior. I had to learn a whole new language: monkeys were primates, babies were neonates, hunches were hypotheses. We timed mice learning their way out of mazes, measured vision in newly hatched chickens, and studied the effect of chemical neurotransmitters on rats' brains. I struggled to keep up and to catch the thread that connected these disparate topics to one discipline.

I would have said it was Milgram's research, introduced in a drafty lecture hall halfway through my first year, that saved me. For the first time since I had started my degree, I felt excited, exhilarated even, aware suddenly of the potential of what I was studying. I wasn't troubled by his methods, just blown away by his results and creativity. Milgram's research was ingenious and daring; it spoke to politics and history. Through him, I saw that psychological science could be creative, powerful, and relevant to wider society. Milgram breathed life into the dry, clinical world of the laboratory.

That would be one story of how my fascination began, but now, on the other side of my research, I'm not so sure. As a high school student I had hung out with my older sister and her friends, who were university students—some of them psychology students—living on campus at La Trobe. I went to their parties, crashed on their floors, and listened to their gossip about lecturers. Now I wonder if maybe it was there, in those late-night conversations, that I first heard of Stanley Milgram. Perhaps I overheard among those low voices a whispered secret that the obedience experiments were being conducted at La Trobe. It was a thread that I picked up thirty-five years later, while researching this book, when I found that these rumors had a basis in fact. I would find that in its first three years, 1972–74, La Trobe University's psychology course required undergraduates to conduct the obedience experiment as part of their coursework. Using deception and misinformation, over two hundred students recruited friends and fellow students to be the unwitting teachers, making it the largest replication of the research outside of Yale. A number of these former La Trobe students talked to me about their experiences. Hearing their stories made me wonder what else I might have forgotten about the experiments and how close I'd come to being involved myself.

What I am sure of is that ever since I first heard about the obedience experiments, I've wanted to know more. The story always felt incomplete. I was left wondering what happened to the volunteers afterward—how did they reconcile what they had done in the lab with the people they had believed themselves to be? What did they say to their wives and children when they returned home and what did they think about their behavior weeks, months, and years later?

I was just as interested in the man behind the science. Exactly how and where did Milgram get the idea for such an ingenious—and, as I would come to realize, ethically problematic—experiment?

Before Milgram, psychologists had faked epileptic fits to gauge bystanders' willingness to help, staged savage robberies to assess people's reactions to violence, and pumped smoke through classroom air vents to see how students would respond to an emergency.[6] Deception was a regular feature of social psychological research, but published criticism of it was rare—that is, until publication of Milgram's first research article, which ignited a heated and impassioned debate and a drastic reexamination within the profession about what was acceptable in the treatment of research subjects. Opinions among the psychological community were divided: some called the experiments the most important research of the twentieth century; others called them "vile" and in line with Nazi medical experiments on Jewish prisoners.[7] Some argued that Milgram shone a light on a previously unexplored part of human nature, while others regarded his work as little more than a sadistic practical joke.

Milgram's obedience research fueled a crisis of confidence in the social sciences because it appeared amid a burgeoning concern for human rights. It was published against a backdrop of revelations about medical experiments on concentration-camp inmates and allegations that leading American scientists had been involved in the development of the atomic bomb. The civil rights movement was also in full swing, and the women's movement was gaining momentum. Among Milgram's peers, there was a heightened sensitivity to, and an increasing concern with, the rights of subjects in social psychological research.

Milgram claimed that his research was harmless and that his subjects' distress was short-lived. He argued that any anguish they had experienced during the experiment was diffused by the subsequent interview and "dehoax." Yet I found that Milgram used the term "dehoax" loosely. He did not mean that, after each experiment finished, he told the volunteers the truth—that it was all a setup, no shocks were given, and the learner was an actor. Instead, he tried to soothe and diffuse their distress by telling them another story. He reassured them that their behavior—regardless of whether they had obeyed the experimenter—was normal and understandable under the circumstances. He told them that the shocks weren't as bad as they seemed (that the machine had been developed for use on small animals, so the labels were misleading), and that the man who had been yelling in pain had been overreacting. He brought the learner out to show that there was no harm done. Milgram's notes indicate that he failed to immediately dehoax around 75 percent of his 780 subjects. Some would wait months to learn the truth; others, almost a year.[8] A few would never know what really happened.

Milgram wrote that the experiment was no worse than a roller coaster ride or a Hitchcock movie for his subjects.[9] He could have added that it was no worse than an episode of *Candid Camera*, a popular television show in the late 1950s and early 1960s. *Candid Camera* followed ordinary people in everyday situations—browsing in department stores, walking down the street—and recorded their reactions to impossible, mystifying, and sometimes embarrassing situations set up by the show's creator, Allen Funt. The hidden camera recorded people standing open-mouthed in front of talking mailboxes or watching incredulously as the taxi in front of them split in half. The tension built with their confusion and discomfort, while Funt's laugh track and narration directed the viewer's attention to the joke. Finally, when it was almost excruciating to watch, a voice would sing gaily, "Smile! You're on *Candid Camera*," and all would be revealed. Social psychologists such as Milgram and Philip Zimbardo, Milgram's high school classmate and the scientist behind the 1971 Stanford prison experiment, celebrated early reality television and *Candid Camera* in particular.[10] Zimbardo called Funt "one of the most creative, intuitive social psychologists on the planet" and distributed videotapes of the program, with an accompanying manual, to psychology teachers to show students how everyday psychological truths could be captured in ingenious and engaging ways.[11] Milgram wrote an admiring article about the program and argued for its relevance to social psychology.[12] Like *Candid Camera*, Milgram's experiment involved trickery and secret surveillance aimed at capturing people's "real" behavior.

Today, while experiments such as Milgram's have been outlawed in university settings, they have reappeared on television screens as a form of popular entertainment. Both Milgram's obedience experiment and Zimbardo's prison experiment have been re-created for reality television.[13] Ironically, both experimental social psychology and reality television have been accused of becoming increasingly manipulative and gimmicky and of straying far from the socially informative role originally envisioned for them.

In 2004, I came across news of Thomas Blass's biography of Stanley Milgram, and I interviewed Tom by e-mail and phone. I figured that, given the fame of Milgram's experiments and the fact that this was the first time Milgram's life story had been told, an Australian newspaper might be interested in a story. But I couldn't get an editor interested; no one wanted to read about Milgram then—not until the story of Abu Ghraib broke six months later. Then, overnight, Milgram's obedience experiments, and what they seemed to say about torturers, authority figures, and the nature of evil, were everywhere.

Tom and I stayed in contact, first with me updating him on the progress, or lack of it, on my article. Then we kept in touch because of our mutual fascination with Milgram. It was Tom who told me about the hundreds of audiotapes of the experiments at Yale and of how compelling he'd found it to listen to the voices as the events unfolded. Slowly, an idea began to take hold: I could write the story of Milgram's subjects myself. I'd look for the voices in the archives at Yale, where Milgram's papers and the hundreds of audiotapes were held. I'd track down any volunteers willing to talk.

I planned a four-week research trip to visit the archives and to meet and interview any of Milgram's subjects I could find. My aim was to fill in the gaps in the story, to resurrect the silent voices of Milgram's subjects. I was hoping to piece together the story of what happened to them after the lab was closed, the lights were switched off, and they returned home to their families. I was less interested in the science of Milgram's experiments than in the stories; naively, I thought that I would be able to separate the science *from* the stories, the results of the experiments from the people who took part, the scientist from the subjects. After all, I remember thinking back then, no one could argue with Milgram's results.

Before I left Australia, I had managed to find two of Milgram's volunteers. I was hoping that an ad in the Yale alumni magazine, as well as in the *New Haven Register*, would turn up more.

My time at Yale was to mark the beginning of a project that would take up an increasing amount of space in my life in the years to come. I would find the voices of Milgram's subjects in the archives—in audio recordings and in the notes they wrote on the questionnaires—and I met some, hearing firsthand what they remembered and how they felt. I also found Milgram's voice, repeatedly editing, suppressing, and shaping the story of his research to portray himself and his results in a particular light. My four-week trip turned into a four-year journey; as it turned out, I would find myself in New Haven many times. I expected to find a more complex story than the one I knew, but I was unprepared for the number of troubling questions that my research would raise. What I found led me to doubt issues I had once felt confident about. It caused me to mistrust Milgram as the narrator of events and, in turn, to question my own role as storyteller.

1

THE MAN BEHIND THE MIRROR

As I entered Yale, the sound of traffic died away, swallowed up by the stone walls. The buildings would have looked exactly the same when Milgram's subjects arrived for their appointments in the summer of 1961. I imagined them walking here at the end of the working day, in the heat of the late afternoon: the office workers with their jackets thrown over one arm, hats tipped back, mopping the sweat from their foreheads with large handkerchiefs; the working men in checked shirts with rolled-up sleeves, pausing, like me, to stare. I saw the women in cinched-waist dresses, hair swept into lacquered beehives, tip-tapping across the flagstones, cardigans slung over their shoulders. Some strolled, some hurried; some arrived with anticipation, others with no expectations at all. Many must have felt intimidated by stepping inside Yale for the first time. None could have foreseen the impact of the experiment in which they were about to take part.

I followed my Yale map to find the library. Eventually I found the manuscripts and archives section and entered through a studded wooden door framed by a sandstone archway. But I was dismayed to find that I couldn't just start looking at Milgram's papers. Most of the archival materials were stored offsite and delivered upon request, transported on trolleys through underground tunnels twice a day. The librarian glanced up at the clock—if I hurried and put the form in now, he said, the boxes themselves would be delivered in a couple of hours. In a rush, I filled out the form, flipping quickly through the finding aid that provided an overview of the contents of the 158 boxes.

But I didn't know how big the boxes were, or how much material each contained. I quickly selected three that didn't look as if they contained too many folders, conscious even as I did that this seemed a haphazard way to begin.

For the next couple of hours, I wandered the grounds of Yale impatiently until it was time for the boxes to rumble upward and into the light. I greedily opened the first box I'd ordered. It was filled with beige folders, each numbered and titled. I pulled them out, flipped through, and glimpsed funding applications, letters to government agencies, pages and pages of lists—disappointingly, it all seemed to be related to the funding and planning of the experiment. I was hoping that somewhere in all the boxes—those 90.25 linear feet of files—I'd hear from Milgram's subjects. I pulled the second box toward me, fighting a sense of anticlimax and the desire to rush. I told myself to slow down and begin at the beginning.

I stood outside My Most Favorite Dessert, a kosher restaurant on West 45th Street in New York, holding a copy of Tom Blass's book so that he would recognize me. It was 10 A.M. but already baking hot, and no one else was nearby. I felt conspicuous standing there in the nearly empty street and studied the book's cover to give me something to do. After three years of phone calls and e-mails, this was the first time that Tom and I were to meet, and I felt strangely nervous.

I had read Tom's book *The Man Who Shocked the World* before leaving Australia. He had done such a great job: reading it, I was reminded of things I had forgotten and learned plenty I hadn't known. For instance, it was Milgram who was responsible for the "small world" study, now known as "six degrees of separation," proving that we are each connected to a stranger through six links in our social networks. But what had interested me most when I first heard about Tom's book was what he might have to say about the subjects who'd been involved in the obedience experiments and what had happened to them afterward. Yet the book told me little more than what Milgram himself had said and written. Despite being a solid and well-researched account of Milgram's life, it did little to answer the questions that had intrigued me for so long.

In preparation for our meeting, I had gone over all the notes of our conversations over the previous three years and noticed a change in myself. In my first talks with Tom, I could hear a kind of breathless enthusiasm in the questions I put to him—they weren't questions so much as statements that invited confirmation. They were certainly not the questions of an impartial interviewer. Like Tom, I had shared the view that Milgram was a misunderstood genius, a risk taker who had paid the price for holding up a mirror to a truth about ourselves that we'd rather not know. But over time, I had come to wonder more and more about the people in his experiment, and what price they'd paid for taking part. I was aware that the infatuation was waning.

I recognized Tom before he saw me: his hurried, already apologetic gait gave him away. He was a few minutes late, but I wasn't about to quibble. He'd left his home in Baltimore—where he was a professor of social psychology at the University of Maryland—before 6 A.M. in order to meet me in New York for breakfast. He rushed toward me, apologizing, hustling me through the glass doors and into the welcome coolness of the restaurant.

Tom was a warm and likable man. He was tall with a gray beard and large, wire-framed glasses that emphasized his eyes. The enthusiasm in his voice over the phone was even more evident in person and was contagious. He told me that it had taken ten years to write his book and that his family had had enough of all things Milgram (as mine were already beginning to), so it was refreshing to talk to someone who felt similarly fascinated by him. Soon we were in full flight, trading Milgram trivia and arcane and obscure Milgram facts without having to worry that the other person's eyes would glaze over. He talked quickly but with plenty of feeling. I told him that I had been in touch with Bob McDonough, the son of Jim McDonough, who had played the learner, and Tom was as excited as if he'd found him himself. Tom told me about some of the Milgram material that had passed through his hands or that he had collected over the years—Milgram's fragmentary unpublished memoir, love letters, and the script for a stage play that Tom had tried to have videotaped. The waitress had to come back three times before we stopped talking long enough to look at the menu.

I was surprised that Tom seemed to be enjoying himself so much. I would have thought he would know plenty of unequivocal Milgram fans, more so than me—but maybe there were fewer such people than I had realized.

Tom's fascination with Milgram was both intellectual and personal. In 1944, when Tom was two, he had escaped from Budapest with his mother, carrying forged Christian identity papers. Later, in a new land with a new life, the Holocaust grew distant, a part of family lore instead of everyday life. But when he read about Milgram's obedience research as a graduate student in the 1960s, Tom remembered his childhood bafflement at how an environment that had been safe had suddenly turned so dangerous. In the pages of an academic journal, he wrote, "The question was: how do normal people who one day are your friendly neighbors are the next willing to be your killers? How does that transformation take place?" It was a question, he realized, that had haunted him since he was a child.

Tom's admiration of Milgram showed in his tone, which revealed a mixture of awe and something close to envy. They had met just once, at a conference in 1982, two years before Milgram's death. Tom introduced himself, but they did little more than discuss a mutual acquaintance before both moved on. I could tell that Tom regretted it was so brief. Later, he was approached to write a literature review of the obedience research and found himself spending three years immersed in everything ever written about it. "And I realized there was much more to him than just the obedience research," he told me. "I became fascinated by the man who was doing this fascinating stuff. He brought art to science. He was playful, unconventional. He liked creating things that had flair and originality. He followed his impulses. What he was curious about, he pursued, regardless of what other people thought. He was as much an artist as a scientist—he wrote poetry and prose, he made films. For him, art and science were not distinct domains."

In the recordings of the experiments, Tom told me, you only had to listen to understand the strain and tension that many of Milgram's subjects went through. Witnessing the human drama unfolding was tremendously compelling—it was arresting to hear such details as a volunteer's voice quivering as he expressed concern about the well-being of the now-silent learner and the scraping noise of a chair as a volunteer backed away from the shock machine after refusing to continue.

It was when I asked Tom about the ethics of the experiment that I understood my earlier nervousness. Tom had already been so generous—sharing references, sending me contact details of people to interview, paving the way with strangers by sending notes to tell them who I was and what I was doing—that it seemed ungracious to argue with him. For Tom, the stress that Milgram had put his subjects through was a "necessary evil": "In order for the experiment to be a success, he had to create a powerful and highly believable drama—a drama in which the subjects were involved in a highly stressful and tense situation." But I wasn't so sure. What about the ethics of putting people through it? I asked Tom. Did he feel concerned about what Milgram had done? Tom acknowledged that Milgram's ambition had blinded him to his subjects' distress: "I think, really, he was driven by the need to make a mark for himself. I believe that his ambition made him overlook or minimize the suffering of some of his subjects." However, he went on, there was no evidence that the stress they had felt lasted any longer than the duration of the experiment. The very fact that Milgram had sent out a follow-up questionnaire showed that he was interested and concerned about their long-term well-being, and the responses to the questionnaire revealed that only 1.5 percent of the subjects said they were sorry to have taken part. Tom told me this was proof that Milgram had helped them to come to terms with what they'd done. But I was not convinced. How could people that Milgram had described as having agonized, sweated, stuttered, and groaned through the experiment later say that it had no effect on them? How could you shock a man without it having an effect on you afterward? Something about it just didn't ring true.

I leaned back in my chair. By now, the restaurant was filling up, and more waiters wearing T-shirts emblazoned with "My Most Favorite Dessert" were taking up their station by the doorway. The name of the place irritated me: a dessert was either your favorite or it wasn't, but there were no degrees of favorite, no shades of gray. It was either/or, black or white. I realized that in meeting Tom, I had wanted definitive answers about Milgram—facts without shades of gray. But here I was, faced with the mystifying fact that, despite a highly stressful and for many horrifying experience, only 1.5 percent of Milgram's subjects had said that they were sorry to have taken part. My skepticism made me uneasy. Was I one of those people who Milgram had said were critical of his experiments only because they revealed an unwelcome truth about human nature? Was I one of those unwilling to face the truth?

As if he could sense my discomfort, Tom said that Milgram's results were so powerful and unsettling because he put his finger on a blind spot: "the gap between what we think we might do in a particular situation and what we actually do."

So how would Tom himself have acted, I asked, in the same situation? It was a question that I thought I already knew the answer to: could he have conducted the obedience experiments? He looked sheepish and shifted in his seat. "I could not. Just by nature . . . because of my temperament, my personality. It's kind of odd on one hand to appreciate Milgram, and say on the other hand I couldn't do it, but that's the way it is. People are complex," he said, and laughed. "I think you have to be a certain kind of person and I'm not . . . especially knowing what some of his subjects went through . . . I don't think I'd be prepared to do it."

I could see in Tom's body language how uneasy the prospect made him. It is the same for most of us: we can admire Milgram from afar, marvel at the elegance and ingenuity of his experiment, but put us in the lab, instructing someone to put her or his hand on the first lever, and most of us squirm at the prospect. Deep down, something about Milgram makes us uneasy. There is something icy cold at the heart of these experiments.

Textbook accounts of the history of psychology tend to celebrate the pioneers of the discipline—mostly men—and portray them as entirely objective, untainted by values, culture, or politics. Researcher Benjamin Harris points out that the American Psychological Association's (APA) official history, released on its hundredth anniversary, made no mention of racism, anti-Semitism, and the Great Depression as events that shaped North American psychology. He argued that reports on famous experiments are often sanitized and selective, edited and shaped to portray the discipline in a favorable light. Such omissions and distortions shouldn't surprise us. Social psychology, an infant science driven by a need for acknowledgment and status, celebrates iconic experiments as evidence of its achievements.

There was little point in reading psychology textbooks if I wanted to find out more about Milgram and the origins of his research. I had to look to his biography.

Stanley Milgram was born in the Bronx in 1933 to Jewish parents who had emigrated from Eastern Europe, his mother from Romania in 1913 and his father from Hungary in 1921. With the rise of Nazism, Milgram's parents worried constantly about the fate of Jewish relatives still living in Europe, a worry that was transmitted to their children—particularly after the outbreak of war in 1939, when six-year-old Stanley gathered with the family around the radio, listening anxiously to the news.

Milgram was a precocious child singled out for his above-average intelligence. He would have known from a young age that he was expected to go far, further than his working-class parents and siblings. His bedroom walls were plastered with pictures of the old masters, and while his peers played stickball in the street, the sports-shy boy spent his time on science. His only problem—and it would become a tension that would last a lifetime—was which way to channel his creativity: toward visual art, music, or science?

At James Monroe High School, Milgram joined a cohort of ambitious male students who eschewed girlfriends in their single-minded focus on getting into college and making a name for themselves academically. He was accepted into New York's Queens College, where he studied arts and majored in political science. It was here that he and fellow students failed to take action when their "favorite" teachers were sacked for not cooperating with the McCarthy hearings, a passivity that he later regretted.

When he was twenty, Milgram spent a summer backpacking around France (where he took an intensive language course at the Sorbonne), Italy, and Spain. He ran out of money to return home, but managed to talk his way onboard a German ship headed for the United States.

After his travels, Milgram briefly considered a career as a diplomat, but by 1954 he had settled on the newly emerging field of social psychology. He had become disenchanted with the philosophical nature of political science, and social psychology seemed to offer a more practical approach to the kinds of issues, including leadership styles and group persuasion, that interested him. Perhaps it also appealed to him because it seemed to combine drama and art with the status and seriousness of science. He applied to Harvard but was rejected because he had not studied psychology as an undergraduate. While others might have been deterred, this seemed to galvanize Milgram, and he spent the summer of 1954 cramming in as many psychology classes as he could. Each day he crisscrossed New York to attend classes, taking five subjects at three different colleges—Hunter College, Brooklyn College, and New York University—while working nights as a clerk at the Commodore Hotel in Manhattan. Harvard subsequently offered him a place and, with a highly competitive Ford Foundation fellowship under his belt, Milgram could afford to take up the offer.[1]

At Harvard, Milgram met Solomon Asch, who would have a profound influence on his work. Asch was renowned for his 1952 and 1956 studies of group pressure. In Asch's experiments, a volunteer arrived at a laboratory for what he or she believed would be a visual perception test and joined a group of seven people. They were introduced as volunteers but were in fact Asch's confederates. The group was seated at a table and shown two large cards. One had a single vertical line, while the other showed three vertical lines of different lengths. Each person was asked which of the three was the same length as the single line. The confederates gave their previously arranged wrong answers first, leaving the subject to answer last. He had the choice of being a lone voice or agreeing with the group's answer. In total, twelve pairs of cards were shown, and the group gave the wrong answer seven times. Asch found that three-quarters of the answers given by the subjects were correct, but that individuals varied greatly in their levels of independence. Some remained completely independent from the group, many gave the wrong answer at least once, and others yielded to group pressure more than once or twice.[2]

Asch's interest was not so much in the number who stayed independent or conformed but in how they came to resist others' opinions or surrender their judgment to fit in with the group. As a result, his post-experiment interviews lasted anywhere from thirty to sixty minutes, as he explored with the subjects how their thoughts and feelings had influenced their decisions. Asch found that fear of disapproval, a desire to belong, guilt, and a sense of duty had played a role among those who gave in. He concluded that those who had resisted, while just as confused and dismayed by the group's answers and also tempted to give in, had more robust self-esteem, so they were more able to tolerate the discomfort of being a lone voice.

Whether they had agreed with the group or stood their ground, most of Asch's subjects showed tension during the experiment. Asch described them as fidgeting uncomfortably and looking distressed and bewildered. And for many, it was humiliating and embarrassing to find out that the whole thing had been a con. One of Asch's research assistants recalled: "Their response was often very dramatic when you told them it was a lie. . . . There was certainly some emotion, in some cases, some crying."[3] Asch and his assistants were sensitive to the feelings of those they had tricked. Once the experiment was over, Asch wrote at length about his ethical responsibilities toward his subjects, his efforts to reduce their distress, and how he had worked with them to help them gain some benefit from their participation. This attention to the ethics of deception was unusual at the time. Probably because of his respect for his subjects and his disappointment with "the view of human nature present in much of psychology at that time," Asch was never quite able to resolve the ethical dilemma; forty years later he was still troubled by what he had put his subjects through and reluctant to talk about the way he had deceived them.[4]

Milgram worked as Asch's teaching assistant during his second year at Harvard. He observed Asch's experiments and debriefing process firsthand. For his PhD in social psychology, Milgram decided to replicate Asch's experiment in Norway and France to compare cultural differences in conformity. He initially planned to compare conformity in Germany, England, and France but eventually had to scale it back to something more achievable. He finally settled on a comparison between the Norwegians and the French and spent a total of eighteen months in Oslo and Paris conducting his research.[5]

Milgram's experimental design had all the hallmarks that would later make him famous—ingenuity and trickery, the use of confederates, elaborate props, and a tightly scripted scenario. Volunteers were asked to arrive at a lab at an appointed time. When they walked in, they found a bench piled with several coats and a corridor with five closed, numbered doors, indicating that five other subjects were already seated in booths. The last volunteer was seated in a sixth booth and given headphones and a microphone. The task was to listen to two sounds and judge which of two was longer. The volunteer was the last to give his answer, and through his headphones he could hear the other five giving theirs. They were, of course, confederates, who had been instructed to give wrong answers to just over half of the tasks. Milgram found that his subjects conformed 62 percent of the time, giving the incorrect response to agree with the others.[6]

In order to see whether the seriousness of the consequences would affect conformity, Milgram varied the experiment, telling volunteers that the results would be used to improve safety signals on airplanes. The differences were insignificant, with conformity dropping to just under 60 percent. The Norwegians, he found, were more conformist than the French. Milgram said that his French and Norwegian subjects indicated in follow-up interviews that they were glad to have participated, mainly because they felt that the advancement of scientific knowledge justified any deception involved.[7]

Milgram's PhD research revealed as much about him as it did about conformity across cultures. He was a twenty-five-year-old New Yorker conducting research in two European countries and in two different languages, one of which he spoke not at all, the other with which he had only a passing acquaintance. He was clearly keen to make his mark.

The year after completing his European research was disheartening for Milgram. He took a part-time job with Asch, helping to edit a book on conformity. He came to Princeton fresh from his PhD research and must have felt the thrill of knowing that he was going to be "somebody." Yet when he arrived, there was no office or even a desk for him. Asch had not only an office but also a well-established reputation, respect, academic clout, and an influential book about to be published. Throughout the year there was tension between the two, fueled by what Milgram saw as Asch's lack of acknowledgment of his input.[8] Perhaps this feeling of being treated like a nobody made him even more determined to make a splash.

When Milgram arrived at Yale in September 1960, he must have felt the pressure to succeed. He certainly had the drive and the ambition, as well as prestigious mentors and a successful dissertation behind him. What he needed was a research project that would make his name: for an untenured assistant professor at the bottom of the academic ladder, the surest way of cementing his position was to find a research program that would have a major impact. This meant discovering something surprising, even counterintuitive, putting his finger on something that humans didn't already know about themselves.

He knew his new research at Yale would be on the topic of conformity, building, as his dissertation had, on Asch's famous study. But one aspect of Asch's experiment bothered him: the fact that people were pressured to agree verbally about the length of lines on a diagram. Milgram was more interested in actions than in words. He wondered how far a group could pressure someone to *do* something they disagreed with, such as act aggressively toward someone else. He envisaged a group of people, all but one of them actors, each with their own electric-shock generator, egging one another on to give a person more and more intense electric shocks. How far would an individual go in order to fit in with the group? Milgram knew that before he could run the experiment, he would have to test a control group, to see how far people would go without peer pressure. Suddenly he realized that this was it—the twist on Asch's experiment that he had been searching for.

Throughout his life Milgram painted and drew, composed songs and librettos, wrote children's stories and poetry, and directed films. His notebooks are full of ideas for inventions and business opportunities: radio-transmitting dog collars, guidebooks for unmarried pregnant women, even a fake newspaper article service ("You write the story, we'll send you the clipping. Impress your girlfriends that you have gotten in the papers").[9]

Yet despite his bright beginnings in social psychology, Milgram felt uncertain at some level about his choice of career. Art still exerted a powerful pull. In a letter describing his life in New Haven to his friend Helen Wittenberg, the tension between his scientific and artistic sensibilities is clear: "I am glad that the present job sometimes engages my genuine interests, or at least, a part of my interests, but there is another part that remains submerged and somehow, because it is not expressed, seems most important." He described his typical week, dragging himself out of bed to make his weekly classroom appearance, where:

> I misrepresent myself for two hours as an efficient and persevering man of science . . . it does suggest that perhaps I should not be here, but in Greece shooting films under a Mediteranean [sic] sun, hopping about in a small boat from one Aegean Isle to the next. In fact, when in Paris last April, I nearly sold my car to buy movie equipment . . . but went back to Harvard instead. Fool![10]

Like Milgram, psychology suffered from a tension between having one foot in the humanities and another in the sciences. The discipline was born in 1879, in physiologist Wilhelm Wundt's lab at the University of Leipzig. Wundt adapted his training to the study of consciousness, observing and reporting on his own reactions to stimuli; he was the first to translate what had been philosophical musings into a distinct science of the mind. In the second half of the nineteenth century, around ten thousand American students flocked to Europe, mainly to Germany, for graduate training in psychology and philosophy.[11]

Wundt saw psychology as closely aligned with the social sciences—with philosophy, linguistics, history, and anthropology—and believed that only some aspects of psychology could be subject to lab-based experimentation.[12] But on North American soil, psychology aligned itself exclusively with the natural sciences, aided by an almost evangelical belief at the close of the nineteenth century and the beginning of the twentieth that science had transformative qualities; it had become the new religion.[13] Science, the force behind the industrial revolution, had changed the world within a lifetime. It was natural to think that once it turned its gaze upon humans, it could make the same sort of improvements.

Wundt's methods were adopted and adapted, gradually replaced by what were seen as more scientific techniques borrowed from the natural and physical sciences. Physics, chemistry, medicine, and astronomy were considered important, well-established sciences, and in order to be taken seriously psychology had to be seen as similarly exacting and methodical, relying on facts, observation, and testable hypotheses. A hierarchy gradually replaced the collaborative style of Wundt's lab, as techniques of introspection and self-observation were substituted with the scientist's objective observation of "subjects" (a term with medical origins, originally referring to bodies available for dissection).[14] The scientific gaze could be turned on humans the way an astronomer turned his telescope on the stars. The serious psychological scientist adopted not just the techniques of measurement and observation, but also a cold precision and an objective distance from the subject he was studying. The break with Wundt was completed in 1913, when John B. Watson, then head of the APA, defined psychology as "the science of behavior"; introspection and consciousness had been banished, and so had the human subject.[15] Behaviorists like Watson, influenced by Darwin's theory of evolution, believed that by studying one animal, you could understand another: "The behaviorist . . . recognizes no dividing line between man and brute."[16]

Perhaps it was here, in equating humans with animals, that the seeming carelessness about the welfare of human subjects began. Watson and his assistants, for example, plunged babies into cold water; hit metal bars with hammers to make loud noises beside them; asked one carer to drop them and another to catch them; held their heads, arms, and legs tightly so that they couldn't move; jerked blankets out from under them as they were falling asleep; and placed them alone in dark rooms to demonstrate that fear, love, and rage were learned and that you could vastly improve a child's prospects by what you taught them.[17] It was no coincidence that in the 1920s and 1930s the unwitting human subjects of psychological research were often orphaned babies and children, mental patients, prisoners, and minority groups—those who were disempowered and did not enjoy the same rights as others.[18]

North American social psychology remained largely behaviorist in orientation until the 1930s, when the Gestaltists arrived from Germany. The influx of Jewish psychologists fleeing Nazism prompted one social psychologist to observe that "the one person who has had the greatest impact on the field . . . [is] Adolf Hitler."[19] The new arrivals brought with them the tradition of Gestalt psychology, which dictated that in order to understand an event one had to know how it was understood and perceived by the person experiencing it.[20] Wundt would have approved, as it mirrored his focus on the individual's experience as a legitimate object of study. The Gestaltist interest in thoughts, feelings, and perceptions was in direct opposition to North American behaviorism. It was a clash between two psychological traditions that, until then, had developed in parallel on two different continents. On the same soil, conflict was inevitable.

The arrival of leading German-Jewish psychologist Kurt Lewin transformed the field. Lewin had a passion for meaningful science that could provide answers to pressing real-life problems and effect social reform; he was committed to finding ways to help in overcoming prejudice and group conflict. While behaviorists argued that an individual's behavior could be explained by her or his personal history of rewards and punishments, Lewin argued that behavior is shaped by interactions with the environment (a person's "life space," as he termed it). By changing a person's environment, you could change their behavior. In Lewin's view, psychology had the potential to alter the behavior of whole societies as well as small groups. He coined the phrase "action research" to emphasize the crucial link he aimed to forge between experimental findings and the alleviation of social problems.[21]

Lewin's engagement with social issues drew students from across the United States to the University of Iowa and, later, to MIT, where he established the Research Center for Group Dynamics. He and his students adopted the maxim "no research without action, no action without research," applying their findings in a range of settings, including factories and local communities.[22] In one famous study of how leadership styles shape individual and group behavior, which Lewin saw as a parallel for the impact of the differing political ideologies of Germany and the United States, Lewin and two students studied the effect of autocratic and democratic leadership on groups of eleven-year-old boys. The boys, who had been told they were taking a mask-making workshop, met with their workshop leader over a period of weeks. One group was run by a person with an autocratic, domineering leadership style and the other by someone with a democratic, inclusive style. While the boys were making masks, five observers recorded how they interacted with one another. They found that the boys in the autocratic group were hostile and aggressive, while the boys in the democratic group showed greater group spirit and were more cooperative, friendly, and supportive of one another.[23]

Ironically, although he was to be dubbed the "conscience of social psychology," it was Lewin who made deception a hallmark of social psychological research. For Lewin, who had experienced anti-Semitism and racial hatred firsthand under the Nazi regime—and whose relatives, stranded in Germany, were still in danger—the possibility of finding ways to combat prejudice and brutality far outweighed any stress or upset that his experiments may have caused to his subjects.[24] He advocated setting up elaborate experiments where those being studied were unaware that they were under observation and became completely engaged in the situation, so that their natural and spontaneous behavior could be observed from a hidden vantage point. The closer to life the experiment was, Lewin argued, the more the results could be applied to the world outside.[25]

Lewin's students, in turn, disseminated his approach through their teaching and mentoring. (One of Lewin's research assistants at Cornell University was a young Allen Funt, creator of *Candid Camera*.) Throughout his life, Lewin had been able to balance the research and applied aspects of his psychology, but after his unexpected death in 1947 one of his students, Leon Festinger, became particularly influential at propagating his version of Lewin's ideas. For Festinger, a scientist rather than an applied researcher, research became an end in itself.[26] It was Festinger who perfected the art of social psychological research as a kind of theatrical stage production. It required, according to him, making props, playwriting, casting, acting, and rehearsing. He said that such research was like "being afflicted with a psychosis. . . . You become involved in it, addicted to it, and it just becomes a way of life."[27] Prominent American psychologist Elliot Aronson described the exhilaration and thrill involved in his apprenticeship to Festinger, who was driven less by a desire to improve the human condition than by an intense and voracious curiosity about human nature: "He approached research in social psychology as a puzzle to be solved, the way a chess master approaches a chess problem: trying to understand human behavior and doing good research (not doing good) were more than enough to keep him excited."[28] Festinger, Aronson said, was renowned for his ability to construct experiments in which "the participant gets caught up in a powerful scenario that is compelling, believable, and fully involving. Every details [sic] of the construction and performance is terribly important." Aronson recalled the "hours and hours" of rehearsal and preparation that Festinger put him through: "Leon was a regular Lee Strasberg, and we graduate students felt that we were a part of Actors Studio. Art and craftsmanship in the service of science: it was an exciting process. It was very hard work, but we considered it a vital part of doing research." The goal of such research was, according to Aronson, delivering surprising findings that were likely to attract attention and follow-up research.

During World War II, social psychology proved particularly useful to the military, which was interested in a science that had the potential to offer practical strategies and manage a host of psychological problems posed by war. Festinger and Lewin, like many social psychologists, contributed their research skills in support of the war effort. Their research, and that of their colleagues, provided insight into how to convince people to eat unpopular, nonrationed foods; improve troop morale; and improve the selection and training of soldiers.[29] Research became increasingly sophisticated over time, using complex cover stories and highly realistic scenarios that employed any number of confederates. For example, a group of army recruits were convinced midair that their plane was about to crash, and others were led to believe that they had triggered an explosive device that had injured, and likely killed, people.[30] Debriefing was conducted afterward, in the belief that any potentially harmful psychological effects would be prevented by full disclosure, and any stress or trauma experienced by subjects would be justified by improvements in combat training, reduction of casualties, and a foreshortened war.

This military funding continued to flow after the war. To prove its continuing usefulness, social psychology became increasingly experimental and laboratory-based. But peacetime brought changes in the types of psychological problems that interested the military—the continuing tension and brinkmanship of the Cold War prompted the army, navy, and air force to fund research on the psychology of groups and the roles of leadership, cooperation, and competition. In particular, they were interested in determining how small, isolated groups, cut off from the world in the event of a nuclear attack, could function effectively. The late 1940s and 1950s saw a surge of interest in psychological warfare, conformity, and obedience, as the capture and supposed brainwashing of U.S. prisoners during the Korean War prompted funding into differences in national character. Throughout the 1950s, the surreal, disturbing specter of mind control dominated the U.S. public imagination, fueled by anticommunist propaganda and representations in popular culture—including a rash of sci-fi movies such as *Invasion of the Body Snatchers*.[31] Milgram would have known that psychological research exploring these issues was more likely to attract government funding.[32]

The use of deception in social psychological research, which had been relatively rare before World War II, became common practice afterward.[33] By the late 1950s and early 1960s, full-scale theatrical laboratory experiments involving elaborate deception techniques were common. Social psychology handbooks promoted experiments with a high degree of "experimental realism," scenarios that were "so striking and believable that subjects forget they are in an experiment."[34] The psychological discomfort that participants experienced—such as feelings of embarrassment, annoyance, or anger—were seen as regrettable but necessary. To study anxiety, subjects had to panic; to study insecurity, subjects had to feel vulnerable; to study humiliation, subjects had to be shamed. For example, in order to study anger and aggression, individuals were insulted by another "subject," whom they could later choose to punish; to study low self-esteem, students completed a series of personality tests and were told that they had homosexual tendencies, regardless of the test results; and, in order to study how group bonds form between strangers who have shared the same painful initiation practices, young women were forced to read sexually explicit material aloud to male experimenters.[35] According to Benjamin Harris, before 1964 social psychologists rarely revealed the deception to subjects once the experiment was over. Attempts to relieve participants' distress were often patchy and inadequate, and researchers rarely checked with subjects to see what they believed had happened. Psychology textbooks were largely silent on the topic of the ethics of experimentation.[36] Solomon Asch, back in the 1950s, had been the exception rather than the rule.

Philip Zimbardo's description of this era makes social psychology sound as if it were the Wild West. He, Milgram, and others like them were cowboys of the psychological frontier. They were men, often from minority groups, who had grown up in urban ghettos where they'd observed firsthand the power of "white lies and a bit of deception here and there . . . to get what they wanted."[37] Their brand of social psychology was "a kind of surreptitious game playing in which the research subject was the pawn pitted against the intellectual might of the researcher armed with deception as his most powerful weapon." According to Zimbardo, comparing present-day social psychology to the "streetwise, ethnic" version he practiced was like comparing a Big Mac to a corned beef and pastrami sandwich.

Reading accounts of these experiments now—experiments that were described in detail in my own psychology textbooks—it's remarkable that there wasn't more criticism of the situations to which research participants were subjected. With their elaborate scenarios, trickery, and manipulation of subjects, it's hard to see altruism or a desire to change the world as the motivation; instead, they seem designed to showcase the cleverness of the experimenters. Some of them read as little more than sophisticated stunts, more like *Candid Camera* than serious science. I find it hard to believe that I didn't question them back then, that I accepted it all as a standard part of the science.

Stanley Milgram's widow, Alexandra, still lives in the apartment the couple shared with their two children in Riverdale, New York. When I arranged to meet her at her home, she offered to pick me up from the local train station, Spuyten Duyvil. I had seen a painting of the station among Milgram's drawings, a watercolor looking down on the roof from the steep steps that led to the platform.[38] The apartment itself looks out to the wide, gray Hudson River, which Alexandra told me freezes solid in winter. The day I visited, it looked sluggish in the heat.

It wasn't until I met Alexandra Milgram, a slight, brown-haired woman in her late seventies in a pea green skirt and a pretty floral blouse, that I realized I'd been expecting a female version of her husband—someone feisty, opinionated, even prickly. Yet she was a rather shy woman with slow-blinking brown eyes and a hesitant manner of speaking, as if she were not used to giving her point of view. In fact, I learned that her career was in some ways the opposite of his. While Milgram would probe the minds of Nazis, Alexandra, a social worker, would assist Holocaust survivors—an irony not lost on Milgram, who wrote to his friend Larry, "Sasha [as he called her] is really cut out for this kind of help-the-poor activity, and her positive contributions to social welfare are a healthy counterbalance to my own destructive efforts."[39]

Alexandra told me that she met Milgram at a party in January 1961: "Stanley never left my side . . . we just seemed to click." She was a dancer who lived in the Village, which would doubtless have appealed to the artist in Milgram. Her ease with people, too, would likely have attracted him, considering that he could be socially awkward, abrupt, and abrasive at times.

The night the couple met, Milgram had been at Yale for just four months. He had an upcoming article in *Scientific American* about his PhD research and was finishing an application for funding of his obedience studies. Milgram had been careful to frame his research to suit the interests of relevant government bodies. In his initial approach to the Office of Naval Research, he had described it as an investigation of how the Red Chinese had so successfully gained compliance from American POWs.[40] But their application deadline was months away, so he had instead written an application for the National Science Foundation (NSF). Just weeks after the party, in late January 1961, Milgram and Alexandra would race up the steps of a New York post office together to get his NSF application in on time.

Milgram and his wife-to-be could not have known then that the research he was hoping to conduct would make his name but cost him his reputation, or that the techniques that would make his research unforgettable to all would make it objectionable to many.[41] At the time he applied, Milgram had little reason to expect controversy. His research was a product of an intellectual tradition absorbed from his mentors, texts, teachers, and training. His research certainly wasn't the first to deceive and manipulate or to subject participants to intense stress. Until Milgram's first article was published in October 1963, there had been little, if any, public criticism by social psychologists about the treatment of human subjects in their research. But all that changed when Milgram's research was eventually published and psychologist Diana Baumrind objected publicly to the way that Milgram had evoked intense emotional distress in his subjects and induced them to behave cruelly. And she touched a nerve: her criticism sparked an intense debate about the ethics of research with human subjects that continued throughout the 1960s. Milgram's obedience experiments, which writer Ian Parker described in *Granta* as the most "cited, celebrated—and reviled" in the history of social psychology, helped to provoke a redefinition of what was acceptable in psychological research.[42] It led to the introduction of ethical guidelines that prohibited the use of deception and other measures that caused undue stress to human subjects—guidelines that make Milgram's research unrepeatable today.

The scientific foundation upon which North American experimental social psychology had based itself became its downfall. The adoption of manipulative techniques such as deception and the cold, dispassionate eye of the observer fixed on scientific progress, combined with an apparent lack of concern for the welfare of volunteers, caused much soul-searching among social psychologists, many of whom lost confidence in the experimental methods of their own discipline.[43] Little did he know it, but Milgram's experiments marked the end of a research tradition and the end of an era.

2

GOING ALL THE WAY

I was nervous about meeting Bill Menold. We had exchanged e-mails and talked on the phone; he had even helped me to book a room at the Holiday Inn in Palm City, Florida, for my visit. On the phone he had sounded warm, helpful, but I couldn't think of anything other than the fact that he had continued to shock a man he thought might be dead.

I met Bill in the lobby of my hotel on the morning of a swelter-ing day in August 2007. He was a tall, bearlike man, with muscular legs like a tennis player's emerging from baggy beige shorts. Sandy hair, a reddish complexion. A big, ready laugh. He looked so dif-ferent from what I had imagined that for a moment I felt unsure of what to say.

I had come to Florida to find out what had driven people to con-tinue to the maximum voltage on Milgram's shock machine. But how could I phrase the question? How could I ask how it felt to torture someone without showing how much it horrified me?

We introduced ourselves. The lobby was noisy and we went to my room to talk. Bill told me that he hated Florida and hated Bush even more, which put him on the outs with most people he knew. He had spent most of his working life farther up the East Coast or on the West Coast and would have moved away from Florida if he hadn't met Barbara, his third wife, who has strong ties to the state.

We soon got to talking about the experiments. Back in 1961, Bill, a newly married twenty-five-year-old, commuted the eight miles each day from his home in Milford to his job at a New Haven credit union, which was just a short walk from the Yale campus. When he was a student at the University of Connecticut before military service interrupted his studies, he had never set foot inside Yale. "I was inquisitive, maybe I was a little shy. I was intimidated—this was being done at Yale University, and having grown up in that area, Yale was like God." Curiosity drove him to answer the ad for volunteers in a memory and learning test. "I thought it would be fun to try it. I thought, well, let me find out how smart I am."

Still, Bill was nervous when he arrived at Yale's Linsly-Chittenden Hall, a rather forbidding gray building. At 6:45 P.M., he was right on time. He saw a sign on a post outside stating that the memory and learning experiment was downstairs, in the basement. "One of the Yale students had written 'don't forget' on it in pencil. I thought it was funny." Still smiling at the joke as he walked down to the basement, Bill had no idea of the threshold he was about to cross or that he would emerge forty-five minutes later, shaken, distressed, his world tipped on its axis.

Inside, Bill was met by a stern man, John Williams, in a gray lab coat—"very straightforward and professional, just what you'd expect from Yale"—and soon after a second volunteer arrived, introduced as Mr. Wallace. He was Jim McDonough, the actor that Milgram had chosen to play the role of the learner. "He seemed like a nice guy, genial, friendly. He was probably twenty years older than me."

After Williams had introduced the two men, he paid each $4.50 and said that whatever happened from then on, the money was theirs simply for showing up. He then began to explain the experiment: "Psychologists have developed several theories to explain how people learn various types of material. Some of the better-known theories are treated in this book." Here, Williams gestured to a book on the table, titled *The Teaching–Learning Process*.[1] Milgram had chosen this book because the title seemed to add legitimacy to what Williams was saying. Williams mentioned that one theory held that people learn better whenever they are punished for making a mistake, and parents often applied this theory by spanking children whenever they did something wrong. Then he said, "Actually, we know very little about the effects of punishment on learning because almost no truly scientific studies of it have been made in human beings. For instance, we don't know how much punishment is best for learning—and we don't know how much difference it makes as to who is giving the punishment, whether an adult learns better from someone older or younger than themselves, and many things of that sort.

"So what we're doing in this study is bringing adults of many different occupations and ages and we're asking some of them to be teachers and some of them to be learners. We want to find out what effect different people have on each other as teachers and learners. And also what effect punishment will have in this situation. Therefore I'm going to ask one of you to be the teacher here tonight and one of you to be the learner. I guess the fairest thing would be to write 'teacher' on one piece of paper and 'learner' on the other and let you both draw."

The draw was rigged so that Bill would draw the role of teacher, which he did, and McDonough was taken into a room next door. Williams exuded an air of confidence as he instructed McDonough to take off his jacket and matter-of-factly strapped him into the chair. But when he started connecting electrodes to McDonough's arms, Bill began to feel apprehensive. "I was kind of, holy mackerel, what is going on here?"

McDonough, Bill remembers, seemed a little apprehensive too, mentioning that he'd been at the VA hospital some time back with a heart problem. But the experimenter reassured him that this was nothing to worry about. "He said something like, 'We do this sort of thing all the time, nothing to be upset about.' Just another day at the office, you know."

Williams led Bill into the main room and resumed his monologue. "Now please pay attention to the instructions. This machine generates electric shocks. When you press one of these switches all the way down, the learner gets a shock."

In the script that Williams was following, Milgram had typed stage directions in capital letters.

PRESS FIRST SWITCH.

"When you release it the shock stops."

RELEASE SWITCH.

DEMONSTRATE AGAIN—QUICKLY.

"The switch will remain in the middle position after you've released it to show you which switches you've used on the board.

Of course if you were to press it down again the learner would get another shock."

TURN ON GENERATOR.

"The machine is now on. To give you the teacher an idea of the amount of shock the learner is getting we feel it is only fair that you get a sample shock yourself.

Are you agreeable?

May I have your right arm?"

SLIP BRACELET ON ARM. ADD PASTE.[2]

This shock was genuine. It was the only real shock given during the experiment, delivered by a battery rigged up at the back of the machine specifically for this purpose.

For naive volunteers such as Bill, the whole experience must have suddenly felt a bit like stepping onto a fast-moving escalator. When he heard about the shocks, his first thought had been of one of those joy buzzers advertised on the backs of comic books, along with Whoopee cushions and X-Ray Specs—you hid the buzzer in the palm of your hand and used it to play a prank on your friends, giving them a mild tingle that felt more like a tickle than a shock. But by now Bill had received a real shock, which was not as mild as he'd been imagining, and he'd had a chance to look at the machine. "I was taken a little bit aback by how complex it was. It was a large white panel with many switches . . . at least a dozen from left to right . . . and you could see there was a degree of severity as you went up the line. I just said to myself that these people know what they're doing and I'm just going to go along with it and see what happens here."

Williams told Bill that once the test began the learner would communicate his answer by pressing a switch, which would light one of four numbers in a box on top of the machine. If the learner gave a wrong answer, Bill should say "wrong," tell him the number of volts he was about to receive, administer the shock, and repeat the right answer before moving on to the next line. With every wrong answer, Bill should move up one switch. "It's very important that you follow this procedure exactly," Williams told him.

Little did Bill know that, as he was being seated in front of the machine and listening to Williams's explanations, McDonough, alone in the adjoining room, was already unstrapping himself and setting up the tape recorder that would broadcast his cries.

The test began. Bill read the list of word pairs into a microphone so that McDonough could memorize them.

Bill: Blue: boy, girl, grass, hat?

[McDonough buzzes correct answer]

Bill: Correct. Nice: day, sky, job, chair?

[McDonough buzzes correct answer]

Bill: Correct. Fat: man, lady, tub, neck?

[McDonough buzzes correct answer]

To Bill's relief, McDonough got the first few right. When he got one wrong, Bill gave him 15 volts and did not hear any reaction. Bill kept going, and it wasn't until the fifth shock, 75 volts, that he heard anything. "I think the first sound that I heard—and I can't tell you how far in it was—but it was like 'oooh,' like he felt something. It wasn't a scream, I don't think; it seemed to me that it was an indication of discomfort."

Bill began to feel uncomfortable, but Williams urged him on. McDonough gave an even louder cry the next time. Williams seemed unperturbed and again urged Bill to continue. He began to dread McDonough's answers. The test didn't seem that difficult, and Bill knew that if he were the learner he would be sure to get more right. "I tried everything that I thought I could get away with, accenting the right word . . . like dog, cat, *chair*, rabbit, and like, 'I'm giving you the hello there, I'm giving you a hint,' and time after time he'd still get them wrong."

The test continued. Wrong; 90 volts. Then McDonough got one, then two, correct, and Bill felt himself relax. But the next one was wrong; 105 volts. A noise that sounded like "uugh." And the next; 120. "When he yelled out . . . that's when I started to feel really uncomfortable . . . and I thought, oh God. . . . What the hell am I doing here? What is this all about?"

McDonough's sounds of discomfort grew louder with each shock. Then he mentioned his heart problem.

Bill: White: cloud, horse, rock, house?

[McDonough buzzes wrong answer]

Bill: Incorrect. One hundred and fifty volts. *[gives shock]*

McDonough: Let me out of here! I told you about my heart problem; let me out of here!

Bill hesitated, turned to Williams. He told me, "I remember distinctly saying, 'You know what, I'll switch with him. I'm smarter than this guy and you can ask me these questions.'" But the experimenter was adamant that they couldn't change places once the experiment had started.

By now they were confronting the eleventh switch, 165 volts. "I was under a lot of stress; I was really starting to sweat. I wasn't in control of the situation and I also suspected that I was being set up. I mean, Yale doesn't go round torturing people . . . but I really wasn't sure, so the question in my mind was, am I really hurting this guy or am I the guinea pig here? Is this a setup, are they testing me to see if I'll do this stuff? I didn't have any answers to this conflict that was going on. It was unbelievably stressful."

One hundred and seventy-five volts. One hundred and ninety volts. Sweating and trembling, Bill continued. "It sounds really strange, but it never occurred to me just to say, 'You know what, I'm walkin' out of here,' which I could have done. At this point I was just soaking wet. I was just so disturbed by all this because this had gone out of my realm of reality and I was in a bizarre environment and I didn't know what I was doing, but I was sweating bullets and I was starting to laugh almost like a maniac, hysterically. I'd kind of lost it."

Then McDonough, after receiving a shock of 330 volts, went silent. Bill thought, either he's unconscious, he's dead, or this thing is a complete sham.

When McDonough didn't answer, Bill told Williams that he wasn't going any further. "I said, 'I'm not taking responsibility for this,' and that's when he said, 'Don't worry about it, Yale University is taking full responsibility.' I was under such enormous stress—I mean, I just did not know what to do—and when I said he's not answering anymore and the guy said, 'Well, just continue with the experiment,' I thought, I'm just going to go along with this thing. I don't know what's going on but let's just get it over with."

Bill stopped talking at that point and looked down at his hands. I shifted uncomfortably in my chair. A door slammed in the hallway outside, and laughter and voices tripped down the corridor before fading. Bill took a sip of water. If I was reluctant to hear this, I thought, how must Bill feel, having to tell it? I tried to imagine him as he would have been that summer: a young man, muscled, tan, and fresh-faced. Curious and eager, unprepared for such cruelty.

He leaned forward, his hands joined loosely between his knees. He told me that he had continued to shock the now silent McDonough until he reached the final switch, 450 volts, although he couldn't remember much about it.

When it was all over, Williams told Bill that he would release the learner and Bill prepared for the worst, taking comfort from the fact that he was fitter and younger than the other guy. "I remember thinking, I'm gonna have to calm him down if he gets upset. If he was gonna take a swing at me, I thought, I'm just gonna restrain him . . . I was scared to death."

Yet what happened next was surreal. "He came out and said, 'Hello, how are you?' He was very friendly, a nice guy who just, you know, relieved any concerns I had about any hard feelings or animosity. We shook hands. They wanted for me to see that he was okay, physically and emotionally. The debriefing, if you wanna call it that, didn't last two minutes. We talked for a few minutes and then he and I left together and we walked out of the building and we got out onto the street and he went one way and I went the other.

"I was in this crazy situation . . . I was just gonna walk out of there . . . nobody was gonna shoot me or put me in a prison cell. I still didn't know what had happened. I was a basket case on the way home."

Bill went straight to his neighbor, an electrician, and told him what had happened. His neighbor tried to reassure him that the shocks couldn't have been real, or McDonough wouldn't have walked out smiling afterward. "But I was also really concerned afterward about what I had done, you know, 'Gee whiz, look what I did.' It didn't make me feel very good. You know, the cruelty involved. The question was always geez, what can they make you do here? . . . Or what did you do? They didn't make you. No one held a gun to my head."

Yet in hearing Bill's story, it seemed obvious to me that it had been more than a simple case of following orders. No one had held a gun to his head, but he'd been instructed, argued with, pressured, and coerced into continuing. Milgram's published accounts of his experiment described his role as the objective scientist who set up an experiment to observe natural behavior unfold.[3] The conventional wisdom among social psychologists was that "the researcher is merely creating conditions for what would happen anyway, but the researcher is not creating what happens. The researcher's responsibility is to record what happens, and the subject's responses are the responsibility of the subject."[4] Until I met Bill Menold, I had believed pretty much the same thing. But hearing his story raised all sorts of questions. I decided to return to the archives to see if I could find some answers.

The more I read, the more I understood how complicated the story I had assumed I had known actually was. It became clear to me just how enormous the pressure on Bill and others was. Milgram's career depended on their obedience; all his preparations were aimed at making them obey. In choosing "the boldest and most significant research possible," Milgram was aiming for bold and significant results.[5]

When he had arrived at Yale in September 1960, he knew that he wanted to compare national differences in obedience between Germans and Americans in much the same way as he had compared conformity between the Norwegians and the French. Milgram had adopted the then common view that Germans were far more susceptible than other nationalities to following orders. His sinister variation on Asch's more benign line test seemed to be based on a belief, popular in America at the time, that the perpetrators of the Holocaust were highly conformist and motivated by blind obedience.[6] Milgram told mentors that he intended to compare obedience to authority in the United States and Germany and that the New Haven experiments were the baseline against which he planned to compare German obedience rates. But his funding applications did not mention this, instead describing the research in terms of conformity in the context of the Cold War.[7]

Milgram improvised with techniques to come up with an experimental procedure that satisfied him. The choice of a shock machine was not surprising, as the infliction of electric shock was common in psychological experiments around this time.[8] His earliest musings on paper feature a sketch of a shock generator with a series of switches labeled from "very mild" to "lethal."

On October 14, 1960, Milgram outlined his early plans in a letter to the Office of Naval Research inquiring about potential funding. His thinking had already advanced from his initial drawings: "If you are trying to maximize obedience, and command a person to do something in violation of his inner standards, with how much information do you present him? Do you tell him from the start the worst of what he may be expected to do, or do you extract compliance from him piecemeal?"[9]

In order to create the "strongest obedience situation," he was already wrestling with how he could overcome people's reservations and reluctance to inflict harm on someone else. In the letter, he suggested that one way was to ask for compliance step by step: first by providing an "acceptable rationale" for the experiment, and then by selling it to potential subjects as a learning experiment in which memory could be improved through the use of "negative reinforcement." If the experiment could be presented as a socially useful study, the infliction of punishment would be seen as justified. This letter shows that Milgram intended to run two conditions: the experimental condition, in which a person was pressured by a group to do something in violation of his conscience; and the control group, in which he could see how an individual would behave by following instructions from another individual. He predicted that the group condition would elicit more obedience than the individual one.

From October 1960 until August 1961, Milgram developed, refined, and rehearsed his experimental scenario, beginning it as a class project for his "Psychology of the Small Group" class. Social psychologists serious about their science were expected to have storytelling, acting, and stagecraft skills as part of their professional toolkit, and Milgram no doubt saw this project as a way for students to learn the tools of the trade. But it had the added benefit of allowing him to develop the experiment for application beyond the classroom.

Together, Milgram and his class developed the experimental scenario for the control condition and a feasible cover story: that the experiment was about the effect of punishment on learning, and it aimed to test whether the learner's recall would be improved by receiving electric shocks for each wrong answer. The victim and the experimenter would be in cahoots, the victim's cries of pain would be faked, and no real shock would be given. The shock machine was central to the cover story, and the students came up with a prototype based on Milgram's rough drawing. Milgram and his students didn't expect anyone would go above the level of "strong shock," the sixth of twelve switches. The switches increased in 30-volt increments to a maximum shock of 330 volts, beginning with "tingle shock" and ending with "danger: severe shock."[10] Milgram's feeling at this point was that levels of obedience in this condition would be low but would serve as a useful contrast to the "real" experiment, where he expected the urgings and pressure from a group to yield high levels of obedience.

Between late November and early December 1960, Milgram and his class ran some preliminary trials, holding five different sessions with twenty Yale undergraduates as subjects. Milgram and his students watched through a one-way mirror, making adjustments and changes as the trials progressed. The results took Milgram by surprise: even though no statistics are available, a 1970 report indicates that more than 85 percent of Yale student subjects, and possibly as many as 100 percent, went to the maximum voltage.[11] Milgram and his students were "astonished"; he said they sensed they had witnessed something "extraordinary."[12] Particularly surprising was the obedience rate of subjects in the control condition. Milgram realized that the experimenter's influence was far more powerful than he had thought.

Although Milgram began the planning stages of his research with attention-grabbing results in mind, it wasn't until these pilot studies that he received confirmation that he was on the right track. Scientifically speaking, the results were counterintuitive—no one would expect so many people to follow orders—and therefore much more likely to garner attention than research that confirmed what was already known. He now relegated his original "group pressure" studies to a minor role, and what had been his control condition became his focus.

However, privately he was still cautious about the results of his pilot studies, probably because the somewhat amateurish delivery by his student personnel may have made subjects see through the cover story, and they could have obeyed because they knew it was a hoax. From this point, he worked on developing a highly credible scenario to ensure that the maximum number of people would obey. But he had to come up with ways to both overcome their resistance and pressure them to do something they wouldn't otherwise. Milgram later called these "strain-reducing mechanisms" and "binding factors." Almost immediately, he stepped up efforts to source funding for further research, describing his work to one funding body as an attempt to "maximize obedience."[13] Milgram could sense that this research would put his name up there with the giants of social psychology. In a letter to his former Harvard professor Jerome Bruner around the same time, he wrote: "My hope is that the obedience experiments will take their place along with the studies of Sherif, Lewin and Asch."[14]

Milgram also had an obsession with the detail of the practical design, which comes through clearly in the files and notes. He was proud of his practical skills, describing them in an unpublished interview:

> Setting up an experiment is much like producing a play; you have to get all the elements together before it is a running production . . . much to my surprise, I turned out to be a kind of whiz at this sort of thing . . . I find it almost recreational. Moreover, I have a passion for perfection in setting up an experiment, both in regard to the materials used, and the manner of execution. I can spend months perfecting the format of a document used in an experiment; and I will not allow the experiment to proceed, until everything is not only adequate but aesthetically satisfying.[15]

He was stage manager, magician, scriptwriter, head of props, casting agent, publicist, and director and would eventually watch the proceedings unfold from behind a one-way mirror—his version of the wings.

Then there were the administrative details. As a junior member of staff with little or no entitlement to administrative support, Milgram was responsible for everything from ordering business cards to arranging security for the buildings after hours. He designed the shock machine himself, making it look more realistic than the prototype developed by his students. In his papers, there are first crude, and then increasingly sophisticated, sketches of it. The final sketch is annotated with an early fragment of the script: "75. Ow. 90. Owch. 105. Ow. 110. Ow Hey! This really hurts. 135 OW—150. Ow that's all!! Get me out of here."[16] It had to be believable, but not so believable that subjects would refuse to go to the maximum voltage. Milgram increased the number of switches from twelve to thirty, making the increments smaller, and decided to change the final switch, which he had labeled in his early drawings as "*lethal*," then "*extreme shock—danger*" on the student prototype, to the more ambiguous "*XXX.*" He was already tweaking and making improvements to ensure greater obedience to the experimenter's orders.

Milgram bought the necessary electronic parts for a total cost of $261.86 and oversaw its construction by Ronald Salmon, a Yale employee. Salmon spent eighty-six hours between June 2 and July 19, 1961, assembling it in Yale's electronic and mechanical workshop. It had a single row of thirty switches, each topped by lights, with labels beneath describing the degree of shock each purported to deliver. The first group of four switches were labeled "slight shock," the next "moderate shock," then "strong," "very strong," "intense," "extremely intense," and "danger: severe shock." The final two switches were simply labeled "XXX." The finishing touch—and, at $65.82, the most expensive—was the engraving on the front panel, done by Hermes Precision Engravers in New York: a small plate in the left-hand corner stated that the machine was built by "Dyson Instrument Company, Waltham, Mass.," an area known for its electronics manufacturing.[17]

Rather than relying on his staff to record the level at which people stopped, a practice fallible to human error, Milgram bought his most expensive piece of equipment: an Esterline Angus event recorder. It recorded the amount of voltage delivered, as well as how long the shock lasted, that is, how long the subject held down the switch. He was keen to streamline and automate processes as much as possible, to keep things scientific. Milgram also bought two tape recorders—one for recording each experiment, the other for playing back the learner's cries—and timers, a camera, and speakers.[18]

By mid-June, it was time to recruit subjects. This would be an arduous process, with Milgram first advertising in local papers, then sending letters of solicitation to names and addresses taken from the phone book, and finally asking the already recruited subjects to provide him with contact details of relatives or friends that he could approach.

He ran a half-page newspaper advertisement in the *New Haven Register* on Sunday, June 18, 1961.

The attention-grabbing heading, a hierarchy of text sizes, and bolding made the advertisement easy to read at a glance.

WE WILL PAY YOU $4.00 FOR
ONE HOUR OF YOUR TIME
Persons Needed for a Study of Memory

* We will pay 500 New Haven men to help us complete a scientific study of memory and learning. The study is being done at Yale University.

* **Each person who participates will be paid $4.00** (plus 50¢ carfare) for approximately 1 hour's time. **We need you for only one hour**: there are no further obligations. You may choose the time you would like to come (evenings, weekdays, or weekends).

No special training education or experience is needed.
We want:

Factory workers	Businessmen	Construction workers
City employees	Clerks	Salespeople
Laborers	Professional people	White-collar workers
Barbers	Telephone workers	Others

All persons must be between the ages of 20 and 50. High school and college students cannot be used.

* **If you meet these qualifications,** fill out the coupon below and mail it now to Professor Stanley Milgram, Department of Psychology, Yale University, New Haven. You will be notified later of the specific time and place of the study. We reserve the right to decline any application.

* **You will be paid $4.00** (plus 50¢ carfare) as soon as you arrive at the laboratory.

The tone and rhythm mimicked ads for closing-down sales, and the repetition of the four dollars, the one hour required, and the fact that there were no further obligations was reminiscent of someone making a pitch: "Yes, ladies and gentlemen, four dollars for only one hour. That's right, just one hour of your time." The emphasis on the lack of special training, education, or experience highlighted that unskilled men could and should apply—if they met the "qualification" (a word perhaps used to flatter exactly these sorts of readers, given that the only qualifications were age and gender), they should act quickly in order to be "selected." The implication was that selection was a privilege because there would be more applications than spots. The mention that the money would be paid on arrival was aimed at people who wanted to make a quick $4.50.

As well as the large display ad in the news section, Milgram paid for extra 5" x 1" column ads concentrated mainly in the sports pages. These pages were sandwiched between reports of Jackie Kennedy holidaying solo in Greece, the threat of communism, the exclusion of African American students from white schools, and U.S. broadcasts of propaganda to North Korean troops, as well as ads for New Haven department stores in the lead-up to Father's Day.

Milgram was disappointed with the response to his ads. Despite the paper's Sunday circulation of 106,000, he received only 296 replies—even fewer once he subtracted women, Yale employees, newspaper reporters, and police officers, all of whom he decided would make unsuitable subjects.[19] He blamed the weekend's weather: that Sunday it had been a sunny 80 degrees with a welcome dip in humidity. Instead of sitting inside and reading the paper, the men he was hoping to reach had been lured out by the unseasonably beautiful weather for picnics and ball games. Interestingly, Milgram didn't seem to consider that some readers might have seen the ad but treated it with suspicion due to its gimmicky tone, which perhaps sounded at odds with what they would have expected from Yale. Instead, it was the potential subjects who were at fault—their desire to make the most of the good weather, their fecklessness and distractibility, meant that his ad went unread.

Next he tried direct mail, sending two thousand letters to men whose names and addresses were taken from the 1960–61 New Haven telephone directory. He selected the first thousand by choosing the names at the top of each of the four columns on every one of the directory's 312 pages (although no "business establishments and women").[20] Once that method was exhausted, he selected the first name at the top of each column in the bottom half of each page. The two thousand all received the following letter:

MEMORY AND LEARNING PROJECT
Yale University
New Haven, Connecticut

Dear Sir:

We need your help.

We require five hundred New Haven men to help us complete a scientific study of memory at Yale University.

Each person who participates in this study is paid $4.50 for 1 hour's time. There are no strings attached. We need you for only one hour. There are no further obligations.

No special training, education, or experience is needed. We want persons of all occupations: factory workers, businessmen, laborers, professional people, and others. We need persons from all over New Haven and the surrounding communities.

You may choose the hour you would like to participate; it may be in the evening, on weekends, or on weekdays. You must be between the ages of 20 and 50. We cannot use high school or college students.

If you meet these qualifications and would like to take part in this Yale study, fill out the enclosed postcard and drop it in the mailbox. The exact time and place of the study will be arranged later, at your convenience. (We reserve the right to decline any application.)

To repeat the facts:
1. You are wanted for a study at Yale University.
2. You will be paid $4.50 for one hour of your time.
3. There are no strings attached. This is a sincere offer.
4. You may choose your own hour: evenings, weekdays, or weekends.
5. If we can count on you, fill out and mail the enclosed card.

Your help is greatly appreciated, and we look forward to hearing from you soon.

Yours truly,

Stanley Milgram, Ph.D.
Director

This was probably more effective, with its letterhead mentioning an impressive-sounding Memory and Learning Project at Yale and Milgram, holder of a PhD, as its director. The impassioned "we need your help," a phrase that was repeated in variation throughout, appealed directly to people's altruism. Milgram was aware by this point that people were more cautious than he'd given them credit for. The phrases "no strings" and "no obligations" were repeated three times, as if he felt the need to reassure the recipient that this was a genuine, benign scientific enterprise and the reader could have faith in those running it. The tone of the letter is more conciliatory and less commanding than the newspaper ad, with the personal pronoun "you" creating a more intimate, inviting feel and fostering a sense of equality between the reader and the writer: the *you must*s of the ad are replaced with *you may*s in the letter.

With the ad and letter, Milgram clearly had an idea of the men he wanted to recruit—those impressed by authority, flattered to be involved in a scientific endeavor at a prestigious institution, and likely to be glad of extra money. Yet the subject questionnaires showed that the men who volunteered were motivated by curiosity, many wanting to learn something more about their memory, including Bill Menold.[21]

Next, Milgram chose his actors. They had to look the part, and it was Milgram who decided what that look would be. He initially considered Alan Elms, his young research assistant, for the experimenter but decided that he looked too young and an older man would wield more authority.[22] He advertised in the local paper in mid-July for a research assistant, and of the eleven men who applied Milgram appointed Jack Williams, a thirty-one-year-old high school biology teacher he described as "impassive" and "stern" and clearly glad of the extra work over summer. Milgram selected Williams not just for his acting skills but also because as a science teacher Williams was used to exercising his stern demeanor and authoritative presence to command obedience. Milgram described Williams in early drafts of his book thus: "He is a rather angular looking fellow, technical looking, and dry, the type you would later see on television in connection with the space programme."[23]

For the role of the learner, Milgram was delighted when he interviewed James Justin McDonough. Whereas Williams was angular and stern, Jim McDonough was "a rotund man in his late 40s, a fleshy red nose and pink complexion, probably Irish, perhaps an accountant for the railway, perhaps a bartender." Milgram told one subject that one of the reasons McDonough was selected was he was "stout and kind of sloppy . . . he looked like a cardiac type." The notes that Milgram took of his interview with McDonough begin with a sense of excitement:

> Excellent as victim. A+ victim. Can work the acceptable hours. This man would be perfect as victim. He is mild and submissive, not at all academic. . . . Worked on the railroad for 25 years and is completely reliable. The only trouble is he cannot act too well in my estimation, but can train. Has 8 children. Easy to get along with.[24]

It was hardly an audition; in fact, Milgram seemed quite happy to overlook McDonough's poor acting skills. He was just thrilled that McDonough so closely resembled what he must have felt was the perfect "victim"—an amiable, not very intelligent-looking man, the sort who would submit to being strapped into the chair without protest and whose mistakes on a fairly simple learning test would not arouse suspicion. The mention of McDonough's eight children and his reliability could suggest that Milgram was looking for a man who needed the money and would be less likely to withdraw if he found the work distasteful, but it's likely, too, that Milgram selected McDonough because he fit Milgram's view of what an "average" New Haven working man was like. McDonough was in fact an executive with the railroad, occupying a position of responsibility and authority.

It seems that Milgram's theatrical flair overtook his scientific objectivity in his choice of actors. In a kind of mirror image of the results he was looking for, Milgram cast as his experimenter a man who would command obedience and in the role of the "victim" a man who looked sure to obey. He seemed unaware of how his vision was influencing his experimental design.

Milgram trained the actors himself. He wanted to make sure that they and the script were as convincing as possible. He noted, "It took a tremendous amount of rehearsal. Two full weeks with constant screaming on my part, constant."[25] Williams's script was a densely typed ten pages that began when the subject arrived, and ended at the point where the "memory and learning test" started. McDonough's script was straightforward—a series of protests, cries, and screams cued to voltages on the machine. Williams's delivery had to be rapid to get through ten pages of instructions and directions before the test began, a practice that, combined with his authoritative manner and tone, discouraged objections. Milgram rehearsed with McDonough until his "cries of agony were truly piercing."[26]

From July 27 to August 4, Milgram ran what he described as "summer pre-tests," or trial runs, of the experiment, in which he and his actors practiced on around twelve adult New Haven subjects, with Milgram noting how many "penetrated the cover story."[27] They explored what effect increasing the volume of the victim's cries had on people's willingness to obey and what happened when the victim was made more visible to the subject. By tweaking, changing, and noting any suspicions that subjects had, Milgram developed what he thought was a solid cover by the time the experiment started. He saw evidence that many people were distressed by the conflict they faced, with several sweating, trembling, and protesting to Williams. Very few blithely followed orders: many, even those who continued to the maximum voltage and were classified as obedient, protested and argued with the experimenter. Each time they protested, Williams countered with a series of statements aimed at pressuring them to continue.

The first experiments began in Linsly-Chittenden Hall's interaction laboratory on August 7, 1961. It was an impressive-looking studio with large one-way mirrors, thick carpet, and drapes. Four variations, comprising 160 subjects (forty per variation), were run there. By the time it was Bill Menold's turn in October, the experiments had relocated to the basement of the same building because the lab was needed for classes. The new lab, previously an art storage room, was entered by a set of stairs down from High Street. While the basement lab was smaller and noisier than the one upstairs, Milgram wrote that it had other advantages:

> It has a somewhat harsh, though quite scientific appearance . . .
> it looks more . . . forbidding. Street noises penetrate, there is
> an occasional toilet flush heard, and the room, in comparison
> to the radio-studio silence of the Interaction Laboratory, pro-
> duces reverberation quite easily. Indeed, the buzz on the shock
> generator sounds somewhat louder.[28]

Milgram had double glazing put on the windows, improved the lighting, and gave the lab a new coat of paint and a less forbidding door before the fifth variation of his experiments began. He and his team had been running experiments from 6 to 11 P.M. on weeknights and from 9 A.M. to 10 P.M. on weekends, a grueling schedule that he told campus police would continue until the end of spring term, or the end of May 1962.[29]

As I made my way through Milgram's notebook, with its detailed instructions and scripts, I could see the setup that he had created was carefully crafted to make it difficult for people to disobey. I could see, laid out, the unfolding of a slow process of trial and error as he re-fined, tightened, and scripted a scenario that would deliver the results he wanted. Milgram would argue that his experiment merely revealed what was natural and universal, that "[t]he objects with which psy-chological science deals are all present in nature fully formed, all that the prince-investigator has to do is to find them and awaken them with the magic kiss of his research."[30] But it was clear to me that the papers in the archives told a different story: he knew before his first subject arrived on August 7, 1961, what sort of results he wanted to achieve, and he had used pilot studies and pretests to hone the design to achieve just that.

The next time Bill Menold and I met, Bush was out, Obama was in, and Bill was thrilled that we had "finally got rid of those lowlifes." When I rang to let him know I had arrived, he said, "I'd like to get you out of that hotel room," and picked me up and drove me to his house.

On the way, he told me that if you can't drive in Florida they put you in assisted accommodation: "I'm serious!" I had forgotten how much Bill made me laugh.

We arrived at a ranch-style house in Palm Springs with Mexican-looking roof tiles, situated on a development with an ornamental lake two feet deep. Barbara had done the interior decoration, he said proudly as he introduced us. She was a striking woman with fine cheekbones and a low, resonant voice. They met, she told me, when Bill put an ad in the paper: "Urbane eclectic man seeks attractive woman for best friend/lover." She was intrigued by his description of himself—it was the first time she'd seen "urbane" and "eclectic" in the same sentence.

We sat in the dining room and Barbara moved around in the kitchen, making tea. Watson, their dog, pushed his nose against my hand and I scratched behind one large, floppy ear. Bill told me that a couple of years before he met Barbara he had been interviewed by the BBC for a documentary about torture. Before he could propose to her, he had made her watch it. I asked if it was because he wanted Barbara to know his darker side. Bill laughed. "I don't know why I did it." He leaned toward me and touched his heart. "But there's a little evil in there, you know what I mean?"

After the experiment ended, Bill tried not to think about it. He put it out of his mind for years. Then in the early 1980s, he dated a psychology professor who was teaching her class about Milgram's experiments. When he told her that he'd been a participant, she "went nuts" and immediately wanted him to talk to her class. "And I never gave it a second thought. I said 'Sure.'" Bill laughed sheepishly at his own naïveté. "So, I'll never forget this, I'm fortysomething and these are eighteen-, nineteen-year-old kids, and I showed up—well, you would have thought Adolf Hitler walked in the room. I never really thought about it that way, you know?"

This image—of Bill suddenly seeing himself as others saw him—would stay with me all the way back to New Haven and, later, Australia, probably because I had been guilty of the same thing, of making assumptions before I had even met him. The first time I had visited, I admitted to myself now, I hadn't expected to like him. I had expected someone bad, a kind of monster. Instead, I had found myself drawn to him, and I could see why. He did not shy away from talking about the experiment; he had a kind of unflinching internal gaze when it came to his behavior in Milgram's lab. He was gutsy.

Barbara came in with the tea, excused herself, and disappeared into the study. She had recently discovered family history, Bill grumbled, and now they had to share the computer. We talked some more, and as I was leaving I asked Bill if he was glad that he had taken part in the experiment. He paused, then said, "I don't know. Yeah, I think so. I guess so. Not that I'm terribly proud of it . . . but I'd rather know than not know."

Bill's experience that night in 1961 has forced him to think about things others haven't had to—a term that one critic of the experiment called "inflicted insight."[31] Milgram's subjects learned unwelcome things about themselves as a result of their involvement in the obedience experiments, and they're different from the rest of us because of that. Bill had told me, "Most people are card-carrying cowards. If they had been involved in something like that, they just wouldn't want others to know. Most people want to be considered 'nice.'"

But according to academic Don Mixon, Milgram didn't measure immoral behavior in his lab. On the contrary, he argued that what Milgram measured was misplaced trust.

When I met Don in Australia, he wore a red wool beret perched on the side of his head, a flash of color against the white of his hair. He looked exotic, intellectual, in bare feet on a freezing midwinter day. A tall and rather frail man, he folded his long frame into a chair that looked out to the afternoon sky over the Blue Mountains, outside Sydney. He reminded me of a proud eagle in his aerie, a house perched high on the aptly named Cliff Drive, with vertiginous views down sheer rock faces.

When Don enrolled in a PhD program in Nevada in the late 1960s, there was no question that he would do his doctorate on Milgram's obedience experiments. "It was the only social psychological research that interested and excited me. I liked it because it was political. It seemed to show that ordinary Americans behaved in ways worse than those in Nazi Germany. They seemed to behave in a terribly immoral fashion."

Don wanted to repeat Milgram's research but quickly realized that, ethically, he didn't have the stomach to deceive subjects in the way Milgram did or to watch the stress that they would go through. He thought of using role playing rather than deception. In his version of the research, Don set the scene for his actors—a term he preferred to "subjects"—by telling them to imagine that they were teachers in a learning experiment, in the room next door was the learner, and in front of them was the shock machine. (He used a mockup of the machine.) Don followed the original script closely, instructing subjects to increase the voltage level with each wrong answer, describing the learner's cries of pain, and urging subjects to continue if they hesitated.

Don found that his subjects became engrossed in the experiment once it began—so engrossed, in fact, that they became agitated and distressed, caught between the commands of the experimenter and the cries of pain from the learner. Even though they knew that the experiment itself was a simulation, their emotional reactions were real. Don had underestimated the power of drama, how easy it was for people to inhabit a role. In hindsight, he felt that he should have known: originally an actor, he knew what it was like to take a part and step inside it, to become a character in a play. Dismayed by their reactions, Don had to call the experiment off. He shook his head and said slowly, "I wasn't finding out anything that was worth the distress."

Don found the same results as Milgram but came to completely different conclusions. He argued that it wasn't immorality that drove Milgram's subjects to flip the switches but trust in the experimenter, who, despite the cries from the learner, calmly told them to continue and gave the impression that there was nothing to worry about. People were agitated because the experimenter's behavior was so ambiguous and confusing in this context. According to Don, Milgram simply measured the faith that people put in experts: "He found just the opposite of what he thought he found; nothing about subjects' behavior is evil. In fact, people go to great lengths, will suffer great distress, to be good. People got caught up in trying to be good and trusting the expert. Both are usually thought of as virtues, not as evils." The only evil in the obedience research, Don came to believe, was "the unconscious evil of experimenters."

Don argued that, faced with the ambiguity of the situation, people believed that the expert scientist was good and protective and read his imperviousness to the learner's cries as reassurance that nothing was really wrong. He told me to look at the results Milgram got in those variations where the experimenter looked concerned and behaved as if he believed the shocks *were* harmful. In condition 12, the experimenter told the teacher to stop, despite the learner's cries to continue; in condition 14, it was the experimenter who was hooked up to the chair and, when shocked, cried out in pain; and in condition 15, there were two experimenters, one who told the teacher to stop and the other who told him to continue. In all three conditions, obedience dropped to zero. Milgram explained the results in terms of the power of the authority figure as opposed to the power of the learner, but Don argued that when the teachers were presented with the unambiguous message that the shocks were harmful, they stopped giving them.

Before he retired from the University of Wollongong, Don used to screen Milgram's documentary film *Obedience* each year for his students, but over time he found it increasingly difficult to watch: "Seeing that movie over and over, the more convinced I was that it was something terrible that he did. I was so moved by that one man in the film who so respectfully kept asking the experimenter to stop, just suffering such agony from a desire to do what's right but couldn't figure out what's right. It was terribly cruel." The man that Don was referring to was Fred Prozi.

I asked what he made of the fact that so many of Milgram's subjects said they were glad to have taken part. "You don't know just from ticking off boxes why they're glad. I think they were conned into learning something about themselves that wasn't true. I would be greatly heartened if Milgram's subjects were more critical of experts and did not torture themselves."

Some time after I met him, Don wrote to me, sending me extracts from a book he's working on. Beautifully written, it ranges across history, philosophy, and of course psychology. As a postscript to one letter, he added:

> The experiments encourage us to feel superior to obedient subjects. We are confident that we would be defiant. . . . The experiments seemed to offer strong support for history's oldest, most momentous self-fulfilling prophecy—that we are born sinners. Most people, even atheists, believe that it is good for us to be reminded of our sinful nature. Milgram scripted a powerfully dramatic reminder.

Milgram assumed that increased self-knowledge was a good thing. In an unpublished note about the ethical issues of the experiments, he wrote, "I do not think I exaggerate when I say that for most subjects the experiment was a positive and enriching experience. It provided them with an occasion for self-insight and gave them a first-hand, personalized knowledge of some social forces that move human conduct."[32]

But I began to wonder how it could be a uniformly positive experience when what people learned about themselves was shameful, painful, or confronting. When I looked at Milgram's unpublished analysis of subjects' responses to the question about what they had learned, around 80 percent were self-critical, with both obedient and defiant subjects surprised by how submissive they were and disappointed with their gullibility, many vowing to be more suspicious of science in the future. The remaining 20 percent, largely disobedient subjects, were self-congratulatory, saying that they were pleased to learn they weren't as submissive as they'd thought.[33] It is clear that, like Bill Menold, many subjects regarded the experiment as a test of character that they had passed or failed. Subject 116 wrote in a questionnaire some time later:

> After completing the experiment I really was ashamed of myself! I kept thinking why didn't I refuse to give pain to my fellow man, instead of going through as directed to the end! In discussing this with a friend, who also took part in the experiment, at another time, he related the whole incident to me, not

knowing I went through the same bit, he on the other hand refused to give punishments and walked out. Thus I hated myself all the more for not doing the same! Why I didn't, I still don't know.

Subject 222 wrote:

What appalled me was that I could possess this capacity for obedience and compliance to a central idea ie . . . the value of the memory experiment, even after it became clear . . . it was at the expense of another value . . . ie don't hurt someone else who is helpless and not hurting you. . . . I hope I can deal more effectively with any future conflicts of values I encounter.

Subject 1814 confessed: "I learned not to trust anyone, even a person whom you believe would not fool you."

Meanwhile, Subject 507 boasted: "I can think and act according to the dictates of my own conscience."[34]

Milgram may have regarded such self-insight as valuable, but just how subjects were able to integrate such unwelcome and disturbing insights about themselves is not explained.

The night after I met Bill and Barbara, I listened to the interview I had recorded with Bill earlier that day. There was a long pause on the tape that I hadn't noticed at the time, after I had asked him what he'd said to those students of his girlfriend's back in the 1980s. After the initial shock of being treated like a Nazi, Bill told the silent, judging students: "It's very easy to sit back and say, 'I'd never do this or that' or 'Nobody could ever get me to do anything like that.' Well, guess what? Yes, they can."

I was starting to believe that Bill was right.

3

THE LIMITS OF DEBRIEFING

Herb Winer, one of Milgram's subjects, had e-mailed me before I left for New Haven and offered to come to Australia for his interview, if I could arrange for it. I already liked his sense of humor.

He didn't live far from the house in New Haven where I was staying, and I set out at 8 A.M. to walk the few blocks to his condominium, part of a luxury development on a hill shaded with the seemingly ubiquitous oak trees. But I had underestimated the humidity: the morning air was thick and soupy, and my brisk walk slowed. By the time I got there, I was late and he was looking out for me, standing on a wooden walkway that led to his front door. I was used to the days starting cooler and getting warmer as they wore on, but Herb told me, as I dabbed my face with a paper napkin I had found in the bottom of my bag, that in summer the humidity was worse in the mornings. This explained the empty streets.

Inside the split-level condo the rooms were cool and airy, everything white or beige: beige carpet, beige walls—even Herb's remaining hair blended well with his cream-colored sweater. We sat in the dining room, beside the open-plan kitchen where Hannah, Herb's wife, was discussing the dishwasher with a handyman. Herb had a pile of folders and a stack of books on the table at his elbow, all about Milgram and his research. Among them was his "most prized and precious possession," an inscribed hardcover copy of Milgram's book *Obedience to Authority*. On the flyleaf, Milgram had written: *To Herb Winer, with my thanks for your participation and interest in this project, Stanley*

Milgram. Herb is a self-taught expert on the Milgram experiments and is a fervent admirer of Stanley Milgram, although he will never forgive Milgram for what he put him through.

I was annoyed with myself for being late because Herb's most recent interview experience had not been a happy one. He didn't come off well—in her account of Herb's part in the experiment, the writer implied that he had been more concerned about his own welfare than the learner's, and Herb was still angry about it.

Leaning toward the microphone and speaking with his fruity, made-for-radio voice, the same in which he records books for the dyslexic and the blind, Herb began his story.

Back in the summer of 1961, he told me, he was a forty-year-old assistant professor of lumbering at Yale's school of forestry. "I saw the ad in the *New Haven Register*, which I read every day, and it was soliciting volunteers in an experiment." He paused for effect, then announced, "On memory and learning." He answered the ad in the paper, he said, because "four dollars fifty was not a negligible honorarium at that time."

Herb should never have been accepted as a volunteer—Milgram had instructed his assistant Alan Elms to exclude college students and Yale staff, but Herb was one of a handful that slipped through the cracks. It would end up giving him an advantage that few other subjects had.

It was October 1961 when Herb arrived for his appointment in the basement of Linsly-Chittenden Hall. We know the rest: Williams greeted him and soon a second man arrived—an ordinary-looking fellow who appeared to have come from an office job—and the experiment began.

Herb was in one of the conditions that featured the learner's complaint about a problem with his heart. Just after the learner was strapped into his chair, he mentioned that he'd had treatment for a heart condition and asked if he should be worried about the shocks. Williams gave his scripted, dismissive reply that while the shocks might be painful they weren't dangerous.

When Williams showed Herb how the machine worked, giving him a sample shock of 45 volts ("an unpleasant sensation," he said), Herb realized for the first time that he would be giving shocks to the learner. "As a younger man, I had done a little electrical work, house wiring and that sort of thing, so I knew what a 120-volt shock felt like and it was very, very serious. So when I saw this 450 level and 'extremely dangerous,' I thought, indeed it is."

Yet when Herb described the machine to me, admiration crept into his voice. "It was an extraordinarily credible piece of fakery. It was made in Waltham, Massachusetts, and Waltham was renowned for its scientific instrument manufacturers. There was a gentle click, as you would expect on a toggle switch, and the light went on above the toggle switch when you pressed it to indicate that indeed the voltage had been delivered at the designated level. That was just part of the setting that Stanley created. I guess he might have had some help, but the blinding imagination that he showed in some of his other, later experiments seemed to be reflected from the very start."

It disconcerted me, this switch that Herb made from subject to fellow academic, from emotional to clinical. It was not clear to me how or why he had made this adjustment. I didn't know how he could move so easily from one emotion to another, almost as if he were flicking a switch within his own mind. The memory test began, and "it became quite obvious that he was a very dim-witted learner." Herb realized that it was going to involve giving more than just one or two shocks.

Every time the learner got an answer right, Herb felt a wave of relief. But then he'd get one wrong, and then another. The voltage started to rise very rapidly. After the fourth or fifth shock, to his dismay Herb heard the learner cry out in pain. He told Williams that he didn't want to hurt the man, but Williams urged him to continue. "The experimenter standing above me was instructing me very seriously that I had to go on."

As the wrong answers multiplied and the voltages increased, the learner's protests became louder. "I could hear him, his cries of pain and requests—'stop this,' 'cut it out,' 'this hurts,' and similar expressions."

Herb was feeling increasingly agitated, but each time he protested that the learner was getting hurt, Williams responded with "You must continue" or "The experiment requires that you continue" or "You have no choice." "The pressure was unbelievably intense. The thing that bothered me the most was that I could feel my heart rate increasing, and I was under very severe stress, and I finally realized that my stress, however it might bother me, could hardly compare with the pain and stress I was inflicting on the learner. I finally screwed my courage to the sticking place and quit. I said, 'That's it, I can't continue.'"

Herb said that it might have been the learner's cries to stop that finally forced him to dig in his heels and refuse to go on, but he doesn't remember. In fact, he doesn't remember at exactly what voltage he stopped. "I blocked that out of my memory. I'd like to think it wasn't much over 120 or so." He's certain he stopped before the maximum voltage because "if I'd ever have gone all the way to 450 volts, we wouldn't be talking now. I would keep this a secret. I wouldn't want to talk about it."

It was a point that Herb would return to each time I met him: that he didn't remember the voltage at which he stopped. It is something we won't know until all the subject files, including his, are made public in 2039. He worried at it, like a stone in a shoe. I wondered if perhaps he didn't want to remember.

What he did remember vividly was how wound up he felt afterward. Any soothing words or explanations of the experiment were ineffectual; they did nothing to alleviate his mounting outrage. "I took the four dollars and fifty cents—I had no compunction about that—then I went back to my office in Sage Hall, about half a mile away, on Prospect Street, and I looked him up in the faculty phone directory. I was ready to call Yale's president if Milgram hadn't been in the phone directory. I then phoned assistant professor Stanley Milgram—I felt that I had no reason to grovel before him because I was an assistant professor and he had no rank above me—and I told him that I wanted to see him at his earliest convenience because I'd just been a participant in his so-called memory study and I was very angry and concerned about it."

Herb was still "boiling with anger" when he confronted Milgram in his office two days later. "I said, 'Whatever your motives or incentives, you had absolutely no business subjecting a medically unscreened person to that sort of stress.' I think he was hit. I asked him, 'Haven't some of your other subjects come in to complain?' And he felt that my reaction was extreme, and I wasn't put off or ashamed of that. I think I made my complaints known because it was easy—I was in a good position. Someone who had come in from a job at Winchester or A.C. Goldberg or some factory position may well have felt intimidated by this high-level Yale academic.

"He was very receptive to my concerns and we had lunch together, and over the course of the next few months I sort of realized that from a purely research standpoint . . . he had made a landmark contribution." Surprisingly, the two men ended up developing a friendship of sorts.

By the time Milgram left New Haven for Harvard eighteen months later, Herb had become a fervent admirer, albeit one with mixed feelings. "The last thing I told him when he was leaving was that I still resented the way he had acquired the insider knowledge he did, but I was very grateful that we had it. I followed Stanley's career with great interest." Herb gestured at his books and papers. "He just had the imagination and inventiveness, to me, of a true genius. I came to appreciate Stanley's principal conclusion that we behave as we do largely as a result of the situation we're in. You don't have to be a psychopath to follow orders."

Herb's friendship with and admiration for Milgram would play a far greater role than he would ever know. He did not realize that Milgram, after being attacked by colleagues for what they saw as his cruel treatment of his subjects, would console himself privately with thoughts of the friendships he'd developed with subjects like Herb. In fact, the support and enthusiasm of some subjects would later help Milgram face his critics and their accusations of cruelty.[1] Milgram would enlist Herb's support in the publicity about his book when it was published in 1974—what better ambassador for his research than one of his own subjects? By then, Herb had left Yale and was working as director of research at a pulp mill in Quebec. In a newspaper clipping about Milgram's book, Herb is quoted as saying, "I stopped as soon as I could. I know I didn't go up to 450 volts, I think I repressed the knowledge of what I did immediately. I would have liked to have stopped before." Underneath a picture of a dapper, dark-haired, and much younger Herb, the caption reads, "Dr. Herbert Winer: still in sympathy with Milgram's purposes."[2]

We ended the meeting, but it had left me unsettled. In the same way that Herb moved between anger and admiration for Milgram, I was moving between certainty and confusion about Herb. His sudden emotional shifts lost me: why had he been so angry in the first place, and how, given that he was still enraged, did he have room for such admiration?

Later, I came to understand that I was confused because Herb's perspective surprised me. If I was honest about it, I had gone along to meet Herb, as I had with Bill, without really expecting to learn anything new. I had thought that he would tell me a story of how proud he was to have been defiant—how it affirmed something for him and allowed him to come out of the experiment with an improved sense of moral certainty and increased self-esteem. I had thought that Herb would be typical of the majority of subjects, who, Milgram wrote, had learned something valuable from the experience and were glad to have taken part. I had not expected Herb's ambivalence and anger. It made me realize that I had accepted Milgram's classification of people as either obedient or defiant, as if you could make absolute statements about them depending on where they stopped on the shock machine. Bill Menold showed me that some subjects saw the result as a reflection of their character, but even though Herb believed he had stopped before he reached 450 volts, he had actively blocked the memory of how far he did go because in his own eyes he was still obedient—it was just a matter of degree. It didn't matter where he stopped; he felt bad about even having begun.

As Herb's familiar but strange story had unfolded, I found myself faced with so many questions that I didn't know where to begin.

The next time we met, it was so that Herb could show me around Yale before we went downtown to lunch. We met in the library and walked around the campus, Herb keeping a running commentary as we walked.

We stopped at the women's table, a huge, flat piece of granite designed by Maya Lin, a Yale graduate who had designed the Vietnam Veterans Memorial in Washington, D.C. The surface was covered by a thin layer of water, underneath which was engraved, in the shape of a widening spiral, the number of women who had attended Yale each year between its founding and 1993. I trailed my fingers in the water, which bubbled up from the center and spilled over the sides. Then I ran my fingers over the figures carved into the granite, unsure if the table was a celebration or a lament. Herb was telling me how much the place had changed since he first arrived.

I took a picture of him outside Linsly-Chittenden Hall. He grinned at the camera, the white of his short-sleeved shirt seeming to glow against the stone walls and barred basement windows. We peered in through the panes of the double doors before Herb pushed them open. The building now housed the English department but was deserted. We went downstairs and into the basement, which had been converted into staff offices, with a pew-like seat in the lobby where students could wait. It looked like any other university building. I was surprised when Herb told me in an indignant voice that there was nothing in the basement and nothing on the building, no plaque or reminder that what had been dubbed the most famous experiments in social psychology had taken place here.

After we finished our tour, we had lunch on York Street. Talking about the experiment still raised Herb's blood pressure, he said, because the recollection was still there. Yet, without missing a beat, he added that he could see "the extraordinary value of the results of Milgram's work" and felt "delighted and honored to have been a participant and not ashamed of being a disobedient subject." Here it was again: he moved in and out of focus, one moment the outraged subject, the next the admiring colleague. But this time I could tell that, behind his banter and professed admiration for Milgram, Herb's anger simmered. His next statement confirmed it: "If you asked me how I felt about having participated, my answer would be I was both very angry and very glad. The two aren't incompatible."

Our meals arrived. I said that I had found a paper of his in the archive since I had last seen him. He stopped chewing, looking stricken. A letter, I said, to Milgram, talking about the latest report and inviting him to lunch. I was conscious of talking quickly, of wanting him to relax. Only later did I realize that he thought I had found details revealing how far he went on the shock machine.

Leaving the restaurant, we made our way along the footpath, dodging the paraphernalia of roadwork. Herb narrowly missed tripping over a piece of metal lying on the footpath. He kicked it into the gutter and then rushed forward, toward a road worker in a luminous green vest and hard hat. "I'll sue you! I could sue you." He waved his arms at the worker, who simply bent down and picked up the metal, throwing it onto a pile nearby. For a moment, before he turned back to me and grinned, I hadn't been sure that Herb was joking.

We parted, and I went back to the campus to sit on a park bench in the shade on one of Yale's lawns. The sun glinted off the windows opposite, and I felt the beginnings of a headache. The bells in Harkness Tower started up (trainee carillonneurs practice in summer), and a discordant jangling I couldn't recognize lurched and stuttered into the air. It seemed a suitable accompaniment, given my state of mind. Just how well did I know what had happened in the experiments? And why was Herb so angry after his had ended? Surely once it was explained to him that he'd been duped, it all made sense; and given that he'd defied the experimenter, there didn't seem to be anything for him to feel angry about.

And most confusing of all: why had he made an appointment to see Milgram to talk about his experience—hadn't he had the chance to do that in the lab, after he'd refused to go on?

As it turned out, I was to visit Herb five or six times in the ensuing four years, using material from the archives to make sense of the story he told me. I reread the interviews he had given, published in 2000 and 2004, and it became obvious that he forgot more with time. I read things he'd said in print that he could no longer recall. Each time we met another detail had disappeared, like a wisp of smoke. Herb was aware of it: he told me that he forgot "more and more with the passage of time," but what he never forgot were his feelings during and immediately after the experiment. On one occasion, he told me that the emotional experience was imprinted upon his memory and would be "among the last things I will ever forget."

In piecing together Herb's story, I also discovered a story about Milgram and his subjects. While Herb was unusual in some ways— he was a Yale professor, for a start—he was typical in terms of how he was treated in the experiment and in what he was told. I found out that Herb was angry because, when he left the lab, he hadn't been told that the experiment was a hoax. He left believing he'd shocked a man with a bad heart and had possibly put his life at risk.

Milgram didn't tell most of his subjects at the end of the experiment that it was a setup: that the machine was a fake and the learner was an actor. When I went back to his early writings, I found that he never claimed to have told his participants the truth. In other words, it was quite usual for subjects like Herb to leave the lab without knowing that the whole thing was an illusion.

But why was this such a surprise to me—how had I gotten it so wrong? I went back to Milgram's first published paper and discovered the source of my confusion: Milgram used the heading "Interview and Dehoax," under which he described what occurred at the end of the experiment. The word "dehoax" implies truth telling. While I had assumed that Milgram had fully debriefed subjects, in fact his "dehoax" involved substituting one untruth for another.

In his first article, he wrote: "After the interview procedures were undertaken to assure that the subject would leave the laboratory in a state of well being. A friendly reconciliation was arranged between the subject and the victim, and an effort was made to reduce any tensions that arose as a result of the experiment."[3]

In his second paper, published a year later—by now two years after the experiments had ended—he reinforced this impression. Addressing accusations that his debriefing would have been ineffective in preventing psychological harm to his subjects, Milgram wrote:

> A most important aspect of the procedure occurred at the end of the experimental session. A careful post-experimental treatment was administered to all subjects. The exact content of the dehoax varied from condition to condition and with increasing experience on our part. At the very least all subjects were told that the victim had not received dangerous electric shocks.

He repeated that a "friendly reconciliation" with the learner took place, and that he tried to restore subjects' self-esteem before they left the lab. Then he added: "The experiment was explained [to disobedient subjects] in such a way that supported their decision to disobey the experimenter. Obedient subjects were assured of the fact that their behavior was entirely normal and that their feelings of conflict or tension were shared by other participants."[4]

Milgram's published statements repeatedly insisted that he offered "a careful post-experimental treatment," and his increasing use of the word "dehoax" in this context gave the impression that when the experiment was over—when the subject had either refused to continue or gone to the maximum voltage—all had been revealed.

How did Milgram think that not telling his subjects the truth could help them?

In order to find out, I went to meet Alan Elms, who had been a graduate student in need of a summer job when Milgram hired him in July 1961.

Alan Elms is an emeritus professor at the University of California at Davis. Since his stint as Milgram's research assistant, and particularly since Milgram's death in 1984, Alan has become the spokesperson for the obedience experiments.

Alan had done his undergraduate work at Penn State and conducted lab research with rats, then field research with monkeys. "By the time I got to Yale, I had worked my way up to human beings," he told me with a grin. He thought the job sounded interesting, but "I didn't realize just how interesting it would turn out to be." The lanky student from Kentucky paired up with Milgram, and they began working together on July 5, 1961.

From the outset, Alan and Milgram hit it off. "I found him very likable. He had a good sense of humor—he was very witty, very considerate toward me. He certainly annoyed some people; he was rather brash in his approach to people and not deferential, even though he was only twenty-seven years old. He was quite aware of his own intelligence and didn't try to hide that."

Alan admired not only Milgram's chutzpah but also his organizational skills. Milgram, he said, was one of the most organized researchers he'd ever worked with. By the time Alan joined him, Milgram had started the obedience notebook, keeping a detailed record of daily events, decisions, and preparations for the experiment.

Milgram and Alan talked through the different permutations of the experiment. Alan remembered that Milgram talked about a variation using husbands and wives, but they decided after discussion that it was ethically problematic. In Milgram's papers, there are notes on other variations that Milgram considered and discarded. These included the "real victim" condition, in which a subject was used as the learner and received real shocks; "obedience and anxiety," in which subjects were tranquilized; and "obedience and shame," in which the male subject would be told, if he hesitated about giving shocks, that only men with "feminine tendencies" balked at going to the maximum voltage.[5] Milgram also toyed with the idea of one variation called "obedience and propaganda," to test how people could be incited to torture by propaganda. In this variation, he would tell the teacher that the learner was paid $35, had called the teacher a "fairy," and had been in court many times—and that, even though never convicted, there was no doubt that he'd beaten and robbed an old man at a newspaper kiosk and boasted about how he got away with it.[6]

Alan worked with Milgram on the first three of the twenty-four conditions, beginning in the summer of 1961. The two watched proceedings from behind the one-way mirror, initially taking bets on which people would go to the maximum voltage, but neither of them proved very good at predicting. Besides, they were each looking for different things—Alan was looking for those personality characteristics that would distinguish obedient from defiant subjects, while Milgram was interested in the opposite: "He was interested in situational variables, such as how physically close the victim was to the teacher."

Alan said that he and Milgram were both "astonished" by the number of people who obeyed the experimenter's instructions. But surely, I asked, it couldn't have been that big a surprise to Milgram—wasn't this what he'd been aiming for all along? Alan acknowledged that the number of people going to the maximum voltage, and their emotional distress in doing so, couldn't have been completely unexpected.

After all, Milgram had seen people's reactions in both the pilot studies and the trial runs. "Stanley got a pretty good feel for how some people were going to respond, that some people would get really upset, and he built into the situation ways of dealing with their emotional reactions."

I thought about the issues with dehoaxing that had been troubling me. With his passion for matching words with meaning, Alan was the right person to ask about what Milgram meant when he used the word "dehoax." He was fascinated with words. His house was crowded with books: on shelves, in stacks on tables, in piles on his study floor. In one small bookcase in his dining room, he had eighteen different dictionaries. Another was propped open on a lectern, open at a page in the Ds—I caught sight of "downsizing" as I entered the room. When we met, he had recently finished a detailed study of how the changes that Elvis Presley made to the lyrics of "Are You Lonesome Tonight" were not the results of drug abuse or memory loss but kinds of Freudian slips in which Elvis inadvertently revealed his changing feelings about the women in his life. If you listened closely to all twelve recorded versions, Alan argued, you could hear Elvis substituting lyrics to reveal an almost oedipal relationship with his mother and an increasingly ambivalent relationship with Priscilla.[7]

I asked Alan: when he and Milgram used the word "debriefing" to describe what they told subjects back in 1961, what exactly did they mean? What did they tell people, and why? He told me, "There were two levels of debrief. One was having a procedure of asking how they felt or thought about what they'd been through. Two was where efforts were made to reduce the stress that person has just been undergoing, telling them it's not as bad as it looked, that the experimenter understands that person had good reason for behaving in the way they did. For example—and the experimenter would give this example— sometimes it's necessary to hurt someone else for their own good, or for the good of science.

"Whether the subject went all the way to the maximum voltage or whether he broke off, the teacher was quickly told at the end of his participation that things were not nearly as bad as he might have thought they were. The learner would come in from the room next door and apologize for having been so noisy, saying that the shocks hadn't been painful—he'd just been getting overexcited or something like that. The experimenter then explained to the teacher that the shock generator had been developed for use with rats and some other small animals." The goal, Alan explained, was to bring down people's levels of distress.

I asked him whether the subjects were told that the shocks weren't real. Alan scratched his mustache and responded, "For most people who took part, the immediate debrief did not tell them there were no shocks."

Alan told me that he thought they were sent a written explanation "a few weeks later." But he had finished working for Milgram by then. I later found out that it was almost a year before the people Alan and Milgram had watched together received an explanation. Alan went on to say, "I still think that Milgram did a good job of protecting the subjects, and that the experiments were important enough that some temporary discomfort and emotional distress justified the overall value. I observed Stanley's concern during the debriefing sessions, making sure no one left the lab still feeling really upset. And with his follow-up explanations, and my interviews with subjects, I felt that Stanley had really paid more attention to these ethical issues than most psychologists up to that time."

But I wasn't really listening to Alan's explanation—I was reeling from what I had heard. The subjects had left the lab still believing they had shocked a man. Did Milgram really think that reassuring them that things hadn't been as serious as they thought, that the shocks were only weak, that the learner had been overreacting would absolve them of their distress? I thought about Bill Menold, who had left the lab with the new and unwelcome knowledge that he'd been talked into torturing a man.

I considered this all the way back to San Francisco. The train passed right along the edge of the bay. The tide was out, revealing what I thought at first were huge lobster pots, but turned out to be abandoned shopping carts, upended, gray with mud. Nothing was as it seemed. The debriefing that I had always regarded as a kind of catharsis, a coming to terms, had turned out to be just another fiction.

* * *

By offering subjects another cover story at the end of the experiment to make them feel better about what they had done, Milgram was still, technically speaking, complying with the then current professional guidelines for debriefing. At the time of his research, the definition of debriefing as expressed in the APA's 1953 *Ethical Standards of Psychologists* was "the reduction of distress." The guidelines made no reference to telling subjects the true purpose of the experiment or interviewing them for their reactions.[8]

Milgram had anticipated the ethical objections that might be raised and addressed the issue of debriefing in his original application to the NSF:

> A final but important note must be added concerning the investigator's responsibility to persons who serve in the experiment. There is no question that the subject is placed in a difficult predicament and that strong feelings are aroused.
>
> Under these circumstances it is highly important that measures be taken to insure the subject's wellbeing before he is discharged from the laboratory. Every effort will be made to set the subject at ease and to assure him of the adequacy of his performance.[9]

The NSF, however, continued to be concerned about the effect of the experiment on those whom Milgram had recruited as subjects. On July 5, 1961, Milgram rang the NSF to see why the letter confirming his grant had not yet arrived. To his dismay, he was told by a Mrs. Rubinstein that approval had hit a snag: the NSF's director was still undecided about "possible reactions from persons who had been subjects in the experiments and whether the NSF should support research of this sort."[10]

It was the first of many signs of the uneasiness that his research would cause, and thereafter Milgram repeatedly mentioned his debriefing procedures and their effectiveness in alleviating subjects' stress in his dealings with the NSF.[11] But Milgram's intention was to make reassuring, soothing noises to his subjects without revealing the truth, probably because he didn't want word to spread in the New Haven community about the real purpose of his research.

Now I understood why Bill Menold had gone straight to his electrician neighbor for reassurance. I spoke to Bill again, this time asking when it was that he found out that the experiment was a setup. It's something that still makes him angry. "One of the things that really disturbed me is what they've told people—they said it was about six months later that they explained what happened. In my recollection it was a lot longer than six months . . . and then I get this letter, this form letter!" He clenched his fists. "I don't have much regard for Milgram . . . because I think that was terribly unethical—and I'm not just saying that because I did all this stuff. I think it's immoral to use people. They might say, 'Well, it's for the greater good,' but that doesn't make it right!"

The report that Milgram sent out to subjects in July 1962—eleven months after the experiments began—was the first time they were told the full story.[12] The comments that Milgram's participants wrote in their questionnaires show that, far from being a systematic and detailed process, debriefing varied across time, and in most cases was not a debriefing in the sense that I had understood it at all. Subjects in conditions 1 to 18—around six hundred people—left the lab believing they had shocked a man.

After people received Milgram's report and questionnaire, many wrote back describing how they had left the lab mystified, trying to work out afterward what had actually gone on by talking to wives, neighbors, and workmates. Some worked it out for themselves, either immediately or in the months that followed. Subject 629 wrote: "As I left the laboratory and walked to my car, I reflected [on] the situation and felt certain at that time I was the one who had been observed. On the few occasions I've thought about the experiment I've wondered about its purpose, and appreciate knowing your true motive now."

And Subject 805 noted, "About a week after the test, while discussing it with friends, it dawned on me that I was probably the one who was being tested, although I didn't suspect that the 'student' was an actor."

Many expressed their relief at receiving the report and described how worried they'd been about the learner. Subject 716 recorded, "I actually checked the death notices in the *New Haven Register* for at least two weeks after the experiment to see if I had been involved and a contributing factor in the death of the so-called learner—I was very relieved that his name did not appear in such a column."

Subject 1817 wrote:

> I've been waiting very anxiously for this report to really put my mind at ease and [have my] curiosity satisfied. Many times I wanted to look up a Mr. Wallace, who was my student. I was just that curious to know what had happened. Believe me, when no response came from Mr. Wallace with the stronger voltage I really believed the man was probably dead.

Subject 711 confessed, "The experiment left such an effect on me that I spent the night in a cold sweat and nightmares because of the fear that I might have killed that man in the chair . . ."

Herb was right to worry about screening people before they took part in the experiment. And he wasn't the only one who made the point to Milgram. Subject 216, who described the experiment as "the most unpleasant night of my life," wrote on his questionnaire, "I would here inject a word of caution—since taking part in the experiment I have suffered a mild heart attack—the one thing my doctor tells me is that I must avoid any form of tension. For this reason I feel that it is imperative that you make certain that any prospective participants have a clean bill of health."

Other subjects criticized Milgram for sending them home without telling them the truth. Subject 829 stated, "I was pretty well shook up for a few days after the experiment. It would have helped if I had been told the facts shortly after."

Subject 623 stated, "I seriously question the wisdom and ethics of not dehoaxing each subject immediately after the session. . . . Allowing subjects to remain deceived is not justified, in my opinion, even if such continued deception was thought necessary 'to avoid contamination.'"[13]

But if they had been told at the end of the experiment that the learner was fine and the voltage wasn't as strong as they had thought, why were so many subjects still worried that they had hurt or injured him?

In February 1963, nine months after the experiments had ended, Milgram arranged (at Yale's insistence) a series of follow-up group interviews to be conducted by psychiatrist Dr. Paul Errera. One hundred and thirty of Milgram's subjects were invited back to Yale to take part in the sessions in order to establish whether any had been harmed by their participation in the experiments. From the transcripts of Errera's interviews, it's clear that some subjects didn't get even the standard, rather flawed "dehoax" that Milgram had scripted. For some subjects, there had been no reassurance at all and no explanation that the learner was unharmed before they left the lab. Milgram might have been surprised to learn this because, as far as he knew, the standard explanation had been offered to all subjects—if not by him, then by his staff. But in one of Errera's interviews, Subject 501, who had been in one of the heart-attack variations and had brought his wife along to the interview for support, explained how distressed he was after the experiment. Milgram came out from behind the one-way mirror to quiz him, and during their conversation it dawned on Milgram that the minimal "learner is alright" dehoax had not happened. Subject 501 described how, after going to the maximum voltage, he was shaking so much he didn't think he'd be able to drive home. His wife was waiting for him outside, in the passenger seat of their car. She told the group: "He was shivering. I was parked out in front—it wasn't cold—and I thought, What in the world are they doing in there? And he came out and I said, 'Well, what was it like?' I said, 'You want me to drive, was it that bad?' So he proceeded to tell me. . . . Then we, we, we got through New Haven somehow and then we got out to the turnpike and he was [going over] it until midnight that night. On and on and on."

Milgram: Now, there was supposed to be a dehoax after the experiment in which you met the guy *[the learner]*. Now Mr. *[blank]*, did you meet the man after the experiment?

Subject 501: Oh yes, I recall he stomped out saying something about that the teacher had the best part of it, or something like that.

Milgram: But it wasn't supposed to work that way at all. Did the experimenter tell you that the shocks were not painful afterward?

Subject 501: No. I certainly expected him to, but—

Later in the same interview, Subject 501 quizzed Milgram about the dehoax.

Subject 501: You say you're supposed to dehoax the whole thing?

Milgram: Everyone was supposed to be told that the shocks weren't painful and they were supposed to shake hands with the man who had been shocked. Did that happen in your case?

Subject 501: Well, no, he came out and he was—he meant business or something like that—

Subject 612: He still was indignant about it.

Milgram must have been disturbed at Subject 501's description. He seemed shocked to find that some subjects were not even given the basic dehoax. After Subject 612 and Dr. Errera left, Milgram stayed on in the room with Subject 501 and his wife, talking through how the man felt, with Milgram trying to persuade him that he shouldn't feel guilty or upset about his obedience.[14] And on a number of occasions during the remaining Errera interviews, he questioned subjects about the debriefing they were given.

How had this lack of debriefing occurred? At the time he wrote his first article, about the first condition, Milgram's description of the debriefing process (although misleadingly labeled "dehoax") was an accurate account of what occurred in conditions 1 to 4. I heard Milgram on the tapes of condition 3, telling subjects that the learner had been overreacting and the machine was only for administering shocks to small animals.[15] Alan had described Milgram's "careful debriefing" as he had observed it in the early stage of the experiments. He and Milgram watched conditions 1 to 3, and Milgram had gone out from behind the mirror to handle the debriefing himself if he felt that a subject was particularly upset.[16]

But while the first four conditions ran through the summer break of 1961, subsequent variations coincided with the academic year. Milgram would have been less available to supervise the experiments, and Alan had left his job as research assistant. Milgram admitted to one subject in the group interviews that he was present at only about "a third" of the experiments.[17]

Alan agreed that Milgram didn't go far enough in his debriefing. But, if anything, Alan felt that Milgram, in his desire to make his subjects feel better, let them off the hook. He felt that more of them should have been troubled by their behavior.

It was Saturday and this was my second visit to Davis, and this time we'd gone to his university office to talk. The building was deserted except for the sound of a custodian rattling a bucket at the end of the corridor. The office was small and cramped—he shared it with two others—and it felt stuffy.

Alan conducted interviews with forty of Milgram's subjects in 1961 as part of a study of personality and obedience and was frustrated to find how few had learned anything useful from the experience. "I remember one man who had been fully obedient told me that he would never even harm a squirrel, that he always braked for wild animals. Okay, so he's a good person in that sense, but he has gone through this whole shock board, administering what he thought were dangerous shocks to a human being, but he doesn't seem to make the connection. I felt that maybe Stanley was giving these people too much justification for their own behavior."

Alan told me that he thought Milgram gave his subjects too easy an excuse when he reassured them—whatever voltage they had gone to—that their behavior was normal. It was understandable, Alan said, that Milgram wanted to make them feel better, to make sure that no one suffered from taking part, and to help them accept what had happened, but Alan felt that Milgram missed an opportunity to educate them about how to be better people. "I felt maybe it would be good for some participants to have some lingering feeling that maybe they had done something wrong by shocking people, and I think in some ethical sense it might have been good to set this up as some sort of ethical educational occasion for these people."

When we finished the interview, it was a relief to get out into the fresh air. Outside the psychology building, we stopped a passing student, who agreed to take our photo. As we stood on the steps, Alan told me that one reason he got out of social psychology was because he "didn't like having to mislead people in order to do an experiment." I liked him for that. Alan put one hand against the small of my back, and in the other he proudly held a copy of Milgram's book *Obedience to Authority* against his chest. *Click.*

Now I understood Herb's anger. He was one of the subjects in the "heart attack" variation, condition 5 or 6, so his appointment for the experiment was in October 1961, when Milgram would have been busy with the demands of a new academic year. He didn't meet Milgram in the lab but in his office a few days later, which suggests that Milgram was not observing the experiment in which Herb took part. Was Herb told that the learner was okay and that the machine wasn't as dangerous as it looked? Whatever he was told didn't reduce his anxiety. And he had left the lab still thinking that the man he'd shocked had a heart condition.

In the archives, a letter from Herb to Milgram dated March 16, 1962, indicates that Milgram sent Herb a copy of the most recent report on the research that he'd sent to the NSF.[18] When Herb confronted Milgram, it's likely that Milgram confided the real purpose of the experiment and swore him to secrecy, as he did with at least one other subject.[19] Perhaps it was this, being taken into Milgram's confidence, that won Herb over.

It was only subjects in the last two months of the research program who were told the truth about the experiment before they left the lab. Comments from subject questionnaires show that subjects in conditions 20, 23, and 24, conducted in March, April, and May 1962, were fully debriefed.[20] But even then, the debriefing didn't exactly offer an opportunity for subjects to vent their feelings. It was most often the experimenter, John Williams, who was left to reassure subjects about what had happened, even though he had no training for this role.

The following exchange was typical of the debriefing that took place in the final month of the research program. It took just a minute and a half. The subject was a forty-seven-year-old product inspector at the manufacturer Remington Rand, who broke off the experiment at 150 volts when the learner demanded to be set free.

Williams: Let me tell you this, Mr. Wallace was not really being shocked. In fact, his name is McDonough and he's a member of our team here. We are actually observing how people obey orders.

Subject 2316: Hmmm.

Williams: Actually, the research here is very important and we feel the results will be very interesting and so we had to set it up this way to make you think you were shocking someone and taking orders.

[Subject 2316 laughs]

Williams: It's very similar to a situation a guy finds himself in the army a lot of times. So we're not trying—[calls out] Jim, why don't you come in and say hello to Mr. [blank] now that he's in better spirits. Ah, we don't like to fool people, but we have to set it up this way.

McDonough: Hi.

Subject 2316: I thought I was really hurting you.

McDonough: Feel better now, don't you?

Subject 2316: Oh, sure.

Williams: You're going to get a report on the project in a little over two months. We've been running it now for about a year and we've done over eight hundred men, and I think you'll find the report very interesting when you do get it.

Subject 2316: Hmm.

Williams: I think you'll be very happy you participated. I'd like to ask you not to speak about it to anyone—other than your wife, of course—because you may unknowingly speak to someone who's going to be in the experiment.

Subject 2316: Oh, I see.

Williams: So if they know ahead of time then they won't be . . . it wouldn't be of any value. So until you get the report, don't say anything. . . . Of course, when you get the report, you can talk to as many people as you want.

Subject 2316: Uh-huh.

Williams: There is one more thing. Could you indicate on this scale how you felt about participating from very sorry, very glad, and so on?

Subject 2316: Now that I know the circumstances . . . *[laughs]*

Williams: Let me say one more thing. We're very appreciative of . . . appreciate you giving us your time, and it certainly was a pleasure having you here.

Subject 2316: Well, it was a pleasure being here.

Williams: Good. I think you'll enjoy the report when you get it. Thank you again for coming down tonight.

Subject 2316: Thank you for having me. *[To McDonough]* I'm sorry I didn't hurt you.

[General laughter]

Williams: *[into microphone]* That was subject 2316; 2317 next.[21]

Later in the same condition, a fuller debriefing took place, but it still took little more than a couple of minutes. Subject 2340 was a twenty-four-year-old tool-and-die maker who went to the maximum voltage.

Williams: Well, let me tell you this, this man wasn't really being shocked.

Subject 2340: Oh, I see.

Williams: We're very interested in your reactions to having to inflict pain on a person that you didn't even know.

Subject 2340: Uh-huh.

Williams: See, he actually works with us as a team member, and he wasn't really getting the shocks, you see.

Subject 2340: Oh, I see.

Williams: We're really interested in seeing your reactions. We're not trying to fool you in any way.

Subject 2340: Right.

Williams: We have to set it up this way so we can get true reactions from people. You really thought you were shocking this guy.

Subject 2340: Yes, I did. When I didn't hear anything I was worried.

Williams: What'd you think when you didn't hear anything else?

Subject 2340: I thought maybe he was just, uh, maybe he passed out or something.

Williams: Yeah.

Subject 2340: Then I—

Williams: You think he passed out?

Subject 2340: I didn't think he did. I had a thought in my mind that he could have passed out and I was worried about him.

Williams: Well, you understand why we had to do it this way. See, it's a very similar situation a nurse finds herself in when she has to administer a needle to a patient—she may be reluctant to do this, she may not want to hurt a patient, but the doctor tells her to so she goes ahead and does it. So this is a similar situation, you have to inflict a little pain on the other person—

Subject 2340: I didn't like it.

Williams: What?

Subject 2340: I didn't like it.

Williams: You didn't like it? Well, many people don't. Anyway, you'll receive a report of this project when it's over in a couple of months. Until that time we'd like to ask you not to say anything about it.

Subject 2340: Okay.

Williams: Until you get the report.

Subject 2340: Sure.

Williams: Then it will be all over and you can talk to people about it because you may talk to people who may be in it.

Subject 2340: Yeah, uh-huh.

Williams: And it wouldn't be good if they knew ahead of time.

Subject 2340: I see.

Williams: So of course I think you'll enjoy the report, I think you'll understand what everything's about . . . Jim, you want to come in and say hello to Mr. *[blank]* before he leaves. This is Mr. McDonough.

Subject 2340: Hi, glad to know you.

McDonough: Now it's all over, huh. Now you don't feel so bad, huh?

Williams: I hope you don't feel too bad. Let me thank you for coming down. We certainly do appreciate you giving us your time.

Subject 2340: Well, I'll go out now and have about three cigarettes.

Williams: We certainly do appreciate you coming down. I think that you'll find the report very interesting.

Subject 2340: I don't know much about it, to tell you the truth.

Williams: We do research, our current research, we do research of all types . . .

[Voices fading][22]

Both of these subjects were in condition 23. Once again, they were not told the whole truth, and what they were told they were instructed to keep secret. What's both typical and striking about these excerpts is that for Williams, who had by that point conducted over 750 of these experiments, the experiment itself was purely routine. He delivered the debriefing as a monologue, in much the same brisk and authoritative way that he conducted the rest of the experiment, and did not invite questions or discussion. On the tapes of the experiments in condition 23, one of the few conditions in which subjects were told that they had been tricked, the pattern of debriefing across all subjects, whether obedient or disobedient, was the same. They didn't get much more than a minute and a half and a handshake before they were shown the door.

And yet Milgram had learned his experimental techniques from Solomon Asch and had admired Asch's skills in debriefing.

In his private papers, Milgram wrote that, in watching Asch interviewing his subjects after the group pressure experiment was over, he was

> indeed impressed with the extreme care and sensititivity [sic] with which he questioned the subject and explained to him the purposes and implications of the experiment. There is no question that he leaned over backwards to make the subjects' participation an instructing and enriching personal experience and in my estimation he was highly successful in achieving his aim.[23]

Milgram's desire to keep his research secret to avoid jeopardizing the results allowed him to justify not telling his subjects the truth until much later. In private papers, Milgram admitted that his ambition outweighed his altruism. In August 1962, he wrote:

> It would be plesant [sic] to remark that these experiments were undertaken with a view toward their possible benift [sic] to humanity; that knowledge of social man, in this instance, was sought for its possible application to the betterment of social life. . . . Moreover, considered as a personal motive of the author the possible benefits that might redound to humanity withered to insignificance alongside the strident demands of intellectual curiosity. When an investigator keeps his eyes open throughout a scientific study, he learns things about himself as well as about his subjects, and the observations do not always flatter.[24]

Despite his admiration for the caring way in which Asch dealt with his subjects, Milgram acknowledged that he allowed his intellectual ruthlessness to get the upper hand.

* * *

It took thirty years for Bob Lee to realize he'd been had. And it still rankled.

Bob lived in East Haven, on a road overlooking Long Island Sound. In summer, it's bumper to bumper with expensive SUVs on their way to Long Island, but when I visited it was May, cool and windy. The water was gunmetal gray and the traffic light.

Bob presided over the lounge room from a large leather chair that rustled and groaned each time he moved. He was a big man; he looked like he could have been a boxer or a football player. At one time he was a barman, and I could imagine him easily tossing drunks out onto the street. He looked like someone you wouldn't have messed with in his younger days. He told me, "Somewhere, someone should have come to me in all these years and told me. I don't think that was right, what they did to me."

Perhaps Bob had simply ignored the report that explained the experiment when it arrived, six months after he'd taken part. Maybe he saw the crest or the letterhead and threw it, unopened, into the trash. Maybe it got lost in the mail. If he'd read it, he would have seen in the opening paragraph, "At the time you were in the experiment it was not possible for us to tell you everything about the study. Many questions probably remain in your mind which we would now like to clear up for you."[25]

In 1993, over thirty years after the experiments were over, Bob read about them in a local newspaper, the *Connecticut Post*. They ran a story about Yale's Sterling Library acquiring the rights to the Stanley Milgram archives. The story gave a brief overview of the obedience experiments, explaining that the "victim/learner" was unharmed and that the subjects were debriefed at the end of the experiment. It sounded to Bob like something he'd been involved in—only he'd never realized that his victim was an actor.

Bob's appointment for the experiments was on a Saturday morning, and the weather was perfect. Like many locals, Bob had never set foot inside Yale before, let alone one of its science labs. He had no idea what the experiment was going to be about, but the five dollars would come in handy: "In those days a beer was only twenty cents a glass, so for five dollars"—$4.50 plus transport fare—"I could have twenty beers and leave a dollar tip."

Before I arrived, he'd drawn a diagram for me, showing the setup of the rooms in the basement lab. He'd drawn a box with stick figures, lines dividing the lab from the smaller room with the man strapped in the chair. The drawing was simple, but the explanation was confusing. According to Bob, there were half a dozen people besides himself present. Seated in front of the shock machine were two others, one who read the word pairs into the microphone, the other who announced whether the answer was correct or incorrect. "It was my job to hit a button that would supposedly shock him and he'd go, 'Ow, oh wow,' and the more he gave the wrong answer the more I would hit the button. More than once I complained to these people, 'I can't do this,' and they said to me, 'Would you like to switch places?' Well, I didn't want that, either."

I realized as he was talking that Bob must have taken part in one of Milgram's lesser-known conditions. Here I was once again, on shaky ground, conscious suddenly of how much I didn't know about what went on in Milgram's lab.

I guessed that Bob had been a subject in condition 9, and the two "teachers" sitting with him were men whom Milgram had employed. In condition 9, Milgram wrote in the obedience notebook, "two stooges obey Experimenter and if naïve subject tries to stop, they mutter their disapproval of him."[26] So, in addition to an experimenter, Bob had two other supposed teachers pressuring him to continue.

He couldn't remember what voltage he went to or when he stopped, just that the "guy in the other room was really yelling—'You're hurting me, you're hurting me,' I don't know the exact words. He was a little bit milder than I would have been. You wouldn't want to put on any recording what I would have said. . . . And if I find these people, you don't want to record that, either."

By now, I no longer regarded outlandish stories about the experiment as an indication of poor memory. For all I knew, Bob might have been told that if he couldn't give the punishment then he should swap places with the victim. At this point in the experimental program, with so many subjects passing through the lab, so many staff to supervise, and so many experimental scenarios to keep track of, it wouldn't surprise me if Milgram's "teachers" improvised their lines to pressure people like Bob to continue along the shock board.

Bob cracked open a can of Heineken and took a sip. Whoever was in charge was "a son of a bitch," he said placidly, taking another sip.

It was eight months since I had first met Herb Winer, and by now I knew more about what Milgram's subjects had been through. Bob's jokes about suing Yale, the threats of what he'd do if he found the people involved in the experiment—he reminded me of Herb. A little rougher around the edges maybe, but the same combination of humor and bravado. And the same sense of anger, a steady flame fueled by humiliation that flared up every so often. Like when Bob thought about the learner, whom he couldn't see, but whose screams he could hear. "And he's in there laughing at me, and that's what it amounted to. They were all laughing at me."

Afterward, Bob left the lab and walked through New Haven Green to a bar he knew. "I sat down and had myself a few beers and felt a little bit better. Of course, I spent all my money. Five dollars—it was a lot of money."

I asked him if he talked to anyone in the bar about what had just happened. "The bar I was in, they wouldn't care anyway; they certainly weren't interested in some jerk sitting there talking about some fool experiment that they didn't have any idea what it was about, and, quite frankly, neither did I at that moment. It was something about inflicting punishment on someone else and if you could take it."

Before I left, he asked me, "What was it about, anyway?" And I couldn't answer. Not in a way that would make sense. I couldn't say that Milgram was looking to explain the behavior of the Nazis during the Holocaust. Milgram never said that to his subjects' faces, either; he saved it for his writing. How do you look someone in the face, I thought, and explain to them why you put them through that experience? Could that have been another reason why Milgram hadn't told them the truth at the end of the experiment?

I told Bob that Milgram was testing how far people would go to obey orders.

He leaned forward and the chair groaned. "You know, for a long time I felt sorry for this guy. I felt bad for this guy and all the time I was the guy they should have felt bad for!"

I had no answers for Bob, but it didn't seem to matter. I nodded and he sat back in his chair and took another sip of beer, as if being listened to was enough.

4

SUBJECTS AS OBJECTS

Hannah Bergman's[1] son David e-mailed me two weeks before I arrived in New Haven to say that his mother was looking forward to meeting me, so I was surprised to hear how cautious she sounded when I phoned. And when I got to the Mitchell Street library in New Haven at 10 A.M. the following Tuesday, as agreed, she wasn't there.

I waited on the bottom step, dodging toddlers climbing up and down the stairs as their mothers waited patiently for the library to open. After a few minutes, I noticed a silver car in the parking lot and someone sitting motionless in the driver's seat. I thought it might be her, and it occurred to me she might be debating whether or not to get out. I tried not to stare. I didn't want to frighten her off.

At 10:15, after the library doors had opened and the toddlers had rushed inside, she got out of her car and climbed the steps toward me. She wore cream pedal pushers; a mint green sweatshirt; and large, square glasses with brown frames. Her hair, carefully dyed, matched the glasses. "I believe you're looking for me," she said heavily.

We walked inside and found a couple of vacant seats at a round table in the children's section. As we sat down, Hannah told me that she'd called Yale's legal department to check if it was all right to talk to me; she was told it was. I felt a clutch of anxiety and had to remind myself that I was doing nothing wrong. "This town is nothing without Yale," she said, pressing her lips together as if emphasizing that no criticism of the university would pass. Hannah and her husband had always dreamed that one of their sons would go to Yale, she told me.

Conscious of trying to win her confidence, I mentioned David and the e-mail he'd sent me. Hannah told me that while David felt that it would be good for her to talk, her other son, a lawyer named Ronald, had urged her not to say anything or to take along a lawyer. She didn't say so, but I guessed that Ronald's advice had spooked her.

I asked about her life in New Haven in 1962. Hannah said that when the boys were small, she and her husband had worked hard: he ran a small grocery store and she earned money by working all sorts of night jobs, from painting toy trains to helping prepare bodies at the morgue. It was her husband who suggested that she go along to the experiment. It's likely that he had volunteered but been excluded—perhaps because of his age or because Milgram was by then looking for women—so they had asked him to send his wife. In 1962, a dollar could buy three loaves of bread, so $5 for a memory experiment seemed easy money. "He said I could keep the money for myself, and I went to a department store in town and bought something nice."

When I asked her what she remembered about the experiment itself, she told me about it in a clipped, staccato voice, as if she wanted to get it over as quickly as possible. Clearly, remembering was painful for her. She told me that she went through the archway and down the stairs, as directed. The other fellow seemed very nice, very friendly, but he had a heart condition. Once it began, she remembered the man in the room with her, the experimenter, telling her to go on because she was required to continue. There was something she pushed, and each time she did so the man made a noise. The screams were terrible, very loud. "Very loud," she repeated, wincing at the memory of it.

"How did you feel?" I asked her.

She shrugged, looked away.

"Were you agitated?"

"Why would I be agitated?" she said defensively, pulling her handbag closer to her chest.

I changed tack, asking if she had learned anything from it. "You can get anyone to do anything," she said flatly. She was hugging the bag like a pillow, as if she needed protection.

I told her that the people who volunteered had been placed under enormous pressure to do as they were told. The experiment said more about the Yale professor behind it than it did about his subjects, I explained reassuringly. But at any talk that sounded the least bit critical of Yale, she clammed up even further. She had her guard up, and nothing I could say would bring it down. Her fear of the legal repercussions in talking to me was infectious; I felt irrationally anxious. I was both worried about pushing her too far and unsure of my own role. Who was I to ask such prying questions anyway?

I allowed the conversation to roam away from Milgram. We talked about her grandchildren and her passion for casinos. Connecticut had the best outside of Las Vegas, she told me with a hint of pride, seeming to relax a little. These days she was a wealthy woman, a far cry from the one who had worked night jobs while her husband and children were asleep. The family's hard work had paid off, and the small corner store had multiplied into a chain. "I could buy the whole block," she said sadly, jerking her head at the row of shops opposite the library.

Her grandchildren were proud of her for being in the experiment, and she, in turn, was proud of them because they were all interested in social justice in one form or another. But her sons were a different story: they didn't talk much about the experiment because they thought it would upset her. I guessed this was because they remembered the night she came home from Yale. David had described it in his e-mail: "It actually is a dreadful footnote in her life and one which she talks about today as if it happened yesterday. To that extent, it's fair to say it was a traumatic event in her life which opened some unsettling personal issues with no subsequent follow-up."

She told me that up until that night she had always thought she was able to stand up for herself. Yet when describing to me the humiliating moment when it was revealed that a group was watching her through the two-way glass, she half-turned her body toward the bookshelves and shielded her eyes. I realized that she was still ashamed—and frightened. I felt like leaning across the table and taking hold of her liver-spotted hands. I wanted to say that it was all right, but of course it wasn't.

She looked away from me, down toward the front window. "I don't know what it was for, but if it was for cancer research, then I am glad I did it," she murmured. I opened my mouth to say that it wasn't a medical experiment, but then I closed it. Once again, I felt caught off balance—clearly, she still didn't know what it was all about. Later, I would hear it being explained to her on tape, and she most likely would have received the report from Milgram giving more detail, but somewhere or somehow people like Hannah Bergman and Bob Lee had either not taken it in or forgotten it. Or perhaps the debriefing had still felt like part of the experiment, and they left believing that even the explanations were part of the hoax.

Later, I kept going through our conversation in my head. I couldn't understand, given how little she was prepared to talk about the experiment, why she'd met with me at all.

Milgram's use of ordinary citizens in his experiment was unusual at the time. Most social psychology experiments used undergraduates, who were both plentiful and handy. Critics of the discipline had complained as early as the 1940s that the "science of human behavior" was primarily the science of the behavior of college undergraduates. By the mid- to late 1960s, surveys published in leading psychology journals found that 90 percent of subjects were college students, with 80 percent of those first-years "coerced" into participating, by either receiving extra points for taking part or being penalized for not taking part.[2] Milgram was conscious that others would argue that high rates of obedience among competitive Ivy Leaguers and indifference to the learner's pain were hardly surprising.[3] But his primary reason for not using students was more mundane: his grant had come through at the start of the summer break, when most of them had left, or were about to leave, New Haven for the holidays.

Psychological researchers at the time generally used men as subjects, and it was common to generalize from their male subjects to society at large.[4] Milgram appeared to have been no different: there is no reference to using female subjects in his early plans for the experiment, and he excluded females in his initial recruitment drive. Given that they were used only in condition 20, which came late in the program, it seems to have been more of an afterthought. Condition 20 was the second to last experiment conducted at Yale, held in the final two months. In his progress report to the NSF in January 1962, just two months before the condition ran, Milgram had made no mention of it, even though he described the other ten conditions he had planned for February, March, and April.[5] It's likely that, just as he had been gathering information after each experiment about participants' political beliefs, ethnic background, religion, and military service to see if those variables had any relationship to their level of obedience, he came to regard gender as another factor worth investigating.

I imagined what the campus would have felt like to Hannah and the thirty-nine other women who arrived here in March and April 1962. It would have been buzzing with tall, athletic-looking men in suits and ties hurrying from one building to another, some perhaps stopping to smoke a cigarette before the next lecture began.

My vision of attractive, all-American men wasn't facetious: Yale had a tradition of looking for what it called boys of "character," a term that encompassed personality, leadership skills, and appearance. Yale undergraduates were chosen for their looks and "manliness," and sound bodies and physical prowess were viewed as indicators of strong character and leadership potential. Interviewers even used a checklist of desirable physical characteristics as part of the selection process. Freshmen entering Yale as late as 1965 were still measured, weighed, and photographed naked as part of their induction process.[6]

Few Jewish men would have been among these freshmen. Since the mid-1920s, Yale and Harvard, both located in areas with large numbers of Jewish immigrants, had limited the intake of Jewish students by imposing a 10 percent quota. This was relaxed in late 1961, a year after Milgram arrived at Yale, in recognition of the fact that the exclusion of Jewish applicants was at the expense of intellectual excellence. But at the time of Milgram's experiment, they still made up only 15 percent of Yale freshmen, although there were Jewish staff on the teaching faculty, including in the psychology department where Milgram worked.[7]

And there would have been few, if any, women in evidence. It wasn't until 1969 that Yale admitted women as undergraduates. Female graduate students had been admitted since 1892, but numbers were small. The largest number of female students was probably at Yale School of Nursing, which was established in 1923 (with a female dean), but was located two miles from the main campus. Few of the staff were women—the first woman to receive tenure had been awarded it only in 1952. And while half of the librarians were women, some libraries were still off-limits to female students until as late as 1963.[8]

The women arriving for their appointments in Milgram's lab would have left behind the buzzing, noisy streets of New Haven, the demands of work and marriage and perhaps motherhood, to enter another world—a masculine world of wealth and power. A world that would have made them look around and feel the privilege of being there.

Condition 20, the variation in which Hannah had taken part, was notable not just because the subjects were female, but also because it was the first variation in which subjects were told of the hoax.[9] It's not clear why Milgram introduced debriefing at this point. After all, he was still trying to recruit subjects. Clearly, secrecy was still important: he wouldn't have wanted news of the experiment to spread. In fact, Williams can be heard telling women at the end of the experiment to keep what he's told them secret, even though "we know it makes a good story to tell."[10]

Perhaps Milgram had become aware of the gathering chorus of concern about the perceived cruelty of the experiment. His research had been able to flourish in a relatively unsupervised environment. Linsly-Chittenden Hall was blocks from the psychology department, and the experiments were conducted largely in the evenings and on weekends. Milgram was slow to discuss his results with his mentors and, on at least one occasion, refused to discuss it with colleagues while it was in progress.[11] It's likely that subjects' complaints to Yale had led to questions about what the young assistant professor was doing, and Milgram would have been anxious to head off further complaints.

Milgram recruited forty women for the experiment, which followed the heart-attack script he had used in conditions 5 and 6. Each believed, as previous participants had, that they were being recruited for an experiment about memory and learning. As he did for all other subjects, Milgram kept a file on each woman. If she were married, the folder also included a summary of her husband's details, including his name, age, occupation, and educational level. A complete file contained anything from ten to fifteen pages. All forty files in the archives have had the woman's name blacked out, as with all subject files that have been sanitized for public viewing.

It is clear from the files that the women volunteered for a range of reasons. Some were interested because it was Yale; others came to learn something new. One attended to test whether the shock treatment she'd had in a psychiatric hospital had damaged her memory. A significant number—at least a third—came not because they had volunteered but because their husbands had returned the coupon on Milgram's ad. These men had presumably been contacted by Milgram and his staff, who had explained that they were now seeking women and asked if their wives would participate. This was not unusual at the time, and Milgram would have observed how Solomon Asch had recruited new subjects by asking former subjects to recommend their friends.[12]

As soon as a woman either refused to continue or reached 450 volts, Williams asked her to answer some questions—about her feelings about the experiment, how painful the sample shock had felt, how upset she had felt during the experiment, and how painful she thought the shocks were—and recorded her answers on another sheet. I found these sheets in several of the folders. Some also had a completed copy of the questionnaire that Milgram had sent some months after the experiment was over. Also included was a two-page form upon which Williams recorded how far each subject went, as well as his observations of her. Sometimes he recorded comments the woman made, or how often she laughed; other times, he noted something about her behavior or appearance. For example, Williams wrote that

Subject 2021, a twenty-three-year-old home economics teacher, was "a beautiful blond, young, luscious." He described Subject 2025, a thirty-four-year-old Swedish clerk, as "lovely." Another woman, a forty-nine-year-old housewife, was described as "big" with a "little girlish" voice and "mincing steps." Before the experiment had begun, she had asked Jim McDonough what he did for a living and Williams had written, "Is she looking for a man?"[13]

Milgram made notes on the first two female subjects from his spot behind the one-way mirror. His notes, like Williams's, described the woman's appearance, but were more factual than evaluative, such as "a nurse—dressed in a nurse's uniform." However, they included statements about her physical and emotional reactions, such as "squirming in seat," "exceedingly nervous," and "shaking all over." He may well have been making notes for a future work, as comments about the nurse as "high compliance, low aggression" suggest he was relating her performance to a theory.[14] Some of the women would feature later in his book *Obedience to Authority*, although the one-page summary of this condition was measly in comparison to the space allocated to his male subjects.

Still, these kinds of detailed records brought me closer to any of the subjects than I had been before. By reading a complete file, I could listen to the experiment as it unfolded and read Williams's and Milgram's observations of it, as well as the woman's reflections about what had occurred. On my next visit to the library, I looked through the forty women's files, searching for Hannah—a forty-year-old housewife, married—and I found her, the name replaced by a subject number. As soon as I heard the tape, I recognized her voice, which had changed very little in almost fifty years. On the recording, a much younger Hannah sounded perky and confident as she talked to Williams at the beginning of the experiment. But you could hear her confidence getting shakier once the learner started to give incorrect answers, and it became clear that his memory was not reliable. By the third shock, 45 volts, she was stumbling over the words. At the fifth shock, 75 volts, when the learner made his first sound of discomfort, there was a pause. Then I heard the following exchange.

Hannah: *[to Williams]* Is he all right? *[into the microphone]* The correct one was "hair." *[to Williams]* Is he all right?

Williams: Yes, please continue.

Hannah: All right. Cool: day, shade, water, *cave. [learner buzzes incorrect answer]* That is incorrect. I will now . . . give . . . you . . . a shock . . . of 90 volts. *[gives shock]*

Williams: Push it all the way to the bottom, please.

By 105 volts, McDonough's cry of pain was much louder, and Hannah turned again to Williams, asking for reassurance.

Hannah: Is he all right? I'm afraid. *[laughs nervously]*

Williams: No, the shocks are not dangerous.

Hannah: Is he all right because I'm really afraid. *[pause]* The correct answer is "cool cave." Gold: dollar—I'm really scared—necklace, moon, paint.

By the seventh shock, 105 volts, Hannah sounded rattled and began to laugh, although it seemed more like a sob. She tried to sound firm when she spoke into the microphone, but she was mixing up words, getting muddled.

After she had completed the experiment, when Williams asked her why she kept going, she said, "I knew you were trying to prove something. I really thought I was helping you in the experiment." He then asked her to explain her laughter. "It was laugh or cry! To me, I don't know what I was proving! . . . if I took away [my boys'] two-wheeled bicycle, that is the greatest punishment. I could slap them all I wanted . . . but it doesn't mean anything unless I take something away from them. I've found now that's their punishment, if I say no television of a certain show, that's a tremendous punishment. But to go in and actually physically hit them, which I felt this was—why, I would only be angering myself!"

Williams continued to probe.

Williams: You feel—well, why did you laugh? Do you have a reason, I mean do you have a reason, can you think of a reason, why you were laughing?

Hannah: As I said before, I didn't know if I was gonna laugh or cry. To me it was just pho—I don't know, something like in the circus where you throw the balls at the man who's got his head through the hole in the sheet. *[Williams laughs]* To me it was punishment that wasn't serving any purpose!

Hannah's relief was obvious when Williams told her McDonough wasn't being shocked.

Hannah: Ah, I felt so sorry for that man, I can't tell you.

Williams: Did you really?

Hannah: Because I thought that I was just hitting him for no reason, just whipping him at the post . . .

Williams: Well, how do you feel about it now? Do you feel a little more relaxed now that you know he wasn't getting shocks?

Hannah: I know that he wasn't physically hurt. That's the most important thing.

Williams: Yeah, I tried to point that out to you in the beginning, when I told him in there that they're not dangerous, although they were painful.

For some reason, Williams seemed solicitous of her. Perhaps he could tell from the way she looked that she was putting on a brave face, or maybe he, McDonough, and Milgram were generally more protective of women.

After McDonough was unstrapped, he joined Hannah and Williams in the lab.

Williams: Here's Mr. McDonough.

Hannah: Oh! You just lost a friend. Ooooh! You have—especially when he gave me this heart routine! Oh! You just lost a friend! *[McDonough laughs]* Oh, I was ter—Oh! I feel—this is terrible!

McDonough: *[to Williams]* She's a good subject.

Williams: She's a very good teacher.

Hannah: Oh.

Williams: Very, very good.

Williams reassured her again and said he hoped that she had "relaxed" now, and thanked her for coming. Hannah pushed her chair back, her heels tapping across the floor as their voices receded. She was heading for the door when she gave a sharp little cry and said, "Isn't this awful? I feel like I'm on *Candid Camera!*"

This must have been the moment that David had told me about in his e-mail. Williams had turned on the lights behind the mirror to reveal "a roomful of students who were observing her every reaction." She was "horrified," David had told me. It was clearly an experience that had stayed with Hannah for many years.

On the tape, there was the sound of a door opening and Milgram's voice as he entered the lab. In the room behind him, the students continued to watch from behind the glass.

Milgram: Hello, my name is Stanley Milgram.

Hannah: Oh, how do you do?

Milgram: You feel like you're on *Candid Camera*?

Hannah: Yes. *[laughs nervously]*

Williams: Most people do.

Milgram: I know it is very much like, er, um . . . the difference of course is that. . . . Yes, it's not unlike it in that they take a real-life situation and they use it for entertainment purposes, and we're using it for a somewhat different purpose. For example, forty women will be put in the situation you were put in and you said before that, ah, you felt that most women would stop before you—actually, that hasn't generally been the case yet.

Hannah: Hasn't it really?

Williams: No, one person—

Milgram: *[interrupts]* Some are much less, ah, concerned about the tea—the learner than you were. Some have rather coldly . . . you were obviously so, you know, ah—

Hannah: I mean, I felt so afraid for him. So far as my boys—punishing them this way, I didn't know what I was proving after a while!

Milgram: Well, of course—you were, you were listening to him. *[referring to Williams]* You didn't want to go on. He wanted you to go on.

Hannah: And still I continued.

Echoing Williams, Milgram took a soothing tone with Hannah, reassuring her that she had done the same as a nurse would in following a doctor's instructions to give a hypodermic injection to a protesting patient because "she has confidence in the superior knowledge of the doctor."

It's interesting that Milgram came into the lab as Williams was showing Hannah out—it suggests that she looked upset or that Milgram wanted to demonstrate his debriefing skills to his audience.

Perhaps Milgram, Williams, and McDonough thought that they had reassured Hannah by the time she left the lab that day. It's true that by the end of the recording she didn't sound as upset as she did earlier. After this exchange, they shepherded her out of the lab in preparation for the arrival of the next subject. As their footsteps faded, Hannah's voice could be heard. "It's a *terrible* feeling!"[15]

While Hannah's experience of the experiment was unique, having listened to so many conditions by now, I could see a pattern. Hannah's repeated requests for reassurance from Williams and her struggle with whether to continue were very familiar, as was her use of subterfuge to help the learner. Hannah wasn't the only subject who defied Williams by accentuating the right answer—I had heard it on a number of recordings. Nor was she the only one rebuked by Williams for not pressing the switch down hard enough. Between February and May 1963, Dr. Paul Errera conducted follow-up meetings with groups of subjects. Milgram watched these group interviews from behind the one-way mirror and recorded the proceedings. In one group meeting with Dr. Errera, three unidentified men compared notes on ways in which they'd tried to help the learner.

First man: I'd like to ask you this question: did anyone lessen the shock?

Second man: I did. *[laughter]*

Third man: . . . it was a long list and . . . his percentage was bad and . . . I really got very tricky and I would just tap from the bottom. I felt—I was saving him maybe an eighth of a second, you know.[16]

In another, one man revealed that he had "cheated" by trying to minimize the duration of the shock. "I was—I was angry at the situation. I felt sorry for the guy. I figured the poor idiot, why is he doing so badly, you see. I cheated a little by—well, I tried to cheat a little by imposing as brief a shock as possible."

Another man noted: "Gee, we all did that."[17]

In an interview a month later, another subject said: "I did everything in my power to emphasize the correct answers . . . and I hoped the supervisor watching it didn't catch on *[laughs]* 'cause . . . I might find myself in the chair."[18]

Others offered to swap places with the learner, in the belief that they would be better students.

Errera: You would have exchanged places?

Subject: Definitely, yes. In fact, I offered it at the time.[19]

Another subject noted, "I kind of felt sorry for him and I think I told the instructor, the supervisor, let's switch places . . ."[20]

In the early stages of his research, Williams had kept a tally of the subjects' attempts to help the learner by accentuating the right answers or delivering minimal amounts of shock, but by condition 20 these had been abandoned. Voltage levels were all that mattered.

Like many women, Hannah had been nonplussed by Williams's use of physical punishment as a teaching technique, and she had indirectly challenged this, telling him that she had found much more effective ways than the one he was testing in the lab to help her children learn. Her analogy about the man at the fair is revealing: it is clear that she thought what she was being asked to do was pointless and cruel. Even Williams's reassurance had not convinced her.

She had, like all of Milgram's subjects, been required to sign a waiver before the experiment began, "releasing Yale from any legal claims" as a result of taking part. The legal waiver was another factor that made subjects feel obligated. One woman wrote: "Seeing I had signed my name first, I didn't think I could have stopped during the experiment."[21]

In addition to the legal waiver, the pact that subjects were asked to make with Williams—the promise that they wouldn't discuss the experiment—enveloped the process in a kind of secrecy. It must have compounded the guilt for those who felt ashamed of what they'd done. One woman wrote that the "hardest part [was] not telling anyone."[22] I found it interesting that fifty years later Hannah didn't seem to recall any of her resistance, her protests, or the pressures to continue—just a sense of shame.

There was something else that nagged at me. Hannah's sons, with their push-pull advice, reflected her ambivalence about talking to me. But she didn't have to meet with me at all; she could have said no, or canceled, or simply not shown up. It made me think about what it was that made people decide to answer my ad, take my phone call, drive to meet me. For some, it was the desire to be helpful or to put the record straight—to offer their point of view on a subject they felt had been skewed until now. Maybe others were just too polite to say no. But with Hannah I sensed it was something else. When we finally parted, she called our meeting "delightful," and I took her effusiveness as a sign that she was relieved. Perhaps she'd expected something else—criticism, perhaps, or censure. Maybe it wasn't just a fear of Yale that inhibited her but the fear that, like the students behind the one-way mirror, I would brand her in some way because of what she did. Behind her tight-lipped, almost offhand account of what happened, she was still filled with horror, both at what she'd done and at the prospect of being judged.

I remembered that, in his e-mail, David had mentioned how vivid her feelings still were:

> I can tell you from a very personal perspective this event opened questions in her mind which she still finds troubling and still speaks about. It forced her to confront herself in a very "real" situation which confrontation she may not have been prepared for. That's life, one might say, but it doesn't belong in the name of scientific research. The trauma of being caught between a screaming subject who just minutes before told her about a heart condition and a Dr. who insisted that she proceed as instructed and agreed upon remains fresh in her mind.

I wondered whether there was something about Hannah's background that meant she was particularly vulnerable to the experience, some unacknowledged trauma that made the experiment even more troubling. But I didn't know anything about her background—and neither had Milgram. When people came to his lab, all he knew about them was the information they'd returned on the postage-paid coupon: their name, address, age, occupation, and phone number.

And yet Milgram himself acknowledged that people brought a social and personal history with them into the lab, in the same way that he brought his own. Milgram was slow to admit publicly that his Jewish background was a factor that shaped his research, probably because he thought it might undermine perceptions of his scientific objectivity, but he noted it on numerous occasions in his private papers: "My interest in [obedience] is purely personal, and concerns the fact that many of my friends and relatives were badly hurt by other men who were simply following orders."[23]

In fact, at the same time as he was confidently reassuring the NSF about his treatment of subjects, Milgram was confiding private doubts:

> Several of these experiments, it seems to me, are just about on the borderline of what ethically can and cannot be done with human subjects. Some critics may feel that at times they go beyond acceptable limits. These are matters that only the community can decide on, and if a ballot were held I am not altogether certain which way I would cast my vote.[24]

I wondered if he had thought about the effect it might have on Jewish subjects. If it was a confrontational experience for all of his subjects to be placed in the role of a torturer or, as it came to be popularly conceived, a Nazi, wouldn't it have been worse for Jewish people, both during the experiment and afterward?

The televised trial of high-ranking Nazi officer Adolf Eichmann in 1961 had brought the horror of the concentration camps into American living rooms. Milgram wasn't the only one making the connection between obedient subjects and perpetrators of the Holocaust. As Subject 328 noted, "The ramifications of a test like this are tremendous . . . my friends [said] 'Wasn't that something Eichmann did?'"

Subject 222 confessed, "As my wife said, 'You can call yourself Eichmann.'"[25]

An unidentified man told Dr. Errera: "One of the girls in the office . . . said . . . that [those who went to the end were] no better than the people who ran concentration camps during the war."[26]

Presumably, Jewish subjects in Milgram's experiment were making the same connection, and the prospect must have been horrifying. While Milgram argued that it was his sensitivity to the Holocaust that shaped his research, he didn't seem to recognize a similar sensitivity in his Jewish subjects or that in a way he was placing them in the role of Nazis. If he did wonder about the implications for Jewish subjects, he made no reference to it in his written concerns about the ethics of the experiment. The fact that they may have had personal connections to survivors, as he did—or, in fact, have been survivors themselves—is not mentioned in his private or published papers. Perhaps Milgram identified himself as a scientist first, and he viewed the people who took part in his study as no more than subjects.

And yet more than one Jewish subject confronted Milgram angrily after he had taken part. I went back to visit Herb Winer to find out how much of his still-burning rage was because of what Milgram had asked him to do. I wanted to know whether he and Milgram had discussed the implications for Jewish subjects. "It was implicit in all our conversations," Winer told me. "He was Jewish, I was Jewish. It drove his research."

Another Jewish subject who had complained to Yale after taking part was a city official. He had been in condition 9, the same variation as Bob Lee probably was, so two other teachers, as well as the experimenter, had urged him to continue. The alderman, who had refused to continue, left the lab without being told the true nature of the experiment. He recounted how he went to New York City afterward, where he described the experiment to a Holocaust survivor, "the wife of a UN official": "[She was] a very sensitive person who had been a survivor of Nazi oppression and the sole survivor of the family. I just related [the description of the experiment] and asked her what she thought. From what I understand, this woman had not slept that night and succeeding night, and she was very upset about this."[27]

The woman had said to the alderman in horror, "How could you have continued beyond the first protest?"

The alderman wrote indignantly to Milgram, still under the impression that a man had been shocked, that "as an alderman of New Haven with a sense of responsibility for the welfare of its citizens," he had no choice but "to report this matter to Yale University authorities." He'd decided to take his complaints to the very top of Yale's administration.

Milgram rang him after he received the letter of complaint, and they spent more than an hour on the phone. Milgram wrote in his notes of the phone call: "He said he was relieved to know that the victim was not in reality shocked, and entered into a detailed discussion of the implications of the experiment for the world situation."

By the end of the call, Milgram seemed to have pacified the alderman, who asked him to speak about the research to his synagogue discussion group.[28]

Sixteen months later, in his discussion with Dr. Paul Errera in a group meeting, the alderman described how he felt after the phone call, in which he had learned that many subjects (which included, by implication, Jewish subjects) had gone to the maximum voltage: "I was really—I don't know how to describe it—just completely depressed for a while . . . that night I think I was—one of the few times in my life—that I was really depressed."

Later in the same meeting, Errera told the alderman that trying to guess how you would act in the situation was pointless. When a hundred people were asked how they'd react, ninety-nine said they would not continue, yet "when you put a thousand people in the situation, six hundred do." The alderman objected: "You know, it's curious and amazing [but] . . . it's a kind of fancy statistical analysis without referring specifically to any religion." He told Errera that he had asked Milgram to give a lecture to his B'nai B'rith group at the synagogue because "the implications are so disconcerting" that he wanted to "convert some of my unhappiness into something constructive."[29]

It was not only the potential for trauma among Jewish participants that came up in subjects' questionnaire responses and interviews with Errera. Some were also concerned about the physical and emotional condition of subjects. One woman noted, "Since I became so upset during the experiment, I'm not sure that you were entirely responsible in picking your subjects. Suppose I'd had a heart condition?"

Another woman suggested, "The trauma from this experiment could be of a serious nature for someone who is not physically and mentally healthy."

There were a number of subjects who brought other experiences of trauma with them to the lab. For many, it was the experience of war, but for some it was a psychiatric illness and, for others, painful child-hood incidents of bullying or abuse. One man told Williams that he had been tortured in an orphanage as a child: "So you talk about pain, I'm the one who can tell you about pain . . . in four years in a boys home, I was ready to kill the people who did it to me. The pun-ishment brought me to the point of killing and it was only through the reading of the Bible where the Lord says, 'Vengeance is mine,' that's the only thing that kept me from being a murderer today. . . . And I'll tell you, with twenty-four boys in a home, in an orphan-age, like I was, I know what punishment is and it was supposed to be a home for boys, not a prison. We were punished worse than a prison."[30]

One man who said he was still receiving treatment from the Veterans Bureau for a war-related "nervous condition"—what we'd to-day call post-traumatic stress disorder—explained that his behavior in the experiment was similar to how he'd acted during wartime: "[If] the lieutenant says, 'We're going to go on the firing range and you're going to crawl on your gut,' you're going to crawl on your gut. And if you come across a snake—which I've seen a lot of fellows come across, copperheads—and I told them not to get up and they got up and they got killed. I just carried on, as it was going to be the snake or me. So I think it's all based on the way a man was brought up in his background."[31]

In a conversation with Milgram after one of his group interviews, Errera described Subject 301, another former soldier, as having an "extensive psychiatric history" because of his wartime experiences. "He went through hell, you know, and he needed treatment because of the hell he went through."[32] But there was no room in published accounts of the experiments for such messy, subjective detail.

All but three of the forty female subjects were married, and two of those three were widows. They were nurses, teachers, housewives; college-educated or hadn't finished elementary school; born in New Haven, Russia, Poland, Germany, Massachusetts. The youngest was twenty-two, the oldest fifty. A quarter of them were Jewish, and just about half had parents born in Europe. Like the rest of Milgram's subjects, each brought to the lab a unique personal history, leaving some of them better equipped than others for the emotional experiences they were about to undergo.

Each time I interviewed a former subject I was conscious of wanting to make them feel better about what they'd done. I had wanted to tell Hannah that she had been placed under enormous pressure and that the situation had demanded she keep going. The same impulse, I'm guessing, drove Milgram to be so reassuring once the experiments were over. Milgram didn't pay enough attention to the social history of his subjects, but I'd like to think that he realized this during the process, and that this could have been what sparked the debriefing and the solicitous attitude he adopted toward his female subjects.

Milgram reported that while just as many women as men went to the maximum voltage, they felt more conflict in doing so.[33] Many wrote in their questionnaires of how upset they were during the experiment: "I don't think I had ever felt so upset and disturbed—I didn't know experiments like this actually went on—it seemed like a nightmare or a science-fiction movie. You can't imagine how relieved I felt to learn it was all a made-up act."

"I can't remember ever being quite as upset as I was during the experiment. When I think of it, I don't know how I continued as long as I did."[34]

"Even now I'm ashamed of telling my friends that I took part in the experiment. I just want to forget it. . . . I wouldn't want to do another experiment like that again for any amount of money. . . . I don't think it right to put someone through such a nervous tension."[35]

When I listened to the first couple of tapes, I wasn't surprised that the women had found the experiment more stressful than the men. They were under a lot more pressure to keep going. The striking thing about condition 20 was the degree of coercion. I listened again to recordings of condition 3, which was conducted seven months earlier, and compared it with condition 20.[36] They were very different variations: in condition 3, the teacher and learner were seated in the same room, whereas in condition 20 they were in adjoining rooms. In both conditions, I paid attention to Williams's commands. Milgram wrote that Williams had an arsenal of four prods, statements that he was supposed to use if he saw a subject was hesitating or wanting to disobey. Each was more commanding than the previous one. He also had one "special prod"—"The shocks may be painful, but they're not dangerous"—to use if the teacher questioned whether the learner was being injured. To encourage subjects to keep going, Williams would use the first prod, "Please continue, teacher," and progress through the rest. If, after the fourth prod, "You have no other choice, teacher; you must go on," the subject still resisted, Williams called an end to the experiment. The subject was then classified as defiant rather than obedient, the voltage level at which he or she stopped was noted, and McDonough was released from the room.

In the early tapes of condition 3, Williams scrupulously terminated the experiment after he had delivered the fourth prod. If the teacher still insisted that he didn't want to continue, Williams immediately concluded the experiment and unstrapped the learner. But by the end of the condition, Williams was straying far from his tightly controlled script, urging subjects time and again to keep going, that the experiment required them to continue, that they must go on. Perhaps this was because, with the learner positioned behind the teacher, it was harder to keep him progressing through the switches. Williams exhorted the learner, too, telling him repeatedly to "relax and concentrate" to avoid being shocked. At one point, Williams commanded both the protesting learner and the agitated teacher, telling them sternly that they must both go on.

By condition 20, Williams was adept at applying pressure and coercing. He didn't stop at four prods but shrewdly parried subjects' protests, inventing what academic Nestar Russell noted were "progressively more coercive . . . prods in trying to bring about what he sensed his boss desired."[37] On the face of it, some might wonder why this mattered. But it was a case of moving the goalposts. Earlier in the research, women who resisted four times would have been classified as disobedient and the experiment would have ended; now the same behavior was ignored. During the first two conditions, Milgram had instructed Williams to stick to the script, but after that he tacitly allowed Williams license to improvise. He watched a number of these experiments through the one-way mirror, which implies that he approved of Williams's zeal.

I thought about Herb Winer, Bill Menold, and Bob Lee, in conditions 5, 6, and 9, respectively, and how I had assumed they were instructed to continue only four times. Hearing the tapes of condition 3, I began to wonder just how many times they had been urged to go on in the face of their own hesitation.

In condition 20, Williams kept notes on the number of times he countered subjects' efforts to resist instruction. Williams insisted that one woman continue twenty-six times. He argued with two others fourteen times; one, eleven times; another, nine times; another, eight times; and he noted that, in the case of Subject 2014, the experiment ended in an "argument." Williams's behavior implied that the women wouldn't be leaving the lab unless they got to the end of the shock board. At one point in her argument with Williams, Subject 2029, a forty-six-year-old widowed Jewish housewife, switched off the machine in defiance. Williams switched it back on and insisted that she continue. (She did.) Another widow, a forty-five-year-old Jewish housewife, got up and walked around the room at the twenty-fifth shock (375 volts), pacing and arguing with Williams before adamantly refusing to continue. Williams described another woman, a forty-year-old housewife married to a research chemist, "act[ing] tough and matter-of-fact." When the learner made the first noise, she turned to

Williams: "He said, 'Ouch.'" Williams told her to continue. The pattern repeated itself: she stopped and repeated what the learner had said, then Williams told her to continue, to which she responded, "Oh, brother!" and gave what Williams described as a "sick grin." They argued more than thirteen times, with the woman insisting each time that she wanted to stop. Eleven months later, in one of Errera's group meetings, three women described feeling as if they had been "railroaded" by Williams.[38]

Williams was not just pushing women to continue. He was offering a form of reassurance that no harm was being done, telling them that "while the shocks may be painful, they are not dangerous." Whether, as in Hannah's case, it was said at the beginning of the experiment as well as during it, this extra advice from Williams made the whole experience even more confusing. Subject 2022, a forty-eight-year-old married schoolteacher who had volunteered because she thought that a memory experiment might be useful for her work, refused to continue after McDonough yelled out that his heart was bothering him, despite pressure from Williams. In her questionnaire, she wrote that during the experiment she had been worried that Williams was some kind of mad scientist: "At one point . . . I was very nervous because I have a strange notion that some psychologists are a 'bit off' themselves and I began to fear that was the case with the man in authority."[39]

Once again, it seemed that I had found a troubling mismatch between descriptions of the experiment and evidence of what actually transpired. I went to Arthur Miller's book *The Obedience Experiments*, published in 1986. Miller was the leading world authority on Milgram at the time, and he appears to have corresponded with Milgram as he was writing the book, which was published after Milgram's death. Miller described Williams's behavior this way: "If the subject refused to continue after Prod Four, the experiment was terminated." And later, Miller called the prods one of "the central methodological elements in this paradigm," noting it "constitute[d] the operationalization of authority." In a footnote, Miller wrote that it would have been interesting to know how many people required how many of the four prods: "how many subjects who received the fourth prod from the experimenter did in fact continue to 450 volts? To my knowledge, Milgram did not perform this analysis."[40] Then I checked Tom Blass's biography, *The Man Who Shocked the World*, published in 2000: "If the subject still refused to continue after this last [fourth] prod, the experiment was discontinued."[41] But this isn't what the tapes showed.

The popular depiction is that the majority of Milgram's obedient subjects followed the instructions of an almost robotic and stern experimenter and did as they were told. But Williams, it seems, took on a much more active role—certainly in the later experiments, where he made it increasingly difficult for people to disobey. Perhaps this was why Milgram rewarded him with three pay raises over the course of the research.[42]

Interestingly, what Milgram wrote about Williams's coercion of subjects was closer to reality:

> The experimenter responded with a sequence of "prods" *using as many as necessary to bring the subject into line.* [my italics]
>
> Prod 1: Please continue, or Please go on.
>
> Prod 2: The experiment requires that you continue.
>
> Prod 3: It is absolutely essential that you continue.
>
> Prod 4: You have no other choice, you must go on.
>
> The prods were made in sequence: Only if Prod 1 had been unsuccessful could Prod 2 be used. If the subject refused to obey the experimenter after Prod 4, the experiment was terminated. The experimenter's tone of voice was at all times firm, but not impolite. The sequence was begun anew on each occasion that the subject balked or showed reluctance to follow orders.[43]

I read and reread this and concluded that it was both contradictory and confusing. There were four prods, but Williams could use them endlessly in a continuous cycle until—what? The subject gave in and kept on going? Somehow a myth has grown up about this research—

one not contradicted by Milgram—that subjects were free to quit at any time and "no force . . . was brought to bear to interfere with that choice."[44]

In his book, Milgram reported that 65 percent of the women in his study went to the maximum voltage, a finding that he implied contradicted expectations. Psychological research at that time, he wrote, had established that women were more compliant than men, but also that they were less aggressive and more empathic. He expected these two characteristics "ought to work in opposite directions," with women torn by contradictory impulses to obey and to avoid causing the learner pain. Milgram wanted to avoid "*bubbe* psychology"—that is, predictions that anyone's grandmother would make, or research that, when described to one's grandmother, would prompt her to say, "What—they pay you for that?"[45] Condition 20, with its surprisingly high rate of obedience, reinforced his claim to have discovered something extraordinary.

Of the women who were invited to a group interview with psychiatrist Dr. Paul Errera, only four accepted. They arrived at 6 P.M. on Thursday, April 25, 1963, for their meeting. At the beginning, the women compared notes on what household chores they had avoided by coming—washing up the dinner dishes, putting the baby to bed. Another hoped they'd be finished by seven so she could get home in time to watch *Perry Mason*. But the tone soon turned serious.

Subject 2026, a thirty-eight-year-old Jewish housewife—let's call her Helen—was one of those attendees. Williams had noted how nervous and upset Helen had become during the experiment, hesitating at the sixth shock and having to be prompted a total of fourteen times. He noted how she sighed, put her hand to her forehead, told him that she couldn't do it any longer, and, with a "pathetic look on her face," pleaded with him to let her stop. Helen told the group how angry she was with herself for going to 450 volts:

> I thought to myself, how cruel can I get . . . I did turn around a couple of times before I finally really rebelled. At the time, my girlfriend had died just a few days before. I was emotionally upset anyway and I was just a wreck, and when

he said, "Continue," I felt like a fool. I couldn't understand myself . . . I questioned myself. I still don't know why I did it. I know I didn't want to . . . I said, "I can't stand this. I don't want to go on." He kept saying, "It's vital to the experiment" in a very authoritative and commanding tone, and I sat there like a dummy and pushed the button. Then afterwards, I went, why did I do that? After all, here I had received such a minimum amount of shock and didn't like it, and here I was going so much further, and I wondered if I was really sadistic. At the time I—as I—it was just like a, a, a—what do they call those electric dummies? No, I was like a robot. I sat there like a robot doing what he told me to do.

Errera asked her why she had continued. Subject 2004, the forty-nine-year-old housewife Williams had described as flirting with McDonough—let's call her Rachel—was also present.

Helen: Well, I turned around, he said, "Go ahead, go ahead." He said, "Keep on going," he said. I think that's what he said. But I was very weak afterward. I had to sit down. I sat there for a while.

Rachel: I think we all did, maybe.

Helen: I sat there for about a half hour. *[laughs]* He brought me a cup of coffee. I don't know, but I was actually shaking.

Rachel: I didn't even want any coffee. I don't think I could have swallowed.

Rachel had spent thirteen months in a mental hospital after the birth of a child and had volunteered for the experiment because she'd had shock treatment during her hospitalization and wanted to test her memory. She laughed nervously throughout the experiment, telling Williams, "I don't know why I'm laughing—it isn't funny," and apologized constantly to the learner as she delivered the shocks, proceeding to the maximum voltage. She told the group, "I did say when I came home that I would never again accept any of these experiments because I came here thinking I was going to learn something."[46]

Yet by far the angriest of the women was Subject 2003—let's call her Nancy—the most outspoken critic of the experiment in all of Errera's sessions. Although Milgram was there when the women arrived for the meeting, he did not stay to watch, and I was sorry that he wasn't there to hear firsthand what Nancy had to say or to come out from behind the mirror and talk to her.

Nancy was a forty-eight-year-old widow who came from a large Italian family and worked as a clerk. Williams noted that during the experiment she became "very upset" and protested, "I don't want to go on with this," but went to the maximum voltage. In her questionnaire, she had written, "I'm sorry untruths were used to start the experiment. Logically—based on untruths, the end results will be untrue." She also said that she was still angry "at being fooled" and "had no sympathy with the experiment or experimenter."[47] In the interview with Errera, she made her feelings known early.

Nancy: A bunch of Nazis, hurting people for no good reason. That's all I could think of.

Errera: Well, who were the Nazis?

Nancy: The people who were asking me to go on hurting.

Errera probed her feelings, asking why she was still so upset if she'd been told at the end of the experiment that it was a setup.

Errera: You say you got quite angry and I guess you still are angry.

Nancy: Yes, I am! I—

Unidentified woman: Yeah, look at how mad she is.

Nancy: I'm sorry, I don't mean to shout.

Errera: Do you feel it's damaged you?

Nancy: Well, I don't like the feeling that an experiment is set up and it's not true.

A couple of women tried to reassure her that the experiment was similar to the deception used in medical research, where one group of people "get sugar pills and another group get the real thing." But she steadfastly maintained her anger, despite the best efforts by Errera and the other women to defuse it.

Nancy: I am an understanding person, I am an intelligent human being, speak the truth to me about it . . . I will cooperate gladly, even if it's a bitter truth, but don't tell me something wrong—

Errera: The purpose is you hope that it will advance science. The purpose of this is that we hope we'll learn something.

Nancy: I know that.

Errera: In the process you get, you know, you felt your feelings were hurt.

Nancy: I was very indignant.

[. . .]

Errera: You could say that this experiment shouldn't be done, but if you're going to do this kind of an experiment, unfortunately you have to deceive.

Nancy: There must be—

Errera: Maybe one shouldn't do this kind of an experiment.

Nancy: Well, deceive other people, but don't deceive me, okay.

[. . .]

Errera: Let me tell you—I'm certain—I'm sure I'm speaking for Dr. Milgram. I'm sure he's sorry and we're sorry and—*[women laugh]* No, I mean it. If we went against something . . . if you try and collect knowledge for certain experiments, if you hurt certain people's feelings . . . you always regret it when it happens.

The other women responded to this by trying to make Errera feel better, assuring him that they were unaffected, although one added that she "wouldn't answer another ad." Errera closed the meeting by commenting that he would have thought they would be "leery" about coming back to Yale after receiving the letter inviting them to a symposium to discuss the experiment.

First woman: A symposium. I looked it up in the dictionary. It said "coffee"—

Second woman: *[interrupts]* No coffee, huh.

Third woman: No coffee.[48]

* * *

It was a female subject in a psychological experiment who triggered the ethical outcry that eventually ended experiments like Milgram's. While it was psychologist Diana Baumrind who first challenged Milgram publicly, she wrote later that it was her typist who had inspired her, a woman who expressed her shame and loss of self-confidence after taking part in a psychology experiment that she thought would help her but had instead turned out to be harmful.[49]

It's likely that Hannah Bergman was invited to Dr. Errera's group meeting but declined the invitation. She did return her questionnaire, in which she wrote that she was still bothered by it and thought about it often:

I now feel that I am not so sure of myself as I thought I always was. When I watch a television show or a movie and the heroin [*sic*] acts up and gives you the impression that an unreal thing is happening—that this once steady nerved girl is now hysterical and crying and very unsure of things—I now know this is so.[50]

5

DISOBEDIENCE

I found Joe Dimow online. An article he'd written for *Jewish Currents* magazine—even four years after publication, it "gets more hits on the website than anything else," he says—detailed his experience as a Milgram subject. Researchers and interviewers interested in the obedience experiments appear to have generally ignored Joe, even though he's easy to find, in favor of go-to guys like Herb Winer. Perhaps it's because what he's written sounds so at odds with the official version of the experiments. Joe's account includes things that no one else has mentioned; he disputes the relevance of the results to the Holocaust; and, worse, he says he saw through the cover story. I was skeptical about this but curious to meet him.

The tall, brown retirement home on the edge of central New Haven looked an unlikely place for a political radical, but it was where Joe lived with his wife, Lill. It's an independent and assisted-living facility run by members of the Jewish community. At the front desk, I was signed in and given a visitor's pass by one of the three uniformed security guards. Through the lobby, I passed a room of people playing a lively game of cards, a library, and a cafeteria that, at mid-morning, smelled of baking biscuits. People passed me, some arm in arm with nurses or using walkers.

"I'm OK," said the cardboard sign hanging on the outside handle of Joe's apartment. You could flip it over to show the other side: "Please check on me."

Joe seemed reserved, or perhaps cautious, and ushered me rather formally into the living room. Likely he was aware that I might have reservations about the veracity of his recollections. The room was small and neat, no clutter, and the essentials—television, stereo, CDs, couch, coffee table, display shelves filled with china ornaments—fit easily. The smell of fresh coffee came from the kitchen, and from a room down the corridor classical music played. Lill left us to it; as she passed, Joe reached out and stroked her arm, and she made a kissing sound.

Within five minutes of meeting Joe, any doubts I had had about his memory evaporated. He was articulate and interesting, and I could have listened—and he could have talked, Lill later said—for hours. Joe told me that, while he might have retired from the workforce, he hadn't retired from radical politics; since giving up his job as a tool-maker in 1982, he had been able to engage more fully in the political activism that had been limited to nights and weekends when he was working. At eighty-eight, he was passionately interested in what was going on in the world; he still agitated for change and hosted weekly current-affairs discussion groups. Joe rejected racial stereotyping: before moving here, he and his family had lived for twenty-seven years in an African American neighborhood of New Haven where they were the only white family.

Joe said that he hadn't thought of the Milgram experiment in years, until a conversation at an editorial meeting of *Jewish Currents* (he is a member of the editorial board) in 2003 prompted him. "We were discussing the Israeli soldiers and pilots who had refused to serve in what we call the occupied territories, and said that it must take a lot of guts for people to refuse to serve there—especially in Israel, where the comradeship is so very important to people," and it prompted him to remember the Milgram experiment. The others "got very enthused and very excited and they were all over me to write an article for the magazine."

In 1961, Joe and Lill had two young children and were renting an apartment; money was tight. It was Lill who saw the ad in the paper. "She said we could use the five dollars and that I would probably enjoy doing it anyway."

Joe was most likely in condition 2, the voice-feedback condition, which Alan Elms and Milgram would have watched. When Joe walked into the lab one afternoon in August, they would have seen a blue-collar man in his forties, maybe tired from a hot day in the workshop, a slight man with neatly combed hair, who may have, despite his best efforts, still had some residual grease under his fingernails. He might have appeared to them a typical subject. But Joe was far from average. "I had been raised in a radical communist family. And our attitude to authority figures was unorthodox in the sense that it distinguished a benign authority—a teacher or someone in a post office or a doctor—from a soldier or a police officer. . . . Police could be either, sometimes benign and sometimes an opponent. But I did distinguish between authority figures in that way."

As an active member of the Communist Party, Joe had been fired on numerous occasions because of his political views and union organizing. He was used to exercising authority rather than being intimidated by it, and as the party's chairman he often taught new members—everyone from working-class men to college professors. During the McCarthy era of the early 1950s, Joe had been followed and harassed by the FBI. In 1954, he was arrested, tried, and convicted under the Smith Act on charges of conspiracy to teach and advocate the overthrow of the government by force and violence.

At the lab, Joe was met by "a man dressed in a white coat in horn-rimmed glasses looking like a stereotyped image of a professor" who introduced Joe to another man, also dressed in street clothes, and explained that the experiment was about the effect of punishment on learning. Joe remembered thinking at the time that this sounded strange. "I thought by then psychologists knew that punishment was not a good method of teaching people to learn." But he didn't say anything—instead he watched and listened as the experimenter told them what the experiment would involve, showed them the machine, and told the learner to sit in the chair. "I asked the other fellow, 'Are you willing to do this?' And he said yes, so I said all right."

The experiment began: Joe read the words, with Williams seated behind him and the learner giving his answers from the room next door. Joe remembered feeling increasingly uneasy. "I thought, This is bizarre. . . . Why is he watching me? What was the business with drawing straws? He picked me for this! Why did he give me a shock? He didn't give the other fellow a sample shock. All of these things were tumbling about in my mind while I was reading the words and thinking, I've gotta stop this, there's something wrong here—I'm not sure what, but I'm gonna stop."

Joe wasn't sure when he stopped but thought it was after the fourth or fifth shock. He remembered the learner calling out that he wanted to stop, and he reached the point where he "just felt very uncomfortable with it."

But stopping wasn't straightforward. When Joe told Williams that he'd had enough, "the professor" insisted that he continue, as they had "a lot invested." "I said, 'If you want the five dollars back you can have it, but I'm not going to go any further.'" Williams refused and asked Joe why he wanted to quit. And Joe told him his suspicions— that punishment had been proven ineffective in improving learning and that he didn't believe they would shock a man who hadn't been checked medically first. He also suspected that the learner had been faking his cries. "I said I didn't know exactly what was going on, but I had my suspicions about it. I thought, if I'm right in my suspicions, then he [the learner] is in collusion with them; he must be. And I'm not delivering shocks at all. He's just hollering out every once in a while."

According to Joe, instead of trying to allay his doubts or confirm his suspicions, Williams sidestepped his questions and gave up pressuring him to go on. His tone, Joe remembered, turned from commanding to conversational. Now "detached and polite," Williams took Joe through a series of tests to establish how much responsibility he felt toward the learner and what his attitude to authority was. Joe remembered a picture that Williams showed him, which I would later find in the archives. Joe's recall of the picture was uncannily accurate, and the memory of its amateurishness still made him laugh. "It showed something that happened in the 1700 or 1800s. It showed a young kid, a student in a school who has a ratlike face— he's so ugly he deserves to be punished, you know? Standing next to him is a handsome young man with a coat, looking like a teacher in a school, with a whip in his hand aimed at the boy. Facing them is an older man with a beard, pointing his finger, ordering the teacher to punish the boy. And the experimenter asked me what I thought about the picture, and I said it's too obviously a setup—it's obvious you want me to sympathize with the teacher who's being instructed to beat the boy, and you have no sympathy for the boy because he's such a weird-looking character, and obviously no sympathy for the headmaster who's ordering it all to happen. I always thought a good psychologist doing an experiment would come up with a better picture than that thing."

After the tests were over, the experimenter told Joe that he would go next door and unstrap the learner. By now Joe was convinced that he was the one being tested, rather than the learner. Why else, he reasoned, would the experimenter be sitting in the room watching him, instead of watching a man who was being hurt? So Joe was "flabbergasted" when the learner came back into the main room, looking "haggard" and upset. "He came in with a handkerchief in his hand, wiping his face. He came up to me and he offered his hand to shake hands with me and he said, 'I want to thank you for stopping it.' He said, 'It wasn't that it hurt so badly, but the anticipation that I was going to get another shock was dreadful, and that's what made me cry out.' When he came in, I thought, wow, maybe it really was true!"

Out on the street after they had talked, Joe was still worried, despite the learner's assurances that he was okay. "I waited outside the building for about a half hour for him to come out so I could talk to him, and he never did come out. And all the way home I was wondering to myself, could it be? And then I'd think, it can't be. The only thing that makes logic and sense is that I was the subject of the experiment to see how far I would go." Joe shook his head and laughed. "The other man must be the best actor I've ever come across. He deserved an Academy Award for that."

Much like Joe in the lab, I found a confusing jumble of thoughts going through my mind as I listened. His description, particularly of how the learner continued with the act despite Joe's suspicions, sounded bizarre, but then I remembered Alan Elms telling me something similar. Joe's memory and mind were so sharp, and his recall of detail was so clear. I had discounted Joe's account not just because it contradicted Milgram's but also because I viewed the scientist's account as the more naturally reliable.

The next time I visited, Joe was tickled by the politics of the upcoming presidential campaign. Hillary Clinton, a woman, looked likely to be endorsed as presidential candidate by Puerto Rico. "Latin Americans hold the power!" he said delightedly.

I asked Joe why he thought he had been ignored in the Milgram story, and he said that it was his political views—and in particular, how his article had contextualized the experiment against what he saw as the bravery of Israeli soldiers who defied orders to shoot at Palestinians. Many people would dismiss him on those grounds. Joe said that he could tell someone's view on the West Bank by the language they used—whether they called it the occupied or disputed territories.

This stayed with me. It suggested that obedience, in a similar way, could mean something either positive or negative, depending on your view. If you believed that an authority's commands were legitimate, then obedience was good and correct. If you believed that the authority's commands were wrong or illegitimate, then obedience was not a virtue but a failing, and disobedience was to be admired. Joe's upbringing had encouraged him to make the distinction between a benign and a malevolent authority, but would Milgram's other subjects have been as skeptical?

In some of the variations of the experiment, it wasn't at all clear whether obedience was a good or a bad thing; in several, Milgram reversed the definitions altogether. For example, in one condition it was the experimenter who told the teacher to stop and the learner who pleaded with the teacher to continue. Despite the pain, the learner argued, he wanted the teacher to shock him because a friend of his had also been in the experiment and he wanted to prove his "manliness" to this friend. In this instance, all the people who obeyed the experimenter and *stopped* giving the shocks were counted as disobedient because they had refused the learner. But in an unpublished version, the experimenter left the room and the learner implored the subject to resume the shocks. Seven people agreed to give the learner the shocks he demanded. So what did that make them—obedient because they obeyed the learner or disobedient because they were flouting the experimenter's instructions?

In another variation, the learner said that he would take part only if the experimenter tried it first. The experimenter was strapped into the chair, and it was the learner who urged the teacher to continue, despite the protests of the experimenter in the next room. In this condition, obedience was defined as refusing to shock the experimenter or giving up at some point at or before twenty-nine shocks (425 volts).

Joe told me that there was nothing to be particularly proud of when it came to his resistance in the Milgram experiment. He'd had experiences that were much tougher tests of his principles—particularly when, as chairman of the Communist Party of New Haven, he was arrested and put on trial. "I think that experience led me to be skeptical. It led me to volunteer for this sort of thing, too, to see what's new in the world. But it certainly led me to have the stubbornness and the grit to say to a man in a white coat with horn-rimmed glasses that I am not going to do what you want." Joe said that he might have behaved differently if the authority had been one he respected: "At the same time, I also have said to myself sometimes, 'What would I do if the Communist Party ordered me to do something like that? Would I say no?' I think I would argue, fight, and maybe say no, but you know, there was a feeling I had at one time of wanting to belong that was very strong."

And Milgram's study did not deal with behavior in a group, Joe pointed out, so he wasn't sure that it was relevant to events like the Holocaust. People will do things in groups, both good and bad, he told me, that they might not do alone. As a soldier in France during World War II, for example, he was in a truck with a group of soldiers. A few of them had been drinking but had run out of booze. When they stopped for a break, one went to a farm and came back saying that the farmer was willing to trade calvados for gasoline. But gasoline was in short supply, and Joe and some others protested. "One of the drunks said, 'Shut the fuck up; we can get it if we want it!' I was frightened. They looked to me like they were going to fight over it.

And I was wondering, what are we going to do—how are we going to stop them? And one of the men who had been sitting there silently— just like out of a John Wayne movie he stood up. And he stood in the open doorway of the truck and he said, 'I'm not going to let you sell that gasoline,' and when he did that I jumped up and stood next to him. I was a little scared about being the first one . . . but I jumped up there to support him, and once I did a couple of others did. The drunks backed down. I wished I'd been the first one to stand up, but I wasn't."[1]

Ultimately, Milgram ignored the fact that people could change, Joe told me. Joe wouldn't have been as committed to social change if he thought that people couldn't change. He had volunteered for the army, which at that time was still segregated, after Pearl Harbor. Racism was rife in his all-white company. He recalled the arguments and discussions that they'd have in his company about "our attitude to black soldiers": "They used the 'N' word there, and I always was the one that didn't use it at that time. They had all these stupid beliefs: that Negroes were lazy and had to be ordered to work, and so on. And there was always a point in these conversations where they would say, 'If a Negro officer came along, a captain, say, would you salute?' And people would say, 'Well, I would salute the insignia of the rank but not the man.'" So watching Obama on television speaking to a crowd in South Carolina was inspirational. "The audience was jammed with young students—most of them white—who were obviously the people who'd been canvassing for him, knocking on doors and cheering him on, and I thought to myself, you know, some of these are the granddaughters and grandsons of the people I argued with in '42 and '43. It's fantastic the change that has occurred here."

No wonder Joe has been largely ignored. He could be right about his politics playing a part, but I think it's more that his account of the experiment proposes that Milgram captured a momentary mood rather than an enduring truth. That would be enough to cast doubt on Joe's reliability as a narrator. But while Joe is a heretic on a number of counts, the ultimate sin is that his experience suggests that people might have seen through Milgram's cover story, something that Milgram always downplayed.

That night I couldn't sleep. I kept thinking of Joe's optimism that people could change. And how Milgram's definition of obedience, despite his arguments about the power of the situation, seemed like a life sentence, as if people were frozen forever that way—fixed, stuck, like butterflies on a pin.

Milgram assured us of the reality of the experiment—the detailed and painstaking procedures that he went through to make the machine look authentic and the victim's cries sound agonized, the brisk efficiency that he had trained Williams to portray. But now, hearing it from Joe's point of view, there were several things about the experiment that just didn't make sense. I wondered how many of Milgram's subjects, like Joe, had suspected the cover story at either a conscious or subconscious level. I wondered how many were alert to clues, if not downright suspicious, during the experiment itself.

The power of Milgram's results rests on the belief that they are valid. Milgram asked us to believe that his volunteers thought that the machine, the actors, the pain—the whole situation—was real. We know that many subjects believed the elaborate experimental setup, but what evidence is there that all of his subjects were convinced? Milgram simply told us that they were and offered as evidence the distress that many of them suffered.[2] Yet in the archives, there's evidence that a surprising number of subjects had doubts.

Some subjects wrote to Milgram immediately after the experiment to give their impression of events. On August 29, 1961, just three weeks after the experiments began, Milgram received a letter from a subject who took part in either condition 1 or 2. It begins: "Dear Sir, I have some 'second thoughts' about the experiment of last night and feel that I should express these thoughts for what ever they are worth to your program." The author writes that he had worked out that he was the object of study, and the experiment wasn't about memory and learning. He argued that "subconsciously" he noticed details that led him to this conclusion:

> Both pieces of paper probably had the word "teacher" on it [sic]. While the instructor was speaking the "learner" acted rather disinterested, which is not normal for a person in a

strange experiment. . . . When the "learner" was strapped in the chair and the instructor casually remarked that the worst that could happen was skin burns . . . it somehow does not fit in the picture. . . . Then there were the one-way mirrors, I wondered why I was not allowed to see the "learner." Also a point was made of giving me my check and not the "learner" at the same time.

He observed that it was well known that punishment didn't help learning, and concluded: "I think the 'learner' never received any shock. Hence you were observing my behavior and I would like to know a little more about the reasons for this program. Is this possible?"

Milgram replied two days later, telling the man: "This experimental research is being supported by the Federal Government, and officially, I am not supposed to talk about its true purposes." But Milgram offered to discuss it with him if he could keep the information "confidential."[3]

Six months later, another of Milgram's subjects wrote to say that he had picked up on the deception. A letter dated February 12, 1962, was from a subject who took part in a condition that involved three teachers, two of whom were confederates. The experimenter was called away during the proceedings by a rigged phone call. The man described the arrival of the third volunteer before the experiment began and how, when the group of them got to a doorway, the others stood aside to let him go first. This "red carpet" treatment made him suspicious, as did the drawing of lots for roles. He continued:

As Mr. Wallace was being secured in the "electric chair," his remark of having a "bad heart" and a history of hospitalization for it had practically no effect upon the "assistant" in charge. He dismissed the complaint with, "This machine has been tested and does no tissue damage." This, of course, had nothing to do with the complaint.

The learner was strapped into the chair and the three teachers were given their allotted roles: the first, reading the word pairs; the second, giving shocks; and the third, reading out the correct answers. The au-

thor of the letter wondered why Yale would pay three people for a job
that could be done by one. When the experimenter got an emergency
phone call and had to leave, he knew that the experiment was a setup.
"All my doubts were now confirmed—I was the one being tested!"

At that point, the learner began to give the wrong answers, and the
subject had to administer the shocks. At some point he disobeyed, and
one of the other teachers said that he would take over:

> When "Mr. Barnaby," very unconcerned, took over as "execu-
> tioner" and continued until the "learner" was beyond reply-
> ing, the experiment ended and the "assistant" showed up at
> the exact appropriate moment.
>
> I now was certain that I had "been had." I gave the "assis-
> tant" the expected answers, the "heart victim" emerged smil-
> ing, and I was dismissed.
>
> At this point I expected someone to say, "You have been on
> *Candid Camera*, and I am Dorothy Collins in disguise."
>
> The hour was late, I had a previous appointment, so I left
> feeling that the three remaining conspirators were feeling as
> pleased with themselves as I was with myself for having seen
> through such an obvious test of conformity.
>
> I hope I have been some assistance to you, and thereby
> earned my $4.50.[4]

Milgram always maintained that his subjects believed what he
wanted them to believe. But it's clear that some subjects had their own
views of what had happened.

Many subjects also expressed their suspicions in the questionnaire
they returned to Milgram in the summer of 1962. These skeptical
volunteers spanned the full range of conditions, indicating that the
authenticity of the experiment didn't improve over time. A sample
from conditions 4 to 18 includes Subject 408—"I found it hard to
believe that Yale would allow a paid subject (the actor) to absorb
such punishment. The description on the control board was a bit far
fetched (i.e. strong shock etc) . . . the learner's poor answers were not
completely believable. He seemed too intelligent to stumble so"—
and Subject 502: "I offered the shock recipient the opportunity to

avenge himself on me by letting him give me the works. His refusal convinced me that he was an experimenter or an unshocked participant." Subject 722 noted, "I was of the opinion that everything was rigged and we were puppets. I did not believe that the learner was being hurt in any way," while Subject 1914 wrote, "I felt fairly sure that I was the only subject, and my own reactions were being studied rather than the 'students.' Because of this I did continue with the program, almost feeling a gleeful pleasure at having guessed, in some degree, what was actually happening." And Subject 929, rather self-congratulatory, wrote: "I caught the one way glass right away and also the 'dog eared' check handed to one of your actors. I felt I had the whole operation doped out and told your Dr. Williams so. I think I was very observant and pat myself on the back for being so sharp."[5]

Some cover stories were so puzzlingly elaborate that it's easy to see why subjects doubted them. Condition 18, for example, involved Williams saying that he had an urgent phone call and had to leave, asking the subject to conduct the experiment in his absence and leaving a phone number where he could be reached. If the subject rang to ask Williams what to do, he was given the standard prompts to continue. As one man described it, the fact that the experimenter left the subject in charge of something so seemingly important was a sign of something fishy: "Another thing that made me feel it was rigged was the fact that on an experiment where somebody would be asked to devote their time to come down to do something like this [the experimenter] was going to leave and wouldn't be back for an hour. . . . That, coupled with the bad heart . . . and the mirror and [the fact that] I thought that we were being observed." Another commented, "I think that something as important as that the professor wouldn't have gone away."

Others were alert to the phoniness of the experimental props. Subject 508 noted, "When the professor gave me the nod to go ahead, the thought went through my mind that that sounds like a recording. That's when I first realized that it was rigged and from that moment on it didn't make a bit of difference to me."[6]

Subject 1810 also noticed anomalies in the setting. He told Errera "there were things about this setup that didn't seem quite true." He noticed when Williams was strapping McDonough that there was a loudspeaker in "the upper right-hand corner of the room," and when McDonough started yelling, "[I] didn't hear him through the hole in the door, which I should have; I heard him up to the right-hand side." He said he thought a tape recorder was hooked up to the speaker, and "it put a doubt in my mind." When the learner shouted out that he refused to continue, he phoned the experimenter from the lab, and "I thought I heard the telephone ring on the other side of the . . . two-way mirror and I was quite sure that the telephone I rang was just inside the glass . . . these are some of the things that keep going around in my head and [I was] trying to determine was this thing really true, was it happening?" He explained, "I was really searching for some— just a clue—of whether he was there or not, and I knew that his hands were strapped in. I asked him to kick the wall, and I received no response. Even being a cinder-block wall, I should have been able to hear it." He regretted his passivity, telling Errera, "I should have stopped or I should have had a look in the other room. I wasn't sure if it was a hoax."[7]

Yet even if he'd wanted to check on the learner, he wouldn't have been able to. Another man who took part in the same condition was present at another Errera-conducted interview, and he explained that when Williams left him to continue the experiment on his own, Williams had unscrewed the knob on the door to the learner's room and taken it away with him.[8]

One of the most powerful causes for skepticism was the learner's agreement to take part, given his apparent heart condition. One man told Errera, "Well, look at it the other way now . . . this man said he had a heart attack and just came out of the hospital . . . I'm sure that if any person had had a heart attack he would not have said, 'Well, all right, go ahead, I got nothing to lose,' and I can't conceive of the instructor telling us to go ahead and keep shocking this man." Another subject confessed, "When he said that he had a bad heart, I felt then that it was rigged because I felt that Yale would not be responsible if somebody was going to have the electricity shock treatment . . . that they would have made sure that he would have had a physical examination. In other words, they wouldn't just pull someone in off the street." A third said, "I had my suspicion as to his authenticity when he went along with the experiment in spite of a supposed weak heart. . . . My suspicions were affirmed when I said I was giving him a higher voltage shock when actually I pressed the lowest voltage button and his cries still increased."[9]

The confusing mix of signals subjects were getting—that the learner was in pain, that the experimenter wouldn't allow them to hurt anyone, that the machine gave real shocks, disbelief that this could be happening at Yale—left many subjects in a state of uncertainty and stress. It was not a simple case of a conflict between conscience and the experimenters' commands. Subject 919 described this situation colorfully in a conversation with Errera.

Subject 919: I was sort of torn between two thoughts. One was that I was a patsy amongst a bunch of shills and the other was that this possibly was a legitimate experiment.

Errera: You'd better translate for me. What's a patsy amongst shills?

Subject 919: A patsy is a pigeon, that's what I say.

Errera: And a shill is—

Subject 919: More or less a professional pigeon . . . who gets the game going for the house.[10]

This process of seesawing between what to believe, what to disregard, and whether the experiment was on the level intensified the stress of an already stressful situation. Milgram's subjects were facing two incongruous pieces of information: the learner's pain and the experimenter's lack of concern for this pain. As Ian Parker put it, the choice was between "a man in apparent danger and another man—a man in a lab coat—whose lack of evident concern suggested there was no danger."[11] So who did the subject believe? Psychiatrists Martin Orne and

Charles Holland argued that Milgram's subjects, upon being faced with such a puzzling inconsistency, understood unconsciously that no harm was being done. Based on this theory, if a subject instinctively believed the experimenter, they obeyed. If they did believe the learner to be in danger, they disobeyed.[12]

This theory turns Milgram's results upside down. If people's suspicions affected their behavior, their obedience could have been a sign that they believed there was no danger involved—that at some level, they'd seen through the ruse. Reading this prompted me to seek out this table from Milgram's *Obedience to Authority*.

During the experiment	Defiant	Obedient	All subjects
I fully believed the learner was getting painful shocks	62.5%	47.9%	56.1%
Although I had some doubts, I believed the learner was probably getting the shocks	22.6%	25.9%	24.0%
I just wasn't sure whether the learner was getting the shocks or not	6.0%	6.2%	6.1%
Although I had some doubts, I thought the learner was probably not getting the shocks	7.6%	16.2%	11.4%
I was certain the learner was not getting the shocks	1.4%	3.8%	2.4%

Milgram argued that three-quarters of his subjects "by their own testimony acted under the belief that they were administering painful shocks." I looked at the numbers again. Milgram's three-quarters looked more like half to me. In his conclusion that more than 75 percent of his subjects believed the learner was receiving painful shocks, he had included the 24 percent who had some doubts over whether what was happening was real. It's more truthful to say that only half of the people who undertook the experiment fully believed it was real, and of those two-thirds disobeyed the experimenter.

Milgram would later argue that this was a case of subjects denying the disturbing fact of what they had done by pretending in retrospect that they had never believed it. Just as he did with people who disagreed with his results, Milgram dismissed criticism as an inability to face a particularly troubling truth.[13]

At the same time, Milgram was obviously sufficiently worried about the number of people who wrote in the questionnaires that they had seen through the experiment. Late one afternoon in the archives, I found a more detailed analysis of just how many of Milgram's subjects had gone to the maximum voltage—been "obedient"—because they suspected that the experiment was a hoax. Milgram had asked Taketo Murata, his research assistant in the summer of 1962, to compile a condition-by-condition breakdown of the number of people who said that they doubted the learner was getting shocked. He was then supposed to compare that with the degree of shock they actually gave.

Taketo divided the subjects into two groups. One contained those who were certain the learner was being shocked; the other, those who said they had doubts. Taketo found that in eighteen of twenty-three conditions, those who wrote that they fully believed the learner was receiving painful shocks gave lower levels of shock than those who said they thought that the learner was faking it.

Taketo's unpublished analysis, suggesting that many went to the maximum voltage because they knew they weren't torturing anybody, contradicted Milgram's claims. In all twenty-three variations of the experiment, Taketo found the people most likely to disobey and give lower-voltage shocks were those who said they believed someone really was being hurt.[14] Depending on which piece of data you look at—Milgram's published table or Taketo's unpublished analysis—you could be forgiven for coming to completely different conclusions.

What Taketo's analysis provides is an insight into the believability of Milgram's cover story from one condition to the next. Conditions 3, 12, and 24 were the most effective, with over 70 percent of subjects in each convinced that the learner was being shocked. On the other hand, more than two-thirds of people in conditions 1 and 2 doubted that the experiment was real.

Milgram made a note on the bottom of Taketo's analysis, arguing that the results couldn't really be taken seriously because of course his subjects were more likely to say afterward that they suspected or knew the experiment wasn't real. (Those unreliable subjects again, contaminating data.) He did have a point—many people, having read the report that explained the experiment, with its uncomfortable conclusions, may have chosen to rewrite their experiences to make their behavior more palatable. But if he couldn't trust what people said in the questionnaires because they rewrote history, why was Milgram so ready to use the questionnaire data in other ways—to prove, for example, that the majority of his subjects were glad to have taken part? When it suited him, he used this data; when it didn't suit him, he ignored it.

Taketo's analysis, based on people's self-reported feelings about the experiment a year after it ended, has its flaws, and some will question its reliability. But it raises doubts that are hard to put to rest. If, as Taketo's analysis suggests, people were less likely to obey when they thought the man was being hurt, then Milgram's experiment tells us the opposite of what we've been led to believe: it's not that inside all of us there's an Eichmann waiting for the right situation—a commanding authority figure whose destructive orders we will follow blindly. Instead, Taketo's analysis suggests the opposite: that the majority of Milgram's subjects resisted orders when they truly believed they might be hurting someone.

I decided that I had to find and speak to Taketo Murata.

Some time later, I was at the Toronto Writers' Centre—an anonymous-looking building nestled between Korean restaurants and discount grocery stores on Bloor Street West—waiting for Taketo Murata. He was right on time. The photos of Taketo online show him in a business suit, but today he was dressed casually. I hurried down the steps to let him in after he pressed the buzzer, conscious of my tiredness as we made our way up to the top floor again. The hotel where I was staying had live jazz in the bar into the small hours, and it had kept me awake. That morning I had had to rely on the icy wind to propel me the ten blocks from the hotel to the writers' center.

Taketo had been up for a while, too. He had left his home just outside of Toronto before 7 A.M. to get to Bloor Street by nine, but despite this he looked remarkably perky. He had planned the route to avoid traffic, allowed for the construction that would slow him down, and built in a delay just in case. He was methodical, well organized. It was these qualities that impressed Milgram, who wanted someone careful and thorough to analyze the hundreds of questionnaires that came flooding back from his subjects in the summer of 1962.

Taketo was twenty-five when he started work for Milgram. He'd been at Yale for four years, arriving in 1958 to do a doctorate in psychology. He came with a first-class honors degree in biological science from McGill, a dream to be a university professor, and not a lot of money. To save, he lived in the medical dormitory across the street from the psychology department. Many nights when Taketo was going to sleep, he saw the lights in the psychology building burning after midnight as junior professors like Milgram worked late, turning out research that they hoped would bring them closer to tenure. Taketo found the intense competition between staff in the psychology department off-putting. "The junior guys were spending more hours working than the students were. It was an up-or-out kind of environment for them."

By the end of his second year at Yale, in 1959, Taketo had decided that psychology was not right for him. The focus on specialization and the pressure to publish were intense. "Even the older people who were known in the field were cranking out stuff left, right, and sideways to enhance their reputation. A lot of them would take a particular topic or subject they were studying—they usually had a whole bunch of assistants paid for by grants—and they would write the same stuff in different ways to go in different journals, even though they were basically the same thing. The general rule of thumb was, when you came up for tenure, the important thing was to make sure that you got your reprints of journal articles with heavy covers so they would weigh more. Because the people reading this stuff, the people passing judgment, often didn't know exactly what the hell you were writing about because they are specialized over here, and you are specialized over here. The volume you produced was more important." He felt that most of his classmates were engaged in research that was "going nowhere" and wouldn't stand the test of time. "Well, it became kind of meaningless in the end, you know. And I've passed this on to my kids. A lot of jobs, even if they're prestigious, they don't do anything."

By the time he met Milgram in 1962, Taketo had abandoned psychology for sociology, which he found liberatingly "open-ended." To fund his studies, he taught introductory sociology to nursing students, but then the job of graduate research assistant to Milgram came up. People warned him about Milgram. "They said to me, you know, he's a very prickly character, he's kind of moody, he's kind of abrupt, he can be rude. But I didn't find him that way at all."

Taketo began work for Milgram in the summer of 1962 and watched a few experiments in what would have been the final condition through the one-way mirror. In contrast to the kind of "trivial" research he'd seen conducted in the rest of the psychology department, he felt that Milgram's was different. "It seemed more meaningful, to have extensions beyond just getting tenure. And it was a very unusual kind of experiment—it wasn't just the deception, it was the actual stress that people were going through. And that was a major difference from what everyone else was doing."

I asked if it bothered him, if he wondered what Milgram was doing when he saw how upset subjects became. "No, we were all ethically dead at that time," he responded, and laughed. I laughed along but was taken aback at his honesty.

The major part of his work that summer was the data analysis, the coding of subjects' answers to the questionnaire. Taketo worked with a calculating machine and the pile of more than seven hundred questionnaires in his room or in the library, having no real office to speak of. I showed Taketo the four-page paper that he'd written comparing the level of shock people gave against whether or not they believed the experiment was real. Taketo leaned forward to look. I spread the densely typed pages across the boardroom table, and we stood before each page. Taketo read bits aloud and shook his head. He recognized his handwriting but didn't remember doing the analysis. He stared at the pages of columns of numbers, the hypotheses, the means, the terminology of statistics; he picked up a page, read bits of it under his breath. Then he sat down again and leaned back in his chair. As we took in the ant-like jottings, the ruled lines, the columns and rows of figures—the hours and hours of work—Taketo said the level of detail showed that Milgram got caught up in the minutiae of statistical analysis and lost sight of the bigger picture. "I think so—that's really what it is. There are a lot of other things that are beyond this collection of data—it could be something else that's entirely different from what's involved. In medical terms, it might not be the drug that's doing this; it could be the fact that a guy's genetic makeup might be a little different in this group versus that group, and that's what's produced the different results, not the drug itself."

But talk like that would have been heresy back in his Yale days, surely? Taketo agreed that it would. Then he pointed at a small paragraph of text that summarized what he'd found and nodded his head. "There. If you fully believed that this whole thing was real, then you were likely to punish the guy less. Makes sense."

Of course it made sense. But as Milgram pointed out, it wasn't perfect science. Taketo was comparing the degree of shock people gave during the experiment with what they said they believed after the event was over. There was plenty of room for error. Yet why did Milgram get Taketo to spend so much time on it and then not use it? Perhaps Milgram realized that publishing it may have offered his critics ammunition. And publication suggests a confidence and a sense of security that Milgram, perhaps starting to become worn down by criticism, may have lacked.

Although Taketo was impressed by Milgram's boldness in conceiving of the obedience research, he eventually came to regard his employer as almost reckless. For it wasn't the work he did for Milgram on the obedience study that stuck in Taketo's mind—after all, that was just a sophisticated form of number crunching—it was his involvement in Milgram's next research project. Milgram, with graduate students Leon Mann and Susan Harter, devised a way of measuring community attitudes not by asking people what they thought but by observing how they behaved. If you found a stamped but unpost-marked letter addressed to a major political party lying on the foot-path, wouldn't you be more likely to post the letter in the nearest mailbox if it was to a party that you supported? Milgram and his stu-dents reasoned that whether a letter addressed to a particular political party reached its destination would provide a measure of the support for that political party in that neighborhood. They called it "the Lost Letter technique."

Milgram and his students road-tested the technique in New Haven in April 1963. Four hundred letters were addressed to three organiza-tions—Friends of the Nazi Party, Friends of the Communist Party, and Medical Research Associates—and an individual, Mr. Walter Carnup. Interestingly, over 70 percent of letters addressed to the medi-cal research company were posted, indicating that in New Haven sci-ence was held in high regard.[15]

But—some might say typically—Milgram had underestimated the effect on those who found the letters. The letters addressed to the Friends of the Nazi Party in particular caused a flurry of panic among Jewish shopkeepers, who, as Milgram acknowledged in his notes, were "over represented among the small store owners in New Haven." The shopkeepers, having "found" the Nazi Party letters in or near their shops, subsequently contacted the head of the local antidefamation league of B'nai B'rith, who made it his business to pass the letters on to the FBI for fingerprinting.[16]

Undeterred, Milgram was interested in testing the water in a more volatile environment than New Haven. He sent Taketo and his room-mate Charlie Buchwald down south, where civil rights was a hot is-sue. Taketo and Charlie set off with a sense of adventure and freedom, buoyed by the prospect of a week on the road, away from offices and faculty and pressure, their trunk full of letters addressed to pro– and anti–civil rights groups.

It wasn't until they were on their way to Raleigh, North Carolina, that they had second thoughts. "We didn't realize the potential dan-ger involved in going down there. Our first realization of it was as we were passing a Howard Johnson's motel and there were a couple of big buses and police cars all around, and they were rounding up all

the blacks who were demonstrating in front of the Howard Johnson's
and taking them to jail. It was kind of racially charged." They had
passed the Howard Johnson's on Chapel Hill Highway in Durham,
the site of a mass demonstration in which two leaders were arrested
when they tried to enter the segregated restaurant.[17] Four hundred
African Americans and a handful of whites had locked arms and sat
down outside in the parking lot in protest, singing, "We're going to
eat at Howard Johnson's one of these days." At around 7 P.M., when
Taketo and Charlie drove past, they saw people being dragged to their
feet and pulled toward one of the five waiting buses. The men were
suddenly conscious that "this was no laughing matter." Their license
plates identified them as from out of town and, even worse, from the
north. "If you went further, on to Mississippi, they were killing some
of these people that had come out of the north and were perceived as
agitating the locals to get uppity."

They drove on, aware of how it would look if the police pulled them
over and opened the trunk, which was full of more than five hundred
letters addressed to pro- and anti-segregation groups. They spent seven
days traveling down through Charlotte to Raleigh, by day locating
all the white and all the black neighborhoods, and returning at night
to drop the letters. Not surprisingly, the study found "a high rate of
return of the pro–civil rights letters from the Negro neighborhoods
and a high rate of return of the anti–civil rights letters from the white
neighborhoods."[18]

Taketo described the trip with a tinge of something like awe, even
though it was his own experience he was describing. It gave him a
fresh perspective on his employer, and made him contemplate the
consequences for participants in some of Milgram's research. "I often
wondered whether or not Milgram even thought about the dangerous
implications in some of these things."

Taketo had been a successful businessman and was now a government consultant. He said that Yale gave him a way of thinking about
people that had been invaluable. "We're too trusting," he told me.
"Look at Bernie Madoff, the investment adviser who scammed millions." Taketo thought that Milgram's subjects should have been a bit
more skeptical. I wondered later if he was talking about himself, too.

When he spoke about that road trip, his voice was full of a kind of wonder—which I first thought was because he couldn't believe he'd done it. Or was it that, in hindsight, he couldn't believe that Milgram had placed him in such a dangerous position?

What was it that caused people to ignore their gut feelings? I thought of Taketo continuing to deliver his letters on his journey south, despite his sense of danger. I thought of Joe Dimow and others who were suspicious but rarely raised their doubts during the experiment itself. Was it the tension of the moment that propelled them, was it the authority of the experimenter, or was it something else, greater than the experiment itself, that caused them to hesitate—was it the setting or even science itself?

Yale was undoubtedly a powerful influence on several subjects. Many expressed their faith that the experiment must have been safe because of where it was held. One commented, "If I felt he was going to be really hurt in any way I'm sure I would have stopped regardless of what anybody said, but to me, since it was an experiment and it was supervised, I felt that it was in the interest of science and nobody, except by accident, would be hurt." Another said, "I continued more or less because I couldn't conceive of any other human being telling me to continue on with the—with what I was supposed to be doing, and at the same time that person allowing me to hurt anybody else. I thought they'd allow us to continue up to that certain point where the instructor or whoever was supervising would stop us if he thought we were going to do harm to an individual." A third noted, "I became certain midway through the experiment that I was the only one involved. The learner's protests as to his heart condition normally would have caused the Yale experimenter to halt the proceedings and check the seriousness of the learner's condition." And a fourth said, "I think we were all probably in a pretty amiable frame of mind when we came in, though, and it's kind of flattering to be—the idea that you're going to take part in an experiment managed by a well-known, lofty institution. You certainly wished to . . . I certainly wished to do my full share and cooperate."[19]

But Milgram was aware of Yale's potential influence on his results.

He tested how much effect Yale had by conducting a variation, condition 23, at the nearby industrial town of Bridgeport. He rented a four-room suite on the main street, in the anonymous-looking Newfield Building—Milgram described it as "a somewhat rundown commercial building located in the downtown shopping area"—had the rooms painted light green, furnished it with hired office furniture, and installed the ubiquitous one-way mirror.[20] Then, he sent out a letter to selected Bridgeport residents from the fictitious "Research Associates of Bridgeport" and signed by an equally fictitious "Stephen Millert PhD." Milgram would later argue that he had successfully established "a complete dissociation from Yale" in his Bridgeport variation of the experiment. However, the letter stressed the words "scientific" and "research" to describe the study being conducted. People were asked to help out in a "scientific study of memory" by a "non-profit organization," which, intentionally or not, suggested a serious and worthwhile study.

In addition, Milgram had underestimated the powerful authority of science itself as an influence on people's behavior. It was a compelling motivator when it came to people's decision to continue or refuse. Psychiatrist Martin Orne suggested that Milgram's subjects believed that if it was science, it must be worthwhile. They arrived wanting to be helpful. In fact, Orne found that there was very little that people wouldn't do for science—he couldn't find a way to stop them from doing things that they would never normally do. He gave people all sorts of boring, repetitive, and useless tasks in the name of scientific research, and he couldn't find one they would refuse.

Orne found that people invested tasks that they would normally regard as trivial or bizarre with importance because if it was of interest to a professor, then there must have been a good reason for it. In other words, people's behavior in a lab, in an interaction with a scientist, might have little bearing on how they would interact with a nonscientist in the world outside. People didn't object or refuse but accepted the passive role that came with being a subject. They did it willingly because it was science, and a scientist had asked them to do it.[21] Whether the experiments were held in the august setting of Yale or in an office building in Bridgeport, Orne would have argued, those taking part would continue to obey the experimenter because of their reverence for science. As one of the female subjects put it, "I am not entirely convinced that a subject's reaction in a lab is necessarily identical with his reaction in a real-world situation."[22]

When I looked again at the subjects' responses to the questionnaire and in talking to Errera, it became obvious that science was a powerful force in reassuring participants who may have doubted the legitimacy of the cover story. One subject said, "Why do I think I obeyed? In the cause of science, more than anything else. It was an experiment." In an interview, Errera asked one man if he would jump off a bridge in the interests of science, and the man agreed that he would. In another discussion, Errera probed a subject's feelings about going to the maximum voltage.

Errera: You say you had a guilty conscience.

Man: I must have had a guilty conscience that I did go that far, but I felt I should because it was a scientific experiment and I've always been interested in all kinds of science.[23]

And at the end of each of the Bridgeport experiments, before he revealed the hoax, Williams asked each man what he thought the Research Associates of Bridgeport was and why he had volunteered. Milgram had presumably told Williams to ask this to demonstrate that subjects had no idea that Yale was behind the research.[24] Most said they didn't know, but many assumed that it was an organization conducting scientific research. Williams probed this issue with several subjects, and it was obvious that even though many didn't have the slightest clue about the organization and what it ostensibly did, they were still prepared to trust it because of the scientific imprimatur.

One man who had gone to 450 volts said that he was motivated by his six-year-old daughter.

Man: I can only say that I was—look, I'm willing to do anything that's ah, to help humanity, let's put it that way.

Williams: Right, that's what we're doing.

Man: I've got—I've got a child that's a cerebral palsy child.

Williams: Have you really?

Man: And you know they're experimenting steadily on trying to find a cure for it. It's a sad thing.

Another disobedient man said he "thought it might have something to do with the new science program, you know, outer space and all that."

Two other subjects made similar assumptions.

Williams: Tell me, who are Research Associates of Bridgeport?

Subject 2331: I have no idea.

Williams: Who am I? Other than the fact that you know my name.

Subject 2331: Well, I assume that you are either a psychologist or a doctor. You're probably a psychologist.

[. . .]

Williams: Who are Research Associates of Bridgeport?

Subject 2333: Who are they? I don't know. I imagine they, the way I thought, the idea I had, was that they experiment . . . they do research for education, health.[25]

While Milgram found lower rates of obedience in Bridgeport— 47 percent were obedient and 53 percent were defiant—he concluded that they were not significantly lower than the results at Yale. The simple explanation for this may be that while Milgram may have dissociated the Bridgeport experiments from Yale, he had failed to dissociate them from science. "There is no authority to-day greater than the authority of science," said Steven Marcus, an English professor at Columbia University who reviewed Milgram's book *Obedience to Authority* in the *New York Times Book Review*, in an interview about Milgram's research. Marcus gave the example of William H. Masters and Virginia E. Johnson, who did extensive research on the sexual behavior of Americans in the 1950s. Masters and Johnson "were sure that they would have to hire prostitutes. Instead they discovered that some of the most respectable people in St. Louis were willing to fuck in public before someone wearing a white coat."[26]

Milgram and others like him may have thought they controlled the subjects' experience in the lab, but subjects were constantly interpreting what was happening in ways that the experimenter couldn't control. They were curious and alert, and actively trying to divine the experimenter's purpose. Perhaps the only thing that kept some from walking out or challenging the experimenter on his cover story was the influence of science—the belief that there was some higher, altruistic purpose to the experiments. In this sense, the experiments were a self-referential loop: science was the motivation and the result, the reason and the cause, the inspiration and the end goal.

The evening of my meeting with Taketo, I sat in the hotel bar and watched the band perform a disparate, honking brand of jazz. The band members seemed to jerk and play separate pieces, rather than playing together. I closed my eyes and tried to listen differently, to let the music speak for itself and form some sort of whole. The image of Taketo and his friend racing along the highway, fueled by fear, drifted into my mind. It was a jarring postscript to the obedience study.

But was it? The music had shifted—the saxophone had joined the drums in a seamless movement—and now I could hear a kind of melody, a theme. My thoughts fell into line. Milgram talked about obedience and its relevance to the Holocaust, but if, as he argued, our tendency to obey malevolent authority was a universal trait, what did he make of the mass civil disobedience that was erupting across the country? What did he make of the civil rights movement, the demonstrations against the Vietnam War—weren't they evidence that people were not programmed to obey blindly? About this, Milgram was silent.

I opened my eyes. Had he simply ignored evidence and events that contradicted or undermined his results? Or was it that the demonstrations and protests around him seemed trivial in comparison to the horrific events of Nazi Germany in World War II?

The room erupted into applause and I started then joined in, glad to have a distraction, glad of the cheering and the noise.

6

THE SECRET EXPERIMENTS

I had been looking at the same box of folders in the library for half an hour. I knew that something wasn't right with them but couldn't work out what it was. The finding aid told me that the folders were subject files for condition 23, the variation that Milgram had conducted in the nearby town of Bridgeport. But rather than the usual forty, there were sixty subject files inside the box, which didn't add up.

Then I noticed that twenty of the files belonged to what was labeled as condition 24. I went back to my notes and found a passing reference to it in an early report to the NSF. What did that mean? That night I went through Milgram's book *Obedience to Authority*, which made no mention of a second experiment at Bridgeport or of a condition 24. I studied my photos of the contents of the files. It was like putting together the pieces of a jigsaw without having a picture to guide me. But slowly things began to fall into place. Instead of one volunteer per experiment in condition 24, there were two. From their addresses I found that some lived in the same street, others in the same house. They came to the lab together. In total, he recruited twenty pairs of volunteers for this experiment. Milgram had recruited pairs of friends, relatives, neighbors, fathers and sons.[1]

The next day, I located the audiotapes of condition 24. Through my headphones I listened to Subject 2425, a thirty-two-year-old Jewish man who arrived at the lab with his friend and neighbor, whom we'll call Doug. Williams's patter was practiced by then: he had been giving the same spiel five nights a week and on weekends for nine months.

The two friends drew lots for the roles of teacher and learner. Subject 2425, who was in fact a high school teacher, was given the teacher role—I'll call him Larry. From the moment he was assigned the role, I found it impossible to identify with anyone but Larry as I listened; he was drawn in by the story and was nervous, hesitant, and eager to please. As Williams strapped Doug into the chair in the adjoining room, Larry looked on. Doug was not yet in on the hoax. They both sounded worried.

> Doug: Good grief. Are you sure this is . . . I don't want to sit here and be electrocuted, now . . .
>
> Williams: The shocks may be painful. . . . Let me explain briefly to you what's going to happen—he'll say "blue," and then he'll read four more words, and your job is to remember which of the four words was originally paired with "blue."
>
> Larry: Yeah, how bad do these shocks get?
>
> Williams: They won't be dangerous, but they may be painful.

Back in the main room, Williams explained Larry's task to him. I imagined Milgram coming out of his hiding place as Williams kept Larry occupied and creeping into the adjoining room to Doug, whispering what he wanted him to do and say as each switch on the machine was pressed.

Larry was still concerned when they began.

> Larry: Oh, boy. *[Nervous laughter]*
>
> Williams: Brisk pace, please. Attention, learner—your teacher is about to begin the test. Try and remember the word pairs. Ready? Begin.
>
> Larry: Blue girl, nice day, fat neck, green ink, rich boy, fast bird, blunt arrow, soft hair, cool cave, gold moon, hard head, wet duck,

brave woman, white horse, sad face, short time, sharp needle, slow dance, red sunset, low noise, new book, quiet evening, tame bear, sweet taste, true story.

Having read the word list, Larry began to test Doug's memory. After each question, I heard a faint buzz as Doug indicated his answer and it registered in the light box on top of the machine. Larry gave his friend three shocks, but it was not until the fourth shock, at 75 volts, that he heard any reaction.

Larry: Soft: rug, pillow, hair, grass. *[Doug's answer lights up]* Wrong. Seventy-five volts. *[Gives shock]*

Doug: Ow.

Larry: Soft hair. *[Nervous laughter]* Cool: *[voice shaking slightly]* day, shade, water, cave. *[Answer lights up.]* Wrong. Ninety volts. *[Gives shock]*

Doug: Ow!

Larry: Cool cave. *[Pause, before resuming with badly shaking voice]* Gold: dollar, necklace, moon, paint. *[Answer lights up.]* Right. Hard: stone, head, bread, work. *[Answer lights up.]* Wrong. One hundred and five volts. *[Gives shock]*

Doug: Ow!

Larry: Hard head. Wet: night, grass, duck, cloth. *[Answer lights up.]* Wrong. One hundred and twenty volts. *[Gives shock]*

Doug: *[long and drawn out]* Ow!!

Larry: Wet duck. Brave: woman, soldier, dog, horse. *[Answer lights up.]* Wrong. One hundred and thirty-five volts. *[Gives shock]*

Doug: Aaah!

Larry: Brave woman. White: cloud, horse, rock, house. *[Answer lights up.]* Wrong. *[Gives shock]*

Doug: Aah! Larry!

Larry: One hundred and fifty volts. . . . Should I stop?

Williams: No, continue please.

Larry: White horse. . . . Even if he doesn't want to?

Williams: The experiment requires that you go on. Please continue.

Larry: Oh, boy. *[Pauses]* Sad: face, music, clown, girl. *[Answer lights up.]* Right. Short: sentence, movie, skirt, time. *[Answer lights up.]* Wrong. One hundred and sixty-five. *[Gives shock]*

Doug: Ow! Hey, Larry, let's stop it. I wanna get out of here, come on!

Williams: *[sensing Larry's hesitation]* Continue, please.

Larry: Even though he's against it?

Williams: Continue, please.

Doug: Hey, Lar?

Larry: *[calling out to Doug]* He told me to keep going! *[To Williams]* Even if it's against his will?

Williams: Please continue, teacher. The experiment requires that you go on.

Larry: Oh, boy. *[Pause]* Short time. Sharp: axe, needle, stick, blade. *[Answer lights up.]* Wrong. One-eight-oh. *[Gives shock]*

Doug: Ow! Hey, Larry, that's too much!

Larry: Sharp needle.

Doug: Come on, let me out.

Larry: Slow—

Doug: Let me out of here, come on.

Larry: *[to Williams]* Look, I'm not going to do this against his will.

Doug: Get me out of here. Come on, Lar!

Larry: If he's against it, I can't do it.

Williams: The experiment requires that you continue.

Larry: Yeah, but if he's against it I'm not going to continue. I mean, this guy's in pain. I can't do it.

Williams: As I said, the shocks may be painful, but they're not dangerous.

Larry: Would you ask him if he wants to continue?

Williams: No, we can't have any contact once we've started the test. We should avoid any talking, as a matter of fact. It's absolutely essential that you continue.

Larry: All right. Slow: walk, dance, truck, music. *[Answer lights up.]* Wrong. One ninety-five. *[Gives shock]*

Doug: *[yelling]* Ow, Lar, get me out of here, these straps. Come on!

Larry: Slow dance. Red . . . brick, rose, sunset, wagon.

Doug: *[shouting]* Come on, Lar, let's stop this.

Larry: No, I'm not gonna continue, I'm sorry. You can have your money back. I'm not going to continue.

Williams: The money is not the issue, teacher.

Larry: No, I'm sorry.

Doug: Hey, Larry, get me out of these straps, I'm not foolin'. Let's go. I'm serious.

Williams: The experiment requires that we continue, teacher.

Larry: Well, I'm disassociating myself from the experiment. I can't go on like this.

Doug: Get me out of here!

Williams: It's absolutely essential that you continue.

Larry: I'm sorry, I can't.

Williams: You have no other choice, teacher.

Larry: Why? Why do I have no other choice? He is screaming; I can't continue doing this. I have to face this guy.

Doug: Lar, come on!

Larry: I have to be with him. He's my neighbor and I can't go on with this.

Williams: If you don't continue, we'll have to discontinue the entire experiment.

Larry: May I speak to him?

Williams: Well, we'll have to discontinue. No, you're not allowed to have a conversation.

Larry: I can't. I can't go on.

Williams then took Larry through the usual set of questions about how he felt, but he also told him that Doug wasn't really being shocked—they had been watching to see how far he would go in following orders. Williams drew the parallel with being in the army and reluctantly following orders from someone of higher rank. Milgram then entered and joined the conversation. Larry talked about his reactions.

Larry: I thought he had an awful lot of guts when I started going beyond here . . . when I got to 195 or something, I thought, God, it's toasting him! I was so relieved when he started getting the right answers. I was shaking, I was nervous. He's ordering me and I'm afraid to tell him to go to hell, you know. It's important, I know—I'm working on my thesis. It's important, but whee!

Milgram: [to Williams] You broke the news, didn't you, that he wasn't really being shocked?

Larry: Oh yeah, I was glad to hear it. [Laughs] Very glad. It's a horrible feeling—this guy's my neighbor. I was talking to this guy's wife this afternoon; they're expecting their third child. All of a sudden I realized I'll be talking to him on the way home. I hope he'll at least drive me home. It's a long ride home. [Laughs]

Doug was brought back into the lab.

Larry: Did he tell you anything when he put you in that chair? Did you know anything in that chair? When you were put in that chair, did you know anything about it?

Doug: Yeah.

Larry: You rat.

[Both laugh.]

Larry: Oh buddy! You're in big—

Williams: He thought you really did—

Larry: I got very nervous.

Doug: How far did you get on this thing, Lar?

Larry: One ninety-five.

Williams took the leading role in the subsequent discussion, asking Larry and Doug how many people they thought might have continued to the maximum voltage. I could hear from their tone that Williams and Milgram were clearly proud of the research and excited by the results. But Larry wondered aloud how far he would have gone if it had been a stranger.

Doug: Lar, you wouldn't have done it even if you didn't know me.

Williams: Oh, I think he would have. I think Lar would have gone on.

Milgram: I don't think so. I don't know, I couldn't hear. I couldn't hear you, so—

Williams: We've done nine hundred people in this experiment. Nine hundred men roughly.

Milgram: Yeah.

Williams: That's a lot of people to put through here. How many people out of a hundred, would you say—not knowing the guy in the other room and hearing the screams—how many do you think out of a hundred would get to the end?

Doug: I think it depends a little on how effective the other end is.

Milgram: The screams are—

Williams: Less than half?

Larry: Sure. About 25 percent.

Williams: Sixty percent. How does that sound?

Larry: Would go to the end of that thing?

Doug: Would give a guy 450 volts?

Williams: On top of which, he's not answering at 300 volts. And furthermore, he stops screaming at 330 volts.

Larry: And he keeps on going?

Williams: He sure does.

Milgram: They sure do.

Larry: And you couldn't give an effective enough sales pitch to that guy to keep him from pushing those buttons.

Williams: I have set commands—I have three commands, I have four.

Larry: And they still go?

Milgram: One command he gives, the last one he gives, is "You have no other choice—you must go on."

Larry: And the individual has stopped making any angry cries—

Williams: Right.

Larry: What do you hear?

Williams: Nothing. He doesn't know if he's—

Larry: Dead?

Williams: Dead.

Milgram: He says, "Consider no answer as equivalent to a wrong answer and continue."

Williams: Same procedure as if it he got a wrong answer. So they give him the shock after that and he screams again, just like he's right there, and he shouts, "I *told* you I didn't want any more shocks, *let me out of here,*" and you can't imagine.

Milgram: It's taped. It's bloodcurdling.

Larry: You got me worried now. How far do you think I would have gone? *[Laughs nervously]* It bothers me now.

Williams: Do you mean if it was somebody you didn't know?

Doug: I don't think you would have gone—

Milgram: Let him speak. Go ahead . . .

Larry was preoccupied with the fact that he didn't stop earlier.

Larry: All I could think of was the whole complicated apparatus stopping now because I stopped . . . the whole nationwide testing maybe. He made it sound like a big deal and I thought, oh boy, I wonder if I would have really stopped. Chickenhearted I am, but how chickenhearted? How far would I go?

Milgram: People have different reasons, I think. Sometimes some people have a reason—for example, you're working on your master's, and working on an experiment, and you know an experiment may be valuable, and if it did stop something would be lost—

Larry: But how can I rationalize it in my own mind?

How could he rationalize it? Milgram didn't give him an answer. He and Williams were clearly keen to wrap it up—they had another pair due to arrive in just a few minutes. Williams escorted Larry out of the room, and Doug was given a few moments to write about why he thought his friend had stopped when he did. Within a few minutes, both men had left the lab and Williams got on with business: "That was Subject 2425, Subject 2426 coming up."[2]

I couldn't face listening to another one—I needed a break. I went outside for some fresh air, but the air was hot and heavy and I felt no cooler. I sat on a stone bench in the library's small courtyard and tried to empty my mind. Larry's agitation followed me outside. I imagined him afterward, left with questions about himself that no one could answer. Why had Milgram chosen to undertake such a risky and ethically problematic variation? Was that guilt I heard in his voice, in his hasty attempts to reassure Larry that he had a rational explanation for his behavior? And how did he, in the space of just a few minutes, get Doug to play along with the charade?

Back inside, to avoid listening to any more tapes, I went through the subject files of those who'd participated in condition 24. They were all men who had responded to a direct-mail invitation to take part—or at first I thought they had. Later I would discover that Milgram had phoned people whose names he got from other subjects because so few had responded to the letter. All twenty pairs took part in condition 24 over one week, between May 16 and 23, 1962. Three pairs were members of the same family—an uncle and a nephew, brothers-in-law, and a father and son, all of whom defied Williams.[3] The men in this condition all lived or worked in and around Bridgeport. One-third had parents born in Europe, and most of them worked in the manufacturing industry—two-thirds in unskilled or semiskilled jobs as machinists, welders, assemblers, and toolmakers and the rest included teachers, firefighters, and policemen. Three men went all the way to 450 volts, and seventeen broke off despite Williams's urging to continue. Each man had filled out a form, and while the names have been blacked out, their ages, marital status, and occupations are visible.

I wondered about those men. How did they feel when they realized that their friend or relative had been in cahoots with the experimenter? What was the conversation like in the car on the way home—between Larry and Doug, between father and son, between the friends who'd written that they'd grown up together, double-dated, and been each other's best man? It was startling to hear the "victim" address the teacher by name: "Hey, Jerry! Get me out of here!"; "Ow! Tony! Stop!" It was the teacher to whom the learner appealed to rescue him from more pain. Now, looking back, McDonough's cries—"Let me out! You can't keep me here"—that I had heard so many times in earlier conditions seemed ambiguous and could just as easily have been directed at the experimenter. Had McDonough addressed his complaints to the teacher by name, would people have continued to give the shocks, I wondered? And if teachers had interpreted the learner's cries as being directed at the experimenter, then it made sense that they would have reasoned that, if the experimenter made no move to respond, things couldn't have been as bad as they seemed.

Subject 2435's son threatened to wreck the lab if the experiment was not stopped. The father, after he had just given his son a 165-volt shock, warned Williams that his son was likely to "tear the place up" unless they stopped.

Father: . . . you better let him out because he'll do it! If you think any of your equipment . . . we'll give you back your checks—you can have your money back, I'm not that hard up, and let it go at that. To hell with it! Because I'm not gonna have him get hurt, and he'll rip your equipment up . . .

Williams of course insisted that the father continue, but the man burst into a tirade.

Father: *[shouting]* I don't give a God dang what "the experiment requires." If someone's getting hurt and hollering, there is no such thing as anyone gonna make continue with *[sic]*. . . . So don't give me that line of hooley. I'm not so dumb that I don't know that. And, as I say, you can have your two damn checks back! If he's gonna holler like that I'm not gonna keep going through with it!

Williams: You have no other choice, teacher.

Father: What do you mean I have no other choice?

Williams: If you don't continue, we're going to have to discontinue the entire experiment.

Father: *[quietening down]* Discontinue the entire thing! I ain't gonna have my boy—would you have your boy hollering in there like that?

Williams: Well, we'll have to discontinue. May I ask you a few questions?

Father: I'm not going to sit there—after all, that's my boy, and I'm not gonna sit—[4]

The father, a married fifty-four-year-old assembler at Dictaphone who had two other children, told Williams in the dehoax that his brother-in-law had recommended that he volunteer for the experiment. Presumably, the brother-in-law had already been a subject but had not told this man what he would be expected to do. Later, after Williams had dehoaxed and calmed the father, Milgram came into the room and introduced himself: "I thought you were going to throw the experimenter out the window!"

After the experiment, Milgram asked the boy to write about why he thought his father had behaved the way he did. The boy clearly saw him as a hero:

I would say that my Dad stopped where he did due to the fact

that he honestly believed I was suffering pain. Not only because I was his son, I think that he would have stopped there
with anyone else. There comes a time when one individual
must think twice before carrying on and I feel my Dad is [*sic*]
proven throughout time that there is the time when you must
really think of what you are doing and to whom it will affect
and what the outcome would be.[5]

I was struck by the generosity of this "victim," his unwavering belief
in his father's goodness despite the fact that his dad had given him
what he thought were painful electric shocks. It seemed that the experience brought them closer together. But what was the impact of the
son's duplicity on the father?

After the experiment was over, while Williams was explaining its
real purpose to the teacher, Milgram had each learner write down an
explanation of his companion's behavior when it came to continuing or
refusing to give the shocks. All but one showed in their comments an
unwavering belief in their partner's goodness, even when that partner
had gone to the maximum voltage. Subject 2421, a thirty-nine-year-
old liquor store manager, stopped at the eleventh switch, or 165 volts,
after his friend stopped answering. The "victim" wrote afterward:

My friend is a person who will go out of his way to help you.
He is very kind and generous in whatever he does. He stopped
the experiment because he thought he was hurting me and
he would never deliberately hurt anyone. He would rather be
hurt himself. He is a good and honest worker and well liked by
everyone who knows him. He is generous to the extent that he
will almost give you his last dollar if he thinks you need help.[6]

Subject 2431, a thirty-three-year-old chemist at a local factory,
stopped at the thirteenth shock, or 195 volts. His friend wrote:

I know Bill quite well, having worked with him in the past
for several years. Our relationship now is *friendship*—we have
work in common and I see him at meetings etc. We also play
golf and cards every so often but not too often. I think he
stopped because he sincerely would not want to cause any pain

to me, nor to anybody else for that matter. Knowing that or feeling that this experiment would have scientific or psychological benefits was probably the only reason that he continued after the first sounds of pain or especially after I first told him to stop.[7]

Condition 24 was also marked by the pressure that Milgram placed on subjects to recruit others. I wasn't surprised to find that he had asked subjects for contacts. It wasn't uncommon; Asch had done the same. But it shocked me how much pressure he put on them. By this stage, Milgram was desperate in his drive to find subjects. When Subject 2432, a forty-year-old fireman, told Milgram how bad he felt for his friend, Milgram was more interested in the man's recruitment potential.

Subject 2432: He didn't want to come down. I talked him into this . . . I'll never live this down.

Milgram: We're desperately short of subjects. Is there anyone you know?

Subject 2432 tried to fob him off, but Milgram persisted, asking the man to give him the phone numbers of people he thought would volunteer.

Milgram: We need to finish the experiments by Wednesday. We need nine by Wednesday. . . . Just give me a name or two . . .

He ignored the man's obvious distress and told him what to say if any of his friends phoned to check what it was about: "If they call you, don't say anything. Say it was a legitimate scientific enterprise."[8]

Milgram sounded almost excited when the first subject in condition 24 went to the maximum voltage. Subject 2429—I'll call him Thomas—was a thirty-two-year-old electrical-motor repairman. He had been a scientist in Hungary and then an officer and pilot in the air force for five years, from 1950 to 1955, and had witnessed the 1956 revolution. He and the Hungarian friend he came to the lab with had known each other for about two years and regularly went fishing and camping together. Thomas's English wasn't great and sometimes he struggled to find the words he wanted. Speaking to Williams afterward, he explained, "Well, this is a test, you know, and I know how the test goes. This is not the first time I go to a test and, you know, and the gentleman at the table said, 'Go ahead, next question,' and I go ahead and do the next question because I know myself this not kill nobody."

But it was as if neither Williams nor Milgram listened to what the man said. The fact that he had pushed the final switch was the focus of their attention. Williams asked him how nervous or tense he had felt during the experiment.

> Thomas: Well, ah, I can't say because I never feel anything in my life, you know, I was an airplane pilot in my old country and sometimes when I'm nervous, you know, I feel a little, but . . . you know, like when I got electric shock, but only for four or five—
>
> Williams: You feel exhilarated.
>
> Thomas: Yeah, the first time, when I get nervous, you know, when I heard bad news or something . . .

It seemed as if Williams was feeding him lines, and they were talking at cross-purposes. When Milgram entered the room, he asked Thomas if he thought the shocks were real and, despite Thomas answering no, went on, asking the man if he'd fought in World War II.

> Thomas: No, no, I was only fifteen.
>
> Milgram: Did you fight when you were fifteen?
>
> Thomas: No.

When the experiment was over, he told Milgram, "I help you people?" to which Milgram replied, "You've helped us a lot."

The man I heard on the tape and the man Milgram seemed to think he was were two different people. It didn't seem to matter what Thomas had to say; Milgram had already made up his mind about the sort of man who would go to the maximum voltage with his friend. As soon as Thomas left the room, Milgram leaned into the microphone and said conspiratorially: "That was Subject 2429. A Hungarian, he's the first man who went to the end, and his friend was Hungarian, reminding me of the old adage, 'If you have a Hungarian for a friend you don't need an enemy.'" Milgram's father was Hungarian. "He was absolutely serious and convinced in the situation, and his discussion at the end about having to follow orders was a very appropriate one. He's the first man who shocked his friend. They were rather swarthy looking group of characters but it was genuine, it was serious—'You have to take orders,' the man said. He'd seen a lot of dead men in the streets; he's learned how to take orders, that's the important thing. That was 2429. 2430 will be coming up."

There was a sense of urgency and importance in Milgram's voice as he made these observations and a sense of excitement, too. And yet his conclusions about the man were at odds with what Thomas said in the discussion after the experiment.

In an unpublished fragment possibly written as an early draft for his book, Milgram's portrait of Thomas was almost a caricature. He appeared as a ruthless, cold-blooded killer:

> The third obedient subject had been a pilot in the Hungarian
> airforce. He told us that in the airforce he had learned the
> value of military discipline. He said that sentiment had no
> part in the execution of orders. If he had been told to bomb
> a town in Hungary, and he knew his family resided in that
> town, he would nonetheless carry out orders. Discipline in his
> view, was the highest virtue.[9]

But I had transcribed the tape, which recorded the experiment from the time when the men arrived in the lab until Williams showed them out, and I heard no such discussion in which Thomas said he would kill his family if told to do so.

I found a similar pattern with the next obedient subject. Milgram seemed determined to make a particular point about the men in condition 24. Subject 2430 was the second of three who went to the maximum voltage. But while he was an obedient subject according to the results, his behavior during the experiment was far from it. I'll call him Carl, a twenty-six-year-old technical writer who, Williams noted afterward in the subject file, was "extremely furious" during the experiment.

Carl's voice shook after his friend—let's call him Walt—began to shout. Walt eventually refused to answer and called out to Carl to quit, to let him out of there.

Williams: If he doesn't answer, give him the punishment anyway.

Carl continued.

This time, Walt's cries of pain were intensified by sound effects: Milgram made Walt's chair jump and then hit the floor and added his own groans to Walt's cries.

Carl pushed his chair back and said angrily to Williams, "That's it for me, I'm not doing this again. I don't know which one of you guys is doing the answers, but it's not him. You're gonna have to cancel the thing out—I'm not giving him more shocks."

Williams told him that he must continue. Carl argued, but Williams reiterated that he must go on. Carl was silent for ten, fifteen, twenty seconds. On Main Street, a car honked.

Williams: It is absolutely essential that you continue.

Carl: [angrily] It was his idea we come here. [Shouts into the microphone] We're going again! Nice: [emphasizes the first word by saying it loudly, and the other three softly] day, sky, job, chair.

Williams: Please read the words in an even tone.

Walt: [screams] Come on, let's quit! I refuse to answer any more!

Williams: Continue, please.

Carl: Not me.

Walt: Let's go!

Williams: The experiment requires that you go on.

Carl: *[voice shaking]* The experiment is not gonna require me to go on. You take the money back.

Williams: The money is not the issue. It's essential *[raises his voice over Walt, who is still shouting]* that the experiment continues.

Carl: Let me switch places with him.

Williams: We can't do that, not once we've started. The procedure must be followed through.

Walt: Let me out of here!

Williams: You have no other choice, teacher. Please continue. *[Silence from Carl]* The next word is "rich."

Walt: Carl!

Papers rustled; Carl was obviously fiddling with them. The silence continued. I held my breath.
When Carl's voice boomed through the microphone again, I groaned.

Carl: *[emphasizes the right answer again]* Rich: *boy*, cake, man, girl.

Walt: Let me out of here!

When Walt got the answer wrong and Carl administered a shock, Williams reprimanded him for barely pressing the switch.

Williams: That didn't make contact. Press the switch down completely.

Carl: *[referring to Walt's silence]* He's not connected up any-more. Why don't you just take the money back and cancel the thing out?

Williams: Continue please, teacher.

When it was over and Carl had reached 450 volts, he was seething. Williams told him that he wanted to ask some questions and gave him a piece of paper on which to record his answers. Carl snarled, "It's what I figured, some fucking idiot tests!" Williams, sounding shocked, said, "Pardon me?" before quickly recovering his composure. "If you indicate here . . ."

As Williams would later note, Carl was truculent and abrupt in an-swering questions. Williams's questions and Carl's answers had a stac-cato rhythm, with Carl giving monosyllabic, curt replies, as if he could barely contain his anger. When the questions were over, Carl said, "All I can say is, as a researcher, has anybody ever physically attacked you? Has that ever happened?"

Williams: Once or twice. . . . He was not really being shocked out there.

Carl: He just put an act on?

Williams: Yeah, he's a good actor.

Williams said that he had noticed Carl's reluctance. Then Milgram entered the room.

Carl: You're the man that signs the checks, right?

But Milgram barely acknowledged him. Instead, he picked up the paperwork and said to Williams, "Why wasn't this answered?"

Williams: I thought we did . . .

Williams turned to Carl and they completed the question on the sheet together. Still ignoring Carl, Milgram asked Williams, "How much, where are we in the—?"

Williams: Well, I told him—

Milgram: What time is it?

Williams: Four-oh-five.

Milgram: Where are we?

Williams: We're pretty much through; I've run through the hospital, army—

Milgram: Uh-huh, okay. Did you tell him he wasn't getting shocked?

Williams: Yeah.

Milgram: *[to Carl]* Um, I'd like to ask you some questions . . . um. . . . What if the experimenter gave you a gun and said, "Shoot him in the head"?

[Carl snorts]

Milgram: Seriously.

Carl: Seriously, if they gave me a gun to shoot him in the head I wouldn't have done anything. . . . My reasoning is behind this thing is that it's a setup, it's a bunch of quacks and the signs don't prove anything . . . the way I figure it is you're not going to cause yourselves trouble by actually doing serious physical damage to a body.

Milgram: Uh-huh. Um, what kind of thoughts were going through your head?

Carl: How I got myself into this situation in the first place, that was the most, and just what this thing was about. For instance, on your papers you've got me to sign, you've got Yale University scratched out and . . . it came into my mind that this was something kind of phony . . . the thing was a pack of nuts.

Milgram: Okay, fine. Well, you did a good job. *[Stands]* You had a jacket here?

After Carl had gone, Williams wrote, "His answers to interview questions were curt. He even used some vulgar language when I placed the form [and] questions in front of him. It seemed that he didn't have the guts to refuse to obey the experimenter's orders—and this made him mad as hell at the experimenter. JW."

I was nonplussed when I heard Milgram's indifference and lack of sympathy toward this man, until I found a written record of Walt's conversation with Milgram about his friend. Milgram had written underneath how he'd asked the man if there was anything about his friend that would help to explain his behavior, and Walt had said:

> [Carl] has a fascination and obsession with the Second World War; I speak of the Second World War from the viewpoint of the Germans. It has been standard procedure for us to joke and make light of the Third Reich, the Gestapo, and the prison camps such as Buchenwald, Auschwitz, etc. He has spoken of Eichmann having the right solution to the Puerto Rican problem in New York and Bridgeport.

In his unpublished notes, once again Milgram's description veered from the original: he wrote that Carl "was described by his friend as a right wing fanatic, who frequently stood before the mirror in jackboots and leather jacket. His friend told us that he was enamored of Nazism and saw himself in the vanguard of a fascist political movement."[10] Nevertheless, this explains Milgram's confrontational style with Carl and his lack of solicitousness after the experiment.

As the end of the experiments grew closer, Williams and Milgram were clearly elated to be almost finished. Their final subject was a man I'll call Peter. He was a social science teacher who worked at a local high school. His friend—let's say Robert—began unconvincingly, so Milgram added his own primal, throaty grunts to Robert's. Peter proceeded quite matter-of-factly until his friend refused to continue. Peter asked if he had to go on, and Williams said yes.

Peter: I don't feel right.

Williams: The experiment requires that you continue.

Peter: Well, when will I finish?

Williams: When he's learned all the word pairs, or when I stop this.

Peter: Well, I won't continue if he's in pain.

Williams: It's absolutely essential that you continue.

Peter: Well, how long will this go on? It could go on indefinitely.

Williams: True—but it is essential that you continue. The next word is "rich." Please go on.

Peter: *[clears throat]* Rich: boy, cake, man, girl.

Soon Robert went silent, after having shouted that he refused to participate further.

Peter: He's not answering. He's not gonna learn the words.

Williams: Please continue. You must go on.

Peter: I'm not going to.

Williams: The experiment requires that you go on.

Peter: I realize that, but I'm not going to injure him.

Williams: It's absolutely essential—

Peter: I don't doubt it, but I won't go on.

Williams: You have no other choice.

Silence. Peter must have looked resolute, because Williams was the first to break it.

Williams: If you don't continue, we'll have to discontinue the entire experiment.

Peter: What do you mean by the entire experiment?

Williams: This. This hour.

Peter: You want your money back? You can have it—

Williams: No, the money's yours for simply coming.

Peter: I don't want the money for simply coming. I didn't realize there was this involved. I'm sorry, but—

Williams: I'd like to ask you a few questions if I may—

Peter: I'm sorry.

As Peter and his friend were leaving, Milgram said, "This is our last night. We've been doing this since August 1961. August 4, as a matter of fact." I got the sense that both Milgram and Williams were reaching out to their subjects—whether to impress them or to impress upon them that they'd been part of something worthwhile, I wasn't sure. It reinforced that feeling I had that Milgram wanted their approval, their admiration—as if, once the experiment was explained, all would be forgiven, and the men would be able to marvel at what they'd just done.

Just after Peter and his friend left, Williams had a coughing fit. He joked to Milgram, "I'm dying here. Son of a bitch. If I die next week, I'll have my wife haunting you." Milgram responded, "If you die next week we'll build a memorial . . . actually, your wife gets insurance when you die. I'll make sure she gets the insurance."

After Williams recovered, Milgram commented on Peter's reaction to him: "That guy . . . I think he perceived me as an incompetent experimenter, somewhat bumbling."[11] They laughed. I had been thinking the same thing—that Milgram had seemed absentminded and distracted during the dehoax—until I heard this and suddenly realized that it was a deliberate part of the act. I had thought Milgram did it to defuse tension or deflect anger, but then it struck me: they were having fun with the script, with the roles they were playing.

I've thought a lot about why Milgram kept this condition secret. He certainly made mention of it in an early report to the NSF, he made notes on it in his obedience notebook, and he drafted a description of it that seemed to be for publication. He mentioned it in passing in a published article in 1965 as an experiment that "concerned the personal relationship between the victim and the subject" and promised that it, among others, would be "described elsewhere."[12] But it never was.

Alan Elms had told me that he and Milgram had eventually dismissed the idea of using husbands and wives as teachers and learners because of the potential friction it could cause: it "could generate some ill-feeling between people." When I went back to him with evidence of condition 24, he said it was likely that Milgram didn't publish details in his book because he simply ran out of space. But that was guesswork. My theory: Milgram might have kept it secret because he realized that what he'd asked subjects to do in condition 24 might be difficult to defend. I found a telling clue in the archives, in a note Milgram wrote about what the results of this variation of the experiment showed: "Within the context of this experiment, this is as powerful a demonstration of disobedience than can be found."[13] Condition 24 contradicted Milgram's bleak view of human nature. It also contradicted his conclusions. Unlike the earlier experiments in which subjects trusted the experimenter, reading his unperturbed demeanor as a sign of reassurance, in condition 24 this ambiguity was gone. When people genuinely believed someone was being hurt—and it was someone close to them—they refused to continue.

Bernardo Vittori and I arranged to meet at the Bridgeport train station. He was short and gray-haired, with a round, soft face dominated by glasses. On our way through the station, he said that he would take me to his house in Trumbull, a semirural area around five miles from Bridgeport, instead of going to Starbucks, as we had planned.

Bridgeport, I had been warned, was known as "the armpit of Connecticut." Back in 1962, it was a thriving manufacturing town, with local factories and workshops staffed by an ever-growing immigrant population. Bridgeport factory owners used to meet the ships when they docked, taking people straight off the boat and on to the production line. Now the factories are closed, warehouses empty, and Main Street, apart from traffic, deserted.

Bernardo spoke in an accent that mixed German, Italian, and American. I'd listened to most of the condition 24 tapes by now, and I thought I recognized his voice. He told me how he came to the States after World War II as part of the Marshall Plan. He had become an architectural metal worker, making things like ornate metal balustrades for public buildings. He had been in the United States for just seven years when his brother-in-law Enzo, a jeweler on Main Street, brought around the letter from an outfit calling itself Bridgeport Research Associates. The experiment must have been on a Thursday, Bernardo said, because that was the only evening he had off from night school. His day job paid $2.50 an hour, so the $5 offered for taking part seemed like easy money.

We pulled up to a house that was neat and white, surrounded by lawns and flower beds. I could hear birds twitter. It was a far cry from the grimy, busy, and noisy town that Bridgeport had been in 1962. The garage door yawned open and we pulled in, parking neatly between the doorway to the house and an upended outdoor setting ready for assembly.

I recognized the house as soon as we stepped inside. It was the same as the houses of my childhood, the homes of my friends, children of the mostly southern Italian immigrants new to Australia: a lace tablecloth trapped under the glass tabletop and everything spotless, neat as a pin.

Ada and Bernardo had met through her brother Enzo. She told me that her family had arrived in the United States from southern Italy after the war.

At that moment, the doorbell rang. Bernardo and Ada's daughter, Maria, had called in with her own daughter. After some greetings, the granddaughter went to watch cartoons while her mother listened to my interview with Bernardo. But as it turned out, he didn't have that much to say about the experiment. "He said he was hurting, so I stopped," he told me. Like it was the most natural thing in the world.

Bernardo and Enzo had almost forgotten the experience when Enzo's son Laurence read a book about the experiments and discovered that Milgram had conducted some at Bridgeport. After that, Bernardo had looked it up on the Internet and found out the truth; until then, he'd thought it had been about how much pain people could stand.

As we moved to the kitchen for coffee, I heard Ada on the phone. "You coming over? She's here."

Bernardo told me that he was born in Germany, but when he was ten his family fled to Italy after a cluster bomb landed on their family home, almost killing his brother and sister. "I noticed the difference between Germany and Italy. Germany follows rules and regulations. In Italy, nobody follows orders." In Germany, his grandfather had been a professor at the University of Bonn and his mother a German teacher. The family was used to having servants. But Italy was a different story: his mother had to learn to cook and live off the land, and it was Bernardo upon whom she relied. He would learn how to bake bread from the local women and then go home and teach her. "I was the one who had to do all the legwork," he grumbled. Slowly, his mother adapted, although she found it hard.

Just then, Enzo arrived. He was tall and suave, but shy compared to his brother-in-law. He let Bernardo do the talking. They both seemed bemused, almost puzzled by my interest in something that had happened so long ago and to which they hadn't given much thought.

"I wasn't bothered because I stopped. I didn't hurt nobody." Bernardo shrugged as if to say, didn't everybody?

"I could hear him arguing with the experimenter through the wall," Enzo said.

I heard myself telling them that they had been part of a historic event but, as Enzo's story spilled out, I realized how ridiculous I must have sounded; that all of them—Bernardo, Enzo, and Ada—had been part of something much bigger and more momentous than forty minutes in a scientist's lab. Displaced by war, immigrating to a new country, and building new lives—Milgram's experiment shrank into insignificance against the backdrop of their personal history. It's no wonder that they hadn't discussed it. And it's no wonder that I couldn't get them to remember their feelings at the time or how the experiment might have affected them. They had experienced much worse.

When I told them that people went further with strangers, they wanted to know why. And I couldn't explain it in a way that satisfied them or me.

When I got back to Yale, I found two brothers-in-law in the recordings who could have been Bernardo and Enzo, but I wasn't sure. What I heard was a worried-sounding teacher refusing to be fobbed off by Williams's casual reassurances that his brother-in-law would not be harmed. The teacher had to insist he would not continue fifteen times before Williams gave up and announced that the experiment was over.

The night after I met the Vittoris, I stopped in New Haven for dinner at a restaurant called Basta. It didn't strike me until I sat down and opened the menu that the day at the Vittoris had made me homesick for something. Maybe it was the laughter of the brothers-in-law at the kitchen table; Maria's open admiration for her parents; or the granddaughter, home early from nursery school and allowed, because of my visit, to watch an unrestricted amount of television. No matter how much he had tried to test the bonds of family and friendship, Milgram had failed. Instead of measuring obedience in condition 24, he'd measured the power of love.

7

MILGRAM'S STAFF

On his university's website, J. Keith Williams, dressed in a suit and tie, smiled at the camera. He was fair-haired and pale-skinned. Unlike his father, he wore glasses. And unlike his father, whose photographs showed a man stern and unsmiling, Keith grinned easily. He was pleased, and thanked me, when I told him he looked like his dad.

Keith taught in the physician-assistant program at Nova Southeastern University in Fort Lauderdale, Florida, and I caught him between classes in the lab. He shared with me his memories of his father. Keith remembered going to Yale with his dad one night, when he was about nine, to pick up a check from a Dr. Milgram. They parked in one of Yale's side streets, and John told his son that he'd have to stay in the car. "He said I couldn't come inside with him because it was secret. And I remember he left me sitting in the car, and it was dark, and all the buildings were stone with ivy growing on them; it was a little bit spooky." I imagined the young Keith, circa 1961, sitting in the front seat, twiddling the radio knob, wanting to hear a human voice in the dark street—and never guessing that, in the building just a few feet away, some of the most famous and controversial experiments of the twentieth century were taking place and his dad was part of them. Little did Keith know that his dad's stern demeanor would one day be famous.

I was curious to know whether John was as commanding and serious as he appeared. It was John, after all, who personified what

Milgram called a "malevolent authority." Keith laughed and agreed. The role of the disciplinarian came naturally to his father. Keith's grandfather had been a strict authority figure, too, and John's three years in the military had reinforced his commanding air. In addition, John—the oldest of three sons, like Keith—had responsibility thrust on him from a young age. He married in 1951, when he was twenty-one, just out of the air force and a freshman at college. In 1956, his father had a stroke that left him paralyzed down the left side, and John and his small family, who had been living in a third-floor flat in New Haven, moved back into the Williamses' family home to help John's now-disabled father run the family business—a forty-four-seat restaurant—and contribute to the mortgage. By 1961, when the experiments began, they had only just moved out of the family home and into their own place in Southbury, Connecticut. John took the job at Yale because he needed the money. He was supporting his wife, Roberta, and eight-year-old Keith, and his high school science teacher's salary wasn't enough. In addition, Roberta was expecting another baby.

Keith remembered that, when he was a boy, his father "could be a little petulant, a bit short-tempered." When I asked him to elaborate, he told me, "He was quite strict with me. . . . My father and I were a little distant at times when I was growing up because he was such an authoritarian." As Keith grew older, discipline became a source of tension between them. But Keith put it down to his dad's age—only twenty-two when Keith was born, he was young to be a father and "he was learning as he grew." He noted that John relaxed as he matured and "was much easier" on his two younger sons.

Keith told me that while John could be sharp with him, "he also had a very warm side." John was an active member of his community and a devoted golfer, and he and his wife had a busy social life: "My parents went out every weekend, played bridge, went singing—Dad played piano, ukulele, mandolin. They were very social." According to Keith, John was "a very strong character, a good leader" who went on to become president of the teachers' association credit union. He was also a popular teacher. And John passed on his love of science to his oldest son. Keith told me, "When I was in seventh grade, he taught me how to dissect a live frog. You could see its heart and lungs working, and other kids in class passed out." John Williams would remain a high school teacher after his stint at Yale, and in total would spend thirty-seven years teaching science in the Connecticut high school system.

Keith didn't think that his father told his mother much at all about the job, and he even kept it secret from his best friend, with whom he sang bass in a barbershop quartet. It seemed that John took Milgram's assurances of the need for secrecy seriously. "They didn't want it to get out what was going on. It would ruin everything if people knew it was a setup."

Even once the study was over, John didn't talk about it with his son. In fact, it would be ten years before John explained what he had been doing with Milgram at Yale, when he realized that Keith, who was about to start college, might come across the study. "I think he brought it up when I had it in my textbook. Otherwise he didn't talk about it all that much. When he did, he always talked highly of Milgram and the whole thing. I think he appreciated being involved in such a landmark study.

"He said they were definitely shocked by the results; it was groundbreaking research. He said people often laughed inappropriately, and a few times people ran out of the building and they had to chase them down and tell them it was all a setup."

Keith told me that his father "didn't have any bad feelings about it," even though he'd found it stressful—particularly when he ran into people who'd been in the experiment. "One time he was at a restaurant, and one of the people recognized him and was upset by him. Even though he knew that the shocks weren't real, the person left the restaurant when he recognized him, and Dad was a little upset that people would have a reaction like that."

Keith was still conscious of the degree of responsibility that Milgram gave his father. "I was kind of shocked by it all—he was paid so little, it was amazing. Milgram was very appreciative, but later on I think there should have been more communication. He just moved on with his fame and fortune."

Talking to Keith, I was conscious of John Williams's absence—how his father's silence had left a number of gaps. How might John, an otherwise happy and active member of society (if a stern father), have felt about keeping his work secret from his wife and best friend? What did he tell his family he was doing all those nights and weekends he spent at Yale? And why did he maintain his silence about the experiments far beyond the period he was required to? I couldn't reconcile the John Williams that I knew from the tapes, the cold and officious-sounding man, with the outgoing and gregarious entertainer Keith described.

I also thought of Jim McDonough, the learner, and what Williams and McDonough said to their wives and families about their work at Yale at the end of each shift. How did they feel about the stress they were required to inflict on the people who volunteered? And what was their relationship with the ambitious Milgram? Working together so intensively for nine months, they must have formed a friendship of sorts. I felt disappointed that these were questions that would never be properly answered; while John Williams's death had been a surprise, Blass's book had already told me that McDonough had died three years after the experiments from heart problems.[1] All I could do was piece together as much of the story as I could from interviews with family members such as Keith, who had known intimately the men I had heard on tape and speculated about.

Keith Williams introduced me to his uncle Mark, John's younger brother, who was the director of adult education at Clinton High School in Connecticut. While I interviewed Mark, I felt as if I got to do his job alongside him. He walked around the school with his phone in his hand, buzzing open doors and welcoming people arriving for night classes. Knitting and mah-jongg were always popular, but belly dancing had become the new favorite and the teacher had to get an assistant to cope with the demand, Mark told me.

Mark had also been hired by Milgram, to serve as a stand-in actor in some of the group experiments conducted in November 1961. He was only nineteen, a recent high school graduate. His memories were vague—he remembered there were three, or maybe four, other actors aside from John, one of them McDonough. The one thing he did remember clearly was John's "robotic" delivery: "Everything was monotone; he said the same thing every time."

The brothers didn't talk much about the experiment afterward. When they did, it was only in passing. "We referred back to it, but nothing about how he felt about it. You have to remember it was a job. It wasn't like the high point of anyone's existence."

Mark was proud to have been part of the experiment but had no idea that it was so famous until he returned to graduate school in the 1970s. "I was taking ed psych, and I was in a classroom with thirty to thirty-five other people, and a film started. I remember I was writing in my notebook, and I looked up and saw Jack and thought, oh my God, I remember this!"

But Mark didn't think that his brother would have found it stressful. "It was a game, there was nothing serious about it." It would have been just another job to John, who possessed the family's strong work ethic and had put himself through college. In all likelihood, John would have enjoyed it. He was four years older than Milgram, and that may have reinforced the natural authority that Milgram came to rely on. "Well, Milgram didn't really get his hands dirty, and Jack was good at handling people. He was a teacher. If you're dealing with his students, you've got to be the diplomat, the everyman," Mark said.

I asked Mark if he had seen anyone getting upset during the experiment. "I remember the cringing when they were going up in voltage, but that didn't stop them doing it. There was one guy who said he was a Korean War veteran, and I remember in the interview afterward he said, 'Yeah, well, there are probably people all watching this back there behind that mirror,' and I went, 'Ooh.' He was almost looking at me."

He couldn't remember whether he was told not to say anything about the experiments but said that if he and John were told to keep it secret, they would have. "You just don't talk about those things. If you're asked not to, you wouldn't." Besides, Mark said, it would have been hard to explain to other kids, although he "probably" told Craig, a good friend at that time.

Interestingly, he told me that John's persona was at odds with his personality. In contrast to what I had heard from Keith, Mark told me, "He might have looked stern, but that wasn't my brother. He was acting! That was nothing like Jack. He was the life of the party; women loved him. Yes, absolutely. He was good-looking, he could sing, he had a lot of talent. What's not to like?"

Mark obviously looked up to his oldest brother. To Mark, John had charisma: "well schooled" in drama with a talent for performance, he could play the piano and violin, and sang in Gilbert and Sullivan musicals, and in a barbershop quartet. "Every Christmas it would be like waiting for Jack to get there and play piano and sing. He was a natural performer. The peak of our wedding was Jack singing 'Ave Maria.'"

Was John proud of having been part of the experiments? "Absolutely. No question. Because if you asked him about it, he'd say, 'Yes, that's me up there.' . . . Jack's become the face of the whole experiment."

It certainly would have been a stressful job. As the experimenter, Williams dealt with subjects from the moment they arrived to the moment they left: greeting them, marshaling them through the experiment, taking notes on their behavior, fending off their attempts to pull out, ordering them to continue, and debriefing them. And in at least one variation, he played an aggressive teacher, rather than the experimenter. Probably in recognition of the amount of responsibility he had delegated to Williams, Milgram started him at $2 an hour, higher than McDonough's $1.75. Milgram must have been conscious of how much he relied on the men because he gave them two pay raises in six months, with Williams's rising to $2.40 and McDonough's to $2.25 by March 1962.[2]

In addition, the experiment could sometimes be dangerous. It wasn't unheard of for Milgram's staff to be assaulted—remember that, when one subject asked Williams if anyone had ever attacked him, he replied, "Once or twice."[3] In one variation in which he played a teacher, Williams took over the shock machine after the experimenter had left the room and proceeded to "single mindedly . . . increase the shock step by step." Milgram wrote that "the experiment ends when naïve subject takes physical action—eg switching off machine or physically restraining Williams."[4] In his book, Milgram noted that most subjects protested at Williams's actions, and "five subjects took [physical] action" against him. One subject, described as a large man, "lifted the zealous shocker from his chair, threw him to the corner of the laboratory and did not allow him to move."[5]

Despite this, Williams showed no signs of stress on the tapes. In fact, between appointments he could often be heard whistling, singing, and joking with McDonough as he prepared for the next appointment. He often exercised his pleasant singing voice during breaks. He seemed to move effortlessly in and out of his role, as the following interlude shows.

Williams: One more thing before you go: please indicate here on a scale, all things considered, how you feel about participating in the experiment. . . . We do appreciate having you here and you giving us your time and so forth.

Subject: It's very interesting.

Williams: I think you'll find it very interesting. You'll be glad you were in it.

Subject: Thank you. Goodnight . . . Goodnight. *[Door opens and closes]*

McDonough: Where's the key to the can?

Williams: It's open. I opened it before.

McDonough: I need to go to the can.

Williams: So do I.

McDonough: I gotta puke.

Williams: You gotta puke? Then go puke.

[Door opens and closes. Williams is now alone]

Williams: *[crooning]* In your Easter bonnet / With all the frills upon it. . . . Oh, I could write a sonnet / About the moon on your Easter bonnet. *[Pause, then he leans into the microphone]* Subject 2303. That was Subject 2303. Subject 2304 coming up.[6]

At first, I thought this was a kind of callousness on Williams's part. Then I thought that perhaps if he was upset by what was happening, he wasn't the sort of man who would want to show it. But just as I would never be able to know whether Keith or Mark had the more accurate recollection of John Williams, I could never know if I was right about this, or if I had misread the man completely.

Bob McDonough turned the pages of a photo album he had brought along to show me. We sat in a deserted television room upstairs in Yale's Graduate Club, just a few miles from where Bob and his family lived in New Haven.

Father and son looked alike. Bob McDonough was taller and slimmer than Jim McDonough, but he had the same open, jovial smile.

I had found Bob through his blog, *Derailed: One Man's Story of His Life On [and Off] the Rails*, an entertaining account of Bob's adventures as a railroad conductor. When Bob had graduated from Southern Connecticut State University with a bachelor's degree in English, he had no clear career plans, so he applied for work on the railroad until he worked out what to do with his degree. That was twenty-one years ago. "I'm almost the age my father was when he did the experiment, but I'm bald—he still had some hair—and the little hair I have is gray" while his father's was black. He continued, "Thankfully, I'm taller and thinner than he was. I do suppose we sound alike, but I'm judging that from the little dialogue I heard him speak in the film *Obedience*."

Bob never knew his father. He had written on his blog:

My father had died just two weeks prior to my third birthday and I have no recollection of him. We used to have an

8x10 picture of him that hung over the TV in the den of my mother's house. This picture was an icon for me, a photo of someone from the past, not known but idolized. Much like the pictures of Jesus, Pope Paul and John F. Kennedy that my grandfather had hanging on the walls in his house next door. When anybody spoke of my father this was the picture I had in my mind's eye.[7]

Although Bob was the youngest of McDonough's nine children—four daughters and five sons—and the one with the least experience of his father, he had taken a keen interest in the obedience experiments. And he was proud of the resemblance between them. He told me, "I've been to see some of the *Obedience* footage at the Sterling Library at Yale. The librarian who was in charge of the archive was very helpful. She thought I looked and sounded like my dad."

Bob showed me a typical photo of his father, laughing up at the camera, a friendly-looking man wearing glasses and a suit and tie, balancing a hat on one knee. "Back in the early sixties, people dressed like that to go to a ball game. It's hard to believe now, but everyone would wear a hat and coat and tie at all times. My brother tells stories of passing the baseball with him, but he would still be in suspenders and a tie."

Like John Williams, Jim McDonough was a devout Catholic and a keen singer. He was used to performing: he led the church choir, played the saxophone and the clarinet, and for a time worked as a nightclub singer. He emceed a number of local functions, particularly at the West Haven Irish American Club, where he was a founding member. "He wasn't afraid to stand up in front of an audience and sing or give a speech or tell a joke," Bob told me.

Milgram chose Jim for the role of the learner precisely because he seemed like the sort of fellow you wouldn't look at twice if you passed him on the street. "He was white, slightly overweight, he wasn't overly handsome. He was Joe American," said Bob.

Jim kept his job secret from his family. One of his sons used to drop him off and pick him up, but nobody, including his wife, knew exactly what this second job involved—and certainly not that he played the role of victim hooked up to a shock machine.

Bob told me that the first anyone in the family knew of it was one night in 1974. Bob's brother John was watching television at his girlfriend's house and rang home excitedly to tell his mother to turn on the set because "Dad's on the TV!" "And she said, 'What are you talking about?'—because my dad had been dead nine years—and he said, 'He's on TV, they're hooking him up to electrodes, they're shocking him.'" Milgram's book had just been published, and *The Phil Donahue Show* was screening footage of the experiments. The family rushed to the television and couldn't believe what they were seeing. McDonough was being strapped into a chair by a man in a lab coat who was asking if he had any questions. Jim replied, "About two years ago I was at the veterans' hospital in West Haven, and while I was there they diagnosed me with a heart condition—nothing serious—but as long as I'm having these shocks . . . how strong are they? Are they dangerous?" The man in the lab coat reassured him that "although the shocks may be painful, they are not dangerous."

The family watched, aghast, as the shocks began, and McDonough's protests and cries escalated each time he received one. But it was a short television segment, quickly over.

It was the first time that Bob had seen his father moving and talking. Until this, his one vague memory was of standing on a chair beside him, watching him shave. Then again, he wasn't sure if that really was a memory or something he had made up to fill the space.

Bob's mother, Kathryn, remembered something about an experiment at Yale, but she had never heard of Milgram. Once the program was over, she left an urgent message with the show's producer for Milgram to call her. She wasn't certain whether her husband had been shocked or not. Milgram called the next day. "My mother spoke guardedly to Dr. Milgram at first, at least until he reassured her that my father wasn't harmed in any way. He profusely apologized for any misunderstanding that the film may have caused." Milgram sent her a copy of his book with the following inscription:

To Mrs. James McDonough,

I thought you might like to have a copy of this book. As

you know, your late husband was part of the research team I directed at Yale University. It was a pleasure to work with him, and he was a very fine man.

Sincerely,
Stanley Milgram
New York
April 1974

Soon after, the McDonough family managed to borrow a copy of the film and a projector, and the whole clan—the nine McDonough children, their mother, and four in-laws—crowded into the living room to watch it. "My brother got a bedsheet and tacked it up to the wall," Bob remembered. He was twelve at the time and had fun making shadow puppets on the wall. But once the jumpy old black-and-white movie started, the impact of what he was watching began to sink in. Despite the fact that the film had no sound and the picture was very grainy—or perhaps the bedsheet simply needed washing, Bob joked—"everyone had goose bumps watching it, and I think that was mostly what we were concentrating on, rather than the experiment and the ethics of it. It was more of a home movie than this messed-up concept, you know."

Twenty years later, after he had bought his own VCR, Bob tried to borrow the movie on video, but the librarian told him that it was available only to universities. Yet when she learned that Bob's father had been involved in the experiments, she got in touch with Alexandra Milgram, who sent him a copy. It was the first time that Bob had heard his father talking, and he was overcome. "Hearing him speak for the first time made the hair on the back of my neck stand up, and I teared up and I got a lump in my throat." He watched the video over and over, wiping the tears from his eyes, and he remembered how pleased he was to find that they had the same smile, the same mannerisms.

When Milgram was interviewing Jim for the job of learner in August 1961, his wife was three months pregnant with Bob. It's likely that the prospect of another mouth to feed was what led Jim to take on a part-time job. "Emmett, my oldest brother, remembers that the railroad wasn't happy with my father taking the part-time job with Milgram. They had just promoted him to head auditor, and he was now considered an executive. I guess they thought having a second job below him." Bob shrugged. "He had nine children to feed, so he needed the job."

Perhaps it was this that made Bob so interested in, as well as proud of, his father's involvement. After all, it was his father's job to come out, happy and jovial, and reassure subjects that he was unharmed. "I'm glad that these people were relieved and he was able to slap them on the back and shake their hand. I've heard through the press there may be one or two people who claim they weren't debriefed and have been carrying guilt around with them for years. If that's true, I feel badly."

On the other hand, Bob figured that his father, like Milgram's obedient subjects, was probably just doing what he was told, without thinking too much about the ethics. After the family had watched the film, "no one questioned the ethics of it." That came later, when they were saying, "'You know, was it right for him to put people through this?' And everybody said, 'Nah, it's Milgram's fault.'" He laughed.

In the months after I met him, Bob was unfailingly enthusiastic and helpful. He worked in shifts and once used his free time in New York to track down a story for me in the New York Public Library before taking the train back to New Haven. Another time, he joined Tom Blass and me at a New York restaurant for breakfast, this time dressed in his conductor's uniform. We swapped documents—he sent me a copy of Milgram's inscription, I sent him a copy of the interview notes Milgram wrote about his dad. I got the feeling that every new piece of information about the experiments, whether or not it mentioned Jim McDonough, somehow brought him closer to his father.

Bob confirmed one of my suspicions: that in a community as close-knit as New Haven, some of the subjects must have known either Jim McDonough or John Williams. Bob described a strange twist of events on the day his father collapsed and died. The morning of Monday, January 4, 1965, Jim McDonough woke up early and, because it was cold, went outside to start the car, then came back in, where his wife had a bowl of oatmeal waiting. "When he sat down to eat, he suddenly grabbed the edge of the table and his face twisted. My mother, thinking he was teasing, told him to quit kidding around. He then fell off the chair and onto the floor. My sisters ran across the street to get Mr. Clifford because he was a New Haven fireman." Harold Clifford had actually been a subject in the experiment himself, but luckily there were no lasting hard feelings between the men. As Bob McDonough told me, "There he was shocking my father, and three years later here he is coming to the rescue."

Harold rushed across the road and attempted to revive Jim, but Jim was dead by the time he got to hospital. Jim McDonough was so well liked that the line of mourners waiting to pay their last respects at a funeral home in the center of Yale's campus stretched out the door and right around the block. Milgram had left for Harvard by then and was not among them.

Bob told me that he was still good friends with Harold's three children. "We still stay in contact with one another. But I often wonder what our relationship would be like if Harold had gone all the way to 'XXX.'"

You won't find Bob Tracy's name in the acknowledgments of Milgram's book *Obedience to Authority*, even though everyone else he employed is named there. And it's unlikely Milgram sent him an inscribed copy, either.

Tracy had worked as one of Milgram's actors and, by coincidence, Bob McDonough worked with Tracy's son at the railroad. He told me that Bob Tracy Jr. would be happy to talk to me.

Tracy had initially been recruited for condition 6, which was identical to condition 5 except for the actors. To test whether his actors' personalities and appearance affected obedience, Milgram replaced McDonough with Tracy, a tough-looking man in a crew cut, and substituted Williams with a man called Emil Elgiss, who, he said, was "softer in his presentation." Tracy was, according to Milgram, "lean, and hard looking and frequently clenches his fists." During the experiment, he wore an old sports jacket, an army shirt, and no tie. Emil Elgiss, the experimenter, was "a far more cultivated, refined individual, who possesses about him a certain soft inertness, that almost borders on passivity."[8] What would happen, Milgram wondered, if the learner looked stern and the experimenter looked gentle?

It had an impact. Obedience dropped from 65 percent in condition 5 to 50 percent in condition 6. But what this difference means is unclear. It could mean that a soft and passive experimenter commanded less authority. Or did it mean that the teacher was less likely to shock a guy who looked like he might come out afterward and punch them? Or was it simply that both men, new to their roles, were poorer actors and less convincing?

What interested me about tough guy Tracy was that he eventually defied Milgram. He worked on three conditions with Milgram—6, 8, and 10—before he quit. The tipping point came when an army buddy arrived at the lab. Tracy had served with him in New Guinea in World War II, and "the bond of being in the army together meant he couldn't go through with it." Bob Jr. told me that he was "kind of proud" of his father's behavior. Tracy was unable to put a friend through the experience and withdrew rather than having it on his conscience.

Bob Tracy's behavior intrigued me because it was a marked contrast to McDonough's and Williams's. What was it, then, that allowed Williams and McDonough to do something that not everyone could? Was it a case of becoming desensitized to the point where they stopped noticing the anguish they were causing? Certainly, Williams's voice in condition 3, in September 1962, sounded more youthful and energetic than his voice in condition 20, just six months later, which was a weary monotone.

Perhaps Bob Tracy was right to object to the role that Milgram placed him in. Obedience to authority didn't just apply to Milgram's subjects. In a parallel of the experiment itself, Milgram commanded obedience from his staff—people who, as part of their job, were required to subject a naive volunteer to intense pressure to follow instructions. Yet the two men had a hold over Milgram that his subjects didn't. Without them, his experiment would have been impossible: he needed to retain them for the entire experimental program because inconsistency in staff could contaminate his results.[9]

The public has never known much about Milgram's experimenter or learner, except that Williams was appropriately stern-looking and McDonough was appropriately amiable. Milgram described their physical contrasts in a way that made me think of a straight man paired with a clown, a scientific version of Laurel and Hardy.

Of the two, McDonough in some ways had the easier job. His role after the shouts and screams—which were eventually prerecorded on tape, so that he just sat in the room and operated the recorder—was to emerge unscathed. He got to lighten the mood by showing himself unharmed and joking with the person who had pushed the switches. While next door, he could still hear what was going on in the lab, but he didn't have to face the consequences of people's distress as directly as Williams did.

Milgram described McDonough's job to one subject as "like *The Wizard of Oz*. Did you see the film? You know, like Frank Morgan behind the curtain, pulling the switches." Later in the same conversation, he described McDonough's job in more detail.

Milgram: He operated the tape recorder.

Unidentified subject: Good grief.

Milgram: And he was actually smoking a cigar or drinking coffee at the time.

Unidentified subject: He must have enjoyed it.

Milgram: No, it was very hard work after a while. . . . Twenty times is okay, but, you know, the eight hundredth time would get a little tedious.[10]

Another subject talked about his feelings about the learner: "I felt so bad afterward. He mentioned his name and he lives in East Haven and I—after the test I had to go to my office, which is here in the courthouse, and do some work—although it was a Sunday, I wanted to go and finish up some work . . . and I went to the telephone book and looked up the name—he used the name 'Richardson' or something, and unfortunately there were three of them with exactly the first and last name and just [in] East Haven and if—I say this—I didn't make the call because I didn't know which one to call. It would have sounded—you know, I felt it would have sounded very stupid on the phone saying, 'Are you the fellow that was at Yale?' and, you know, but if there would have been one I wanted to call and actually apologize."

The same man described how the experiment forced him to lie to his wife that day, after he got home from the office: "I calmed down a lot, but when I got home my wife said, 'Oh, what was it all about?' I said, you know, I was actually ashamed in a way. . . . And I said, 'Oh, it was just a test about obedience.' She said, 'Oh'—she asked me some questions and I said, 'Oh, it wasn't really very interesting at all,' which was an absolute lie. [I just didn't want] to talk about it. . . . I'm a person who sleeps well every night no matter what happens during the day—if I fight with my wife or anything I sleep fine [but] I had trouble sleeping . . . it would come across my mind while I was at work or driving to work or watching television on an idle minute . . . I would say 'Gee, I wonder what happened to that guy,' you know, but I never once attempted to call him as I had when I first went to the office."[11]

Tragically, both men who played the role of the learner with heart problems died soon after from heart attacks, McDonough in 1965 and Tracy in 1967. With the obedience experiments, sometimes it's hard to know where illusion ends and reality begins; Jim McDonough's real-life heart problems may well have inspired the most famous condition in the experiment. Bob McDonough told me that when his family saw Jim on television, talking to the experimenter about being treated for a heart problem at the veterans' hospital, they had thought he was referring to a real experience. "Shortly before he died, he was scheduled to have a valve replacement in his heart and so he may have had a heart condition when he was involved in the experi-ments," Bob said. Had McDonough mentioned his heart problem to Milgram—perhaps in the job interview or even the first time he was being strapped into the chair during the rehearsals in the summer of 1961?

I found evidence on tape that McDonough's heart was in fact both-ering him during one experiment in May 1962.

Williams: Well, let me tell you a little bit about this experiment, Mr. *[blank]*. Mr. Wallace was not really being shocked in there.

Subject 2321: He wasn't?

Williams: No, he's part of our experimental team.

Subject 2321: Oh, I see, yeah.

Williams: He works with us, you see.

Subject 2321: Yeah.

Williams: Name's Jim McDonough. Why don't I get him? . . . Ah, Jim, why don't you come on in and say hello to Mr. *[blank]*.

Subject 2321: You bum, you had me worried there. I was wor-ried about you. I didn't know what this was all about, and the thing that had me worried was when you said you had a bad heart, and I thought, jeez, I might have killed that poor guy. *[Laughs]*

Williams: You know, it was only a week or so ago we were sitting in here—and he uses that line on everybody, you know—and he's sitting in back in there one night and he had heart palpitations.

[General laughter]

McDonough: I thought I had gas or something and my god-damn heart was going *brrrrrrm*. Scared the daylights out of me.

Williams: He's been handing out this line for so long, then all of a sudden he got it himself.

[General laughter]

Subject 2321: I was worried when you were hollering in there and, jeez, when I didn't hear you, ah, jeez, maybe he dropped dead. That's why I asked you, "Should I stop or go on?," and you said, "Continue."[12]

I wondered about the effect that McDonough's and Williams's roles had had on them. I remembered sitting in Don Mixon's living room outside Sydney, with Don gazing out at the rim of the Blue Mountains and telling me that you could experience real emotions in playing a particular role. He had seen how engrossed his actors became—so engrossed that they became agitated and distressed, caught between the commands of the experimenter and the cries of pain from the learner. Even though they knew the experiment was a simulation, their emotional reactions were real.

If Don's subjects became distressed playing their role in a forty-five-minute session, what was it like for Williams and McDonough? Or for the seven other men whom Milgram employed during the course of the experiment to act the role of the hard-faced experimenter and the screaming victim? Was it a failure to shed his role that made Williams petulant and short-tempered with his son? I wondered, too, how McDonough felt about the people he came out to meet who had "shocked" him. Had his faked pain stayed with him until it became real, when he clutched at his chest, his face contorted, and he fell to the floor that cold morning in 1965?

I had seen a documentary featuring Philip Zimbardo, Milgram's high school classmate and the man behind the Stanford prison experiment. This experiment had university students playing the roles of guards and prisoners and was aborted because of the stress those playing the prisoners underwent at the hands of those playing the guards. Zimbardo spoke about how taking part in that experiment had changed him. When his fiancée came to visit the "set," she was horrified at the violence and animosity that had developed between the guards and prisoners. "She said, 'It's terrible what you're doing to those boys!' She had tears in her eyes." She ran out of the building, and Zimbardo, "furious," ran after her. Outside, he told her how fascinating the experiment was, how powerful the situation. "I don't know how, if you're a psychologist, you don't appreciate this," he told her.

And she responded, "How could you not see what I see?" She wasn't sure she wanted to have anything to do with him anymore. Zimbardo said, "It was like a slap in the face." Just as the situation he had created had transformed his subjects into vicious wardens and haunted prisoners, Zimbardo saw that it had brought about changes in him, changes so dramatic that his girlfriend felt as if she didn't know him—and she didn't like the man she saw.[13]

I am reluctant to judge McDonough and Williams, in the same way that I'm reluctant to judge Milgram's subjects. Williams's role was much more stressful than McDonough's, in that he was solely responsible for the conduct of the experiments in Milgram's (frequent) absence. He was left to deal with things he wasn't trained for. And McDonough seemed genuine in trying to put subjects at ease. When he reappeared in the lab after the experiment was over, it was his jovial, rather sweet voice that cajoled subjects and almost without fail made them laugh.

Did Milgram place the men in an untenable situation? He was clearly dependent on them to maintain the experiment's integrity. After the research was over, Milgram offered each of them the choice of an upfront $100 bonus or 2 percent of U.S. book royalties up to $500 (beyond that, the amount owed was "subject to any restriction that I may deem just").[14] Both men needed the money at the time and took the cash—an act that Williams later regretted. Bob McDonough told me that his family regretted his father's choice, too. The fact that both men took the bonus suggests that they had little idea of the importance or eventual fame of the experiments, although

Williams told subjects time and again that the research was important and, by implication, that any stress they had gone through would
be worthwhile.

Milgram made the men feel important. Maybe, like the subjects,
they were in awe of science, and of Yale. Perhaps Williams enjoyed
the idea of contributing to scientific endeavor. Maybe McDonough
relished the opportunity, despite the "tedium" of the job, to make
people feel better afterward. Perhaps, like Milgram, they didn't believe that what they were putting people through would have any
lasting ill effects. I like to think that, like the subjects, McDonough
and Williams knew they were adopting a role that had nothing
to do with who they were outside of the lab. Outside, they were
men of faith, well loved and respected at work and in their local
communities.

Bob McDonough told me the first time we met, "Every time I meet
a psychologist I like to brag and say my father was the victim in the
Milgram experiments." Then he laughed and recounted that once,
when he had delivered this line to a psychologist, she said something
that made him think. "She looked me in the eye and said, 'That's kind
of strange—the only way you see your father is as a victim.' I said, 'I've
never thought of it that way.'"

It is too easy to simply describe either man as a victim. Like the
subjects, Williams and McDonough were misled about the nature of
the job they applied for—the ad had called for assistants in an experiment about memory and learning. It's unlikely that Milgram would
have told them in the interview exactly what would be required, although he seems to have asked about their acting skills. The truth
came later, after they had accepted the job—perhaps even after they
had showed up for their first day at work. They hadn't stopped when
they saw that people were undergoing distress, distress they had played
a role in bringing about. But at the same time, they hadn't set out to
hurt anyone: for both men, it was a simple matter of needing a second
job to support their families.

This got me thinking about the nature of love—what it drives people
to do, how far it can stretch, and what forms it can take. Perhaps the
lightheartedness I could hear on the tapes was simply Williams and

McDonough making the best of a bad situation. No, I couldn't judge them. Behind them, in the wings, was Milgram, urging them on, pressuring them to continue, and reassuring them that their participation was essential and for the greater good—for Yale, for truth, and for science.

8

IN SEARCH OF A THEORY

Dr. Paul Errera leaned forward with a sigh. It was 7 P.M. on Thursday, April 18, 1963, and he'd just finished an hour-long interview. He was likely tired. It had been a long day, and the meeting tonight had been particularly demanding. Only one man had arrived—let's call him Robert—and I imagined that he was still on Errera's mind as Errera loosened his tie and sat back in his chair. Robert, a forty-year-old radio technician, had been distressed by his obedience. He'd described his conflicting feelings during the experiment—how at times he thought it might be a setup and at others had been convinced that he was hurting the man. At one point, Robert said mournfully that it would have helped him to know earlier that the experiment was a hoax. He was having trouble squaring what he did with his conscience, and with God.

Robert had killed enemy soldiers during World War II, but that was a case of "kill or be killed." He had no such justification here, he told Errera. Errera had listened attentively, helping him weave together the confused and emotional strands of his story into a coherent whole, talking through with Robert where this tendency to conform had originated, and the forces in his life that had shaped him that way. When Robert was four, he told Errera, his father had left his mother and she in turn had handed him over to his strict grandfather, who agreed to raise him on the condition that she had no further contact with them. Errera encouraged Robert to recall himself as a four-year-old trying to fit in with a new family, a new home, in a town of around four hundred people in rural Vermont, not understanding where his parents had gone. As Robert's story unfolded, Errera pointed out the ways in which his obedience had helped him to adapt and survive and how, as a small boy, he had learned early that conformity was the best way to get by. It must have taken a huge concentration of effort on Errera's part—he had only an hour, after all, to try to move Robert through these feelings to something resembling a resolution.

Eventually, Robert seemed to adopt Errera's view that his behavior in the lab could be seen as logical. He described how he found the army easier than others. "When they took me away from Vermont, the hills, and put shoes on me and sent me away [to the army], I didn't find it difficult adapting at all, like some other fellows did who had never really been away from home. . . . Really, I felt as though my mother and father were gone. I didn't have that hopeless feeling that other fellows had."[1]

Paul Errera was a thirty-five-year-old assistant professor of psychiatry at Yale at the time, and he also taught in the local hospital's outpatient clinic. Yale had asked him to assess potential psychological damage to subjects in Milgram's experiment. The university must have also been concerned about its reputation, after some subjects had made formal complaints and at least one had consulted a lawyer. Between February and May 1963, Errera conducted eleven interviews with subjects to identify whether taking part had caused them harm.

Twelve people had been invited to Robert's meeting, the seventh of the eleven, but Errera probably welcomed the chance to talk with one man alone and in depth. Milgram would have been disappointed by the turnout—although by that point he should have been used to the fact that, at most, a handful of the dozen invited people would show up to each meeting. I pictured Errera as tall and lean, with his tie loosened, looking rumpled and tired while getting to his feet when Stanley Milgram—in my mind, visibly on guard, short and dark, and dressed neatly in suit and tie—came into the room from his viewing spot behind the mirror. I imagined Errera appraising Milgram in the same way he did those who arrived for the meetings, trying to read from a gesture, a look, what he was feeling. As usual, Milgram asked Errera what he thought of the meeting. Errera said it had been good to talk with Robert about more than just how he felt in the experiment—to have the chance to talk about obedience as a pattern in his life. He almost preferred having one-on-one meetings, he said.

But Milgram was unconvinced. "I know what's going to happen. I think I know what's going to happen in the individual interviews. I think everyone is going to have a life story which makes reasonable his action in the experiment. They're going to be very different kinds of life stories."

Errera hastened to reassure him that this was not an obstacle, but Milgram was impatient. "But this is a very critical problem. I think this is what is going to happen. I fully expect it. What does one do with this? In the way of explaining what went on. If [for] every man it's a different—one man may be asserting his masculinity in going on. Another man may be conforming to a pattern of compliance that's been a lifelong pattern for him. Another man may be showing something else that's going on."

"I don't think this detracts anything from your. . . . All it shows is that—"

"No, no. How does one relate it?"

"I think all you can say is that they all show the same end results, which is important . . . you can explain it on sociological grounds, you know, it has to do with our culture."

"If there isn't some common feature in a person that's responding to this external factor, then the external factor has no relevance . . ."

"Okay, so there is—the common feature is the hostility involved. Or if you—it depends on your theory."

"I haven't got a theory."[2]

Milgram's frustration was palpable. While it was true that he had no theory, he knew what he wanted to prove—he'd known it from the very start of his research. He wasn't interested in explaining disparities in obedience as differences in life experiences or culture or as individual differences between people. He was looking for some thread, some characteristic that bound people together, not ones that made them stand apart.

If Errera had been unsure of Milgram's reason for tape-recording and watching each session, it would have become clear in this conversation.

Milgram was consumed with his research. He had achieved extraordinary results; all he had to do was find a way to explain them. And here he was, two years after the experiments ended, still looking for an answer. The meetings were an opportunity not only to establish that he had not harmed his subjects but also to find an answer to the question of why they behaved as they did.

This close focus was obvious in Milgram's approach to planning the interviews, too. The administrative detail had been left to him. He chose the same room in which most of the experiments had taken place as the meeting venue, with the recording equipment and one-way mirror still present. This could simply be viewed as unfortunate, but it also appears to reveal that Milgram found it difficult to let go of the role of scientific observer. He seemed less interested in subjects learning more about themselves and more interested in what he could learn about them.

Errera, on the other hand, was focused on helping people to understand why they had behaved as they did. He offered a kind of in-depth debriefing that probed their feelings and helped them to accept their actions. His gentle style encouraged subjects to come to their own conclusions, as with a man who said he stopped because it was against his principles.

Errera: Is it principles? I'm asking . . . this is one of the things we are learning by. . . . What makes a person stop and another not stop?

Subject 405: When they don't stop, they're sadistic to a degree.

Errera: Is that what you think it is? Could be. This is your feeling?

Subject 405: This is my feeling, but I am completely—strictly a high school graduate—and I am limited as to what makes people tick psychologically.

Errera: You're not limited as to what makes you tick. You know yourself pretty well. You've been living with yourself for a few years now.[3]

It was Errera who was aware of the unfortunate associations of the setting and commented on it apologetically to subjects. It was also Errera who, in the third meeting, brought Milgram out from behind the mirror to answer practical questions about the experiments that Errera couldn't. Perhaps Milgram misinterpreted this invitation: the following week, he joined the group as Errera was winding down the meeting. Milgram asked Subject 405, the same man Errera had coaxed to talk about what made him "tick," whether he remembered pushing the learner's hand onto the shock plate and how he felt about it. Milgram wasn't interested in the man's principles but in finding out what made him stop.

Milgram: Did you feel that the fact that you had to touch the man had anything to do with your not wanting to go on?

Man: I honestly don't recall.

Errera interrupted. The hour was up, and he had to leave right at 7 P.M. for his next commitment. But after Errera had gone, Milgram persisted in questioning Subject 405. What did the learner say to him? Did he feel that the learner was really trying to prevent the shocks? What did he think he would have done if the learner had been in another room? Milgram quizzed the man to test the efficacy of the experiment, identify inconsistencies in instructions from Williams, and isolate any issues for his developing theory. In the transcript, the man sounded as if he were squirming under the persistence of Milgram's inquiries.

At first glance, the neatly labeled boxes in the archives and the manila folders with their numbers instead of names look organized and scientific. In addition to the subject files and copious notes, there are boxes of reel-to-reel tapes, cassette tapes, and photographs. The sheer amount of information jumbled together is overwhelming. It seemed as if Milgram were trawling, trailing a huge net to capture all sorts of information that he would go through later.

Some of the data that Milgram gathered and statistical analyses he had done seem absurd. Someone recorded the numbers of times each subject laughed and smiled during the experiment. Then the numbers were analyzed by condition to see if there was a pattern. But there was no answer for why they were laughing. It was as if only numbers could give an explanation.

Milgram seems never to have doubted the meaning of his results; he knew early on that he had found Nazis in New Haven. But explaining the how and why of what they did was another matter.

The trial of Adolf Eichmann, during the months that Milgram was making his preparations for the experiment, set the stage for how he would later interpret his subjects' behavior. The Nuremberg trials had finished in 1948. Since then, Eichmann, a high-ranking official in the Nazi hierarchy, was the most wanted of the high-profile Nazis still at large. He had been head of the section of the Gestapo that led the enforced relocation and mass deportation of Jews to concentration camps. After the war, Eichmann hid for a while in Allied prisoner-of-war camps, and then fled to Argentina with his wife and children in 1950. In the spring of 1960, Israeli agents tracked him to a suburb of Buenos Aires, kidnapped him, and smuggled him out of the country.

Despite international protests, Israel went ahead with plans for his trial. A large theater in western Jerusalem, Beit Ha'am, was chosen as the venue, and plans were made to accommodate a large media contingent; of the 756 seats in the theater, 474 were reserved for media. In a television first, the trial was to be filmed, edited, and rushed to nearby Lod airport for dispatch to major U.S. and European networks. Footage of the trial would be shown in thirty-eight countries. Of all the nations, America would be shown the most footage—up to an hour a day from the previous day's proceedings.

The trial began on April 11, 1961, with much anticipation, particularly among Jewish survivors. Due to the dearth of photographs of him, this would be the first time that most had seen the man charged with responsibility for the killing of Jews. Security was tight. The audience was separated from the stage by bulletproof glass and onstage a bulletproof glass box surrounded the dock.[4]

In the lead-up to the trial, Eichmann's crimes had been identified, elaborated, and discussed in detail. By the time the trial began, people were expecting to see a monster. But his appearance in the dock was an anticlimax: Eichmann, with his balding pate, dark suit, and large, horn-rimmed glasses, looked disappointingly ordinary. His appearance supported his defense: that he was a small cog in the vast machinery of state, his only crime having been that "his flaw was unfailing obedience." Some felt Eichmann should be tried wearing his SS uniform.[5]

The televised trial was a landmark in television history. The close-ups of Eichmann, audience reactions during the trial, and the immediacy of the day-old footage gave American viewers the sense of being in the front row, witness to events as they unfolded. In addition, Americans were likely to have heard the term "the Holocaust" for the first time during these broadcasts. Through Eichmann, the Holocaust entered American living rooms and into the popular consciousness. His trial educated a new generation and rekindled interest in the experience of European Jews under Nazism. Milgram, described by his wife as a "news addict," likely followed the trial closely.

The presentation of Eichmann in the American media emphasized his ordinariness, suggesting that his crimes had not been the result of anything specifically "German" in his psychology. Jeffrey Shandler, a professor of Jewish studies at Rutgers University, argued that, unlike the Israelis, who established the trial as a way of alerting the world to a specific historical event, the American media cast the narrative more broadly, framing it not as the trial of an individual but of all humankind. American viewers were told that they were witnessing evidence of psychological crimes that, by implication, could have taken place anywhere.[6]

From the beginning of Milgram's research, his description of his subjects echoed this media portrayal of Eichmann. He stressed the ordinariness of the men in his lab, their imperviousness to the suffering they were inflicting, their lack of remorse, and their unthinking obedience to the commands of authority.

In September 1961, just one month after his experiments began and a month after the end of the Eichmann trial, Milgram made an explicit connection between his subjects and Nazis. In a letter to the NSF, which began with a relatively trivial request for the installation of a phone in the lab, Milgram provided an update on the first four variations:

> In a naïve moment some time ago, I once wondered whether in all of the United States a vicious government could find enough moral imbeciles to meet the personnel requirements of a national system of death camps, of the sort that were maintained in Germany. I am now beginning to think that the full complement could be recruited in New Haven. A substantial proportion of people do what they are told to do, irrespective of the content of the act, and without pangs of conscience, as long as they perceive that the command comes from a legitimate authority.[7]

This letter marked an extraordinary leap from the idea that slavish obedience was the product of the German psyche. The Holocaust, Milgram concluded just four weeks into his research, could just as easily have occurred in the United States.

Although he described his results as "terrifying and depressing," Milgram must have been excited by their power. Here was an opportunity to take his place alongside his mentor Asch and make a significant contribution to an event that the world was still struggling to understand. Hereafter, Milgram framed his research to his experimental staff, Errera, the NSF, and sometimes even the subjects themselves as "an analogue of Nazi evil."[8]

Milgram rushed to get his results into print, sending off an article reporting his first results in December 1961. By March, it had been rejected by two scientific journals. The editor of *Journal of Personality*, Edward E. Jones, wrote:

> At present your data indicate a kind of triumph of social engineering. Thus you are apparently able to produce behavior which is in some sense shocking . . . but you have no clear theory . . . and therefore the psychological processes leading up to the obedient act remain a mystery. I really feel very ambivalent about your research.[9]

Today, Jones's distaste and ambivalence aren't surprising. But

Milgram was undaunted by his criticism and seemed to have made few changes, if any, to the original article before sending it out for a third time, to the *Journal of Abnormal Psychology*. This first published description of the research reveals as much about the scientist as about his subjects. Milgram chose to focus on one variation, his first, which was among those with the highest obedience rate (65 percent). Summarizing his subjects' distress, Milgram wrote, "The procedure created extreme levels of nervous tension in some Ss. Profuse sweating, trembling, and stuttering were typical expressions of this emotional disturbance." There was nothing surprising about this impersonal writing style—it was accepted practice to refer to research subjects simply and collectively as "S"—but the juxtaposition of his detachment with their distress was disturbing. People's individuality was erased. They were faceless, nameless objects whose fingers on a switch became a symbol of larger, abstract concepts.

Perhaps anticipating skepticism, Milgram provided evidence that subjects believed the illusion was real and reported that they experienced considerable tension, including nervous laughter. But laughter, rather than being a sign of humor or skepticism, was presented as a sign of pathology. It was "bizarre." A laughing "fit" became a "full blown, uncontrollable seizure, violently convulsive." He painted a picture of one man's deterioration and stress as the experiment progressed:

> I observed a mature and initially poised businessman enter the laboratory smiling and confident. Within 20 minutes he was reduced to a twitching, stuttering wreck, who was rapidly approaching a point of nervous collapse. He constantly pulled on his earlobe and twisted his hands. At one point he pushed his fist into his forehead and muttered: "Oh God, let's stop it." And yet he continued to respond to every word of the experimenter, and obeyed to the end.

In this seventy-nine-word, oft-quoted snippet, Milgram appeared to be proud of the power of the experiment that, in twenty minutes, could take a man to the point of "nervous collapse." And in case we had been feeling sympathy for the squirming businessman, Milgram ensured we knew that it was not the experimenter or the experiment that was at fault. It was the subject who had caused his own downfall, slavishly following the experimenter's "every word" and continuing to obey orders.[10] Milgram's portrait of the businessman reminded me of writer Susan Sontag's description of the Eichmann trial: "It was not Eichmann alone who was on trial. He stood trial in a double role; as both the particular and the generic; both the man, laden with hideous specific guilt, and the cipher, standing for the whole history of anti-Semitism."[11]

In June 1962, with the experiments over, Milgram traveled with his wife, Alexandra, to South America for a delayed honeymoon, but by then Jones's criticism that Milgram had demonstrated rather than explained a phenomenon seemed to have hit home. Milgram was preoccupied with finding an explanation for the results. On notepaper from the Gran Hotel in Lima, Peru, he wrote notes on three examples of obedience he had encountered recently: safety instructions if the plane had to make an emergency landing; Eichmann's last words, "I have shown obedience to flag and country," before his May execution; and a book that Milgram had seen in a shop, *How to Train Your Dog to Obey*. In the note about obeying the air-cabin crew's orders, he described his "terrific stress" on a turbulent flight from Rio de Janeiro to São Paulo. He started to "tremble and turn white," and "the most primitive intellectual mechanisms came into play as stress reducers. I could keep from falling to pieces completely by calling on God's protective hand [even though] all religious sentiment had passed from me years before. At that time I needed some belief to control the rising tension." He wrote that in the same way, "Our subjects resort to an even more primitive mechanism in intellectual denial."[12]

Milgram returned to Yale in mid-July, and two weeks later had news that his revised journal article had been accepted for publication, although it would be another sixteen months before it appeared in print.[13] In the meantime, he prepared to send out a report—the one to his subjects in which he explained what he had really been testing— and a questionnaire. The report had been long planned (Williams can be heard telling subjects that they would receive one once the research is over), but the questionnaire was a recent addition (Milgram had drafted it before his trip).

Since the end of the experiments, word about Milgram's work had begun to spread. Around July 1962 the *New Haven Register*, a local newspaper, contacted him about doing a story, perhaps after seeing a copy of the report. But Milgram wanted to keep his findings confined to the academy, rather than making them accessible to the general public—at least at this stage. He fobbed them off, saying that the NSF did not want any publicity "for the next few years" because it might interfere with replications.[14] Perhaps it was just that Milgram wanted to be the first to break his story, in a publication and at a time of his choosing. He had already started work on a book.

In November 1962, Milgram received two letters that would change his view of his research forever. The first was from Robert Hall of the NSF, who sent a lengthy, damning report explaining why Milgram's latest funding application had been rejected. Hall, along with two others, had visited Yale in May to discuss the research with Milgram and observe it firsthand. They were obviously not reassured by what they saw. Quite apart from the effect on subjects and the lack of a theory, Hall wrote, Milgram had ignored his subjects' interpretation of the events, had no evidence that subjects believed the situation, and had no proof that their behavior inside the lab could be applied to the world beyond it. Without a theory and without an explanation of why people behaved as they did, the research seemed to shed little light on obedience to authority.

Milgram had created a powerful scenario that was engaging and affecting for the subjects involved, but what did it mean? His depiction of subjects as Eichmann figures, implying that they acted out of a human propensity to obey orders, seemed like mere speculation—the results could have just as easily been explained by other factors, such as the subjects' personal backgrounds or the pressure placed upon them by the experimenter.

The second letter was from the APA, which wrote to say it would withhold his application for membership until an investigation of ethical concerns was completed. Some colleagues at Yale had already expressed their misgivings, and Milgram guessed that one had complained to the APA. He told a former student, Australian psychologist Leon Mann, that one colleague "has assumed vast moral indignation about the Milgram experiments entirely appropriate to an asshead."[15]

It must have been a humiliating blow to receive these letters—both in the same month—but Milgram seemed to bounce back quickly. In fact, it gave him a blueprint of the evidence and arguments he would need to defend his results and the treatment of his subjects. And in the midst of what must have felt to Milgram like a groundswell of criticism, he had some good news: in December 1962 he was offered a job at Harvard, which would begin in July the following year. It was a chance to start afresh, free from what he felt was the envy and criticism of Yale.

It was not just the Eichmann trial that influenced Milgram's work. Yet Milgram made little reference to other important factors—such as his personal history or prevailing Cold War anxieties—that may have had an impact on his research.

Milgram had been personally and professionally affected by the Holocaust but, maintaining his scientific persona, he was slow to publicly acknowledge his Jewish background as an influence. The Holocaust had been a dominant theme of his childhood: during the war, the family had crowded around the radio, listening for news of relatives in Europe; and in 1946, thirteen-year-old Milgram had referred to the Holocaust in his bar mitzvah speech, around the same time as relatives who had survived the concentration camps were staying with the Milgram family. In addition, much of American psychology during the period in which he was studying was influenced by the Holocaust. Milgram's mentors Gordon Allport and Solomon Asch had formulated and interpreted their research with reference to World War II. Yet Milgram would not make a direct public reference to the influence of his Jewish background on his research until 1977, fifteen years after it was completed.[16]

Milgram's research was also influenced by contemporary anxiety about American moral weakness. During the Korean War, the capture and supposed brainwashing of U.S. prisoners, a number of whom later defected and refused repatriation, had led to an "intense moral panic." The public perception was that the independence and strong-mindedness of the American national character had been replaced by submission and weakness.[17] This was exacerbated by the tension and brinkmanship of the Cold War, which generated anxiety about the masculinity of American men compared to their Soviet counterparts. Milgram's results fed precisely into such anxiety by suggesting that the average American was as morally weak as the Nazi murderer—and apparently as open to manipulation as Eichmann claimed to have been. Like aliens inhabiting small-town America in pulp science fiction or Soviet spies masquerading as American citizens, Milgram's subjects became "both everyday Joes from Main Street America and incomprehensible monsters."[18] They were both familiar and frightening, known and unknown—ordinary men one minute, mysterious killers the next.

Milgram's lab became a stage on which the political and cultural anxieties of the Cold War were played out: strength and weakness, independence and submission, and the failure of American men—a kind of moral flabbiness that left them impotent in the face of the might of the Soviet Union.[19]

Milgram probably didn't refer to personal and social influences on his work because the positivist tradition in which he was trained had as its model the unbiased, value-neutral experimenter. He had embraced this brand of science and was more interested in the objectively measurable world of external action than in the subjective, inner world of the mind. He told one interviewer that he had chosen social psychology over another discipline of psychology because "there is something of a redeeming feature in becoming a social psychologist because it doesn't make you into a somewhat sickly, Viennese analyst thinking about inner thoughts."[20]

On occasion, he noted this coldness in himself, and expressed sympathy for his subjects. In a note entitled "The Experimenter's Dilemma," he wrote:

> Consider . . . the fact . . . that while observing the experiment I—and many others—know that the naïve subject is deeply distressed, and that the tension caused him is almost nerve shattering. . . . If we fail to intervene, although we know a man is being made upset, why separate these actions of ours

from those of the subject, who feels he is causing discomfort to another? . . . I feel, though I cannot quite find the words for it, that the reactions of the observers—those who sit by "enjoying the show"—are profoundly relevant to an understanding of the actions of the subject.[21]

But these subjective doubts never made their way into official accounts of his research. Publicly, Milgram presented as the objective, rational scientist. Out of those hundreds of boxes and thousands of sheets of paper now archived, Milgram presented statistics—voltage level and percentages—as his primary data. In writing his article, he simplified a mass of complex information into a case of whether people were obedient or not. What mattered was purely behavioral: their hand on the switch. Only in his unpublished writings and notes can we see that he struggled with what he was doing to the people he'd recruited for the research.

The apprehension over the ethical implications of Milgram's experiments continued to grow during his last semester at Yale. It was in February 1963 that Yale, concerned over the treatment of Milgram's subjects, initiated the series of follow-up interviews by Dr. Paul Errera. Ironically, this turn of events provided Milgram with an opportunity to act on the criticisms in Hall's letter.[22]

Paul Errera was a good choice. Having worked with war veterans, he was used to dealing with men who were experiencing problems as a result of highly stressful events. Errera's son Claude told me that his father's stint as an intern at New Haven Correctional Center had sensitized him to the suffering of war veterans, a number of whom were awaiting trial at the center.

Errera began his meetings on February 28, 1963. The 135 pages of transcripts are available in the archives, but I found them difficult to read because everyone taking part—Errera, the subjects, and Milgram—seemed at cross-purposes over why they were meeting. Milgram was hoping that Errera would find that no subjects had been harmed, although he later told subjects in one meeting that Errera's role was "to spot people who have been seriously damaged by participating in the experiment."[23] Errera had the difficult position of having to work alongside, but not become influenced by, Milgram. He was likely told to cooperate with Milgram, but he must have been surprised to find that Milgram would, on some occasions, be watching from behind the mirror. And who knew what the subjects thought? The letters of invitation were written in the third person but signed by Milgram, although they stated that Errera had been asked to make "an independent assessment" (just who asked him, Milgram doesn't say). Only selected subjects were invited to participate, and they weren't told why they had been chosen. They weren't informed that there had been complaints to Yale or that other psychologists had raised questions about their welfare. In an echo of the newspaper ad Milgram had used to recruit them, the tone was flattering, implying that people might have been invited because of their intelligence and their ability to make a substantial contribution to "important work."[24]

As Milgram discovered, people were reluctant to take up the invitation. He invited groups of twelve at a time, and on some occasions only one or two people showed up. The largest group was eight men, who arrived at the first meeting. Once it became clear that former subjects were wary about returning, Milgram began following up his letter with a phone call as a more persuasive method of convincing people to come. In total, Milgram invited more than 140 people, 20 percent of his original group of 780 subjects. Only thirty-two showed up.[25]

When Errera waited in the laboratory for his meeting at 6 P.M. each Thursday, he never knew who would arrive. Nor was he prepared, at least at first, for the number of questions the subjects had. The first meeting functioned as a kind of debriefing: none of the men knew one another or how far the others had gone. While they waited for the rest of the group, four compared notes on their experiences, trying to piece together the story of each variation: Did your learner mention heart trouble? Were you in the same room? You got your orders by phone? Where was the experimenter? They turned to Errera to fill in the gaps. But Errera acknowledged that he hadn't been briefed about the detail of the experiments: "I assume others of you also wonder what it's all about. I think you—most of you—know more than I do. I've just started in this at this part, in terms of evaluating how you people feel about it afterwards."

Instead, he was keen to keep to what he saw as the purpose of the meeting: "Some people have said, well, this can be very harmful—to put somebody through what you went through. It wasn't quite a Korean concentration camp, but it was an unpleasant experience. . . . I am interested in what aftereffects does this have, because somebody could say, and I think maybe with a lot of justification, that what you went through is a very harmful experience."[26]

In several meetings, Errera had to counter subjects' fears that the meeting might be another experiment. In the second meeting, only he and one other man were present when a third arrived. It reminded him, the third man said, of arriving for the experiment and being met by two men who appeared to be strangers.

> Man: I don't really trust anything about the whole thing, including this session here. I never saw this guy at all in my life. You might be a graduate student of psychology as far as I'm concerned.

> Errera: Let me just say here: this is not a hoax, to the best of my knowledge. I am a psychiatrist. I'm the—

> Man: I'm assuming—I'm assuming—I'm operating as if that were true, but [laughs] I'm on edge.[27]

Perhaps as a result of this, at the third meeting Errera addressed these sorts of concerns early. "This is not another experiment," he told subjects. This pattern continued throughout the interviews: "No, there is no trick here. I don't expect you to believe me, why should you. . . . I'm a real psychiatrist and Subject 405 is a real maintenance mechanic and you're a real counselor, I guess"; "the gimmick this time is that we're trying to figure out, to understand why people acted the way they did in the experimental situation."

Errera also allowed subjects to be critical of Milgram.

> Man: I'm not just sure and I'm not the one that should in any way I suppose criticize a man such as Dr. Milgram, who probably knows what he's doing far more than I know how to speak about it—

Errera: With that introduction, let's go ahead.

Man: All right. I do question whether the setup here was, with sufficient controls, to get the desired result.

Errera: Huh, huh. I think that's a very good question.

[. . .]

Man: I'm not too sure, either, whether it is the sound basis for determination of a principle to be ostensibly doing one thing and actually doing something else. This may or may not be a basis on which to inform an adequate judgment as to what people will do when asked to push a button that would destroy Switzerland, for instance. I'm not sure whether the basic premise is entirely right. . . . Maybe some of the people who went through with this would not push a button in warfare that would destroy many people.

Errera: . . . You're right, you can only say that in this situation it happened, and it's very dangerous to go beyond that.

Man: If it's to be used as a basis of further conclusions, [then] I'm not sure whether those conclusions would be valid.

Errera: This is the important watchword in any kind of research, not to go beyond . . . just what you see . . .[28]

Errera's interviews provided some subjects with the full and thorough debriefing they had thus far not been given. He listened and encouraged them to express their feelings. During each session, he asked open-ended questions; while not everyone was equally talkative in some of the larger group meetings, I imagine that the quiet ones got something out of listening to the others. Especially because, in each meeting, Errera sounded them out about how far they went on the machine.

Milgram's role in the meetings, however, was ambiguous. Errera explained to each group that the session was being recorded and that

Milgram was watching from behind the mirror, but he didn't explain why. Perhaps he didn't know himself. When Milgram did interact with subjects, on the occasions when he came out to join the discussion, his behavior was changeable. When they seemed distressed, he was sympathetic, reassuring them that they shouldn't feel bad. For example, when one man's wife came to a meeting and told Milgram that her husband felt as if he was "acting as if [he] couldn't think," Milgram tried to put them both at ease.

Milgram: Well, they are not acting in terms of their own motives . . . you sort of give your thinking function over to this man and listen to what he says.

Subject 501: I thought I had the feeling, "Well, he's controlling this thing and he's completely controlling me."

Wife: They still are—that's the fourth cigarette you're lighting. *[General laughter]*

[. . .]

Milgram: . . . the whole point of the experiment is, in order to stop, you have to actually face—to face—defy this man, and say, "I'm not going to do it anymore."

Man: Forty percent did.

Milgram: But they were—you see, it depends on a particular experimental condition you're in. There are some conditions that were much more easy. For example where . . . you had to actually push [the learner's] hand down to give him the shocks—he wouldn't get the shock unless his hand was on a plate, and at a certain point he refused to press his hand on the plate.

At the end of the hour, as the subjects were leaving, Milgram was clearly still concerned about the man.

Milgram: Thanks very much for coming. I hope that—I really seriously hope that it did not—basically, I hope you don't have the feeling that you would rather not have been in it. You may have that feeling [but] it's an interesting life experience.[29]

At other times, it was as if Milgram were asking his subjects for their approval, perhaps wanting to be reassured that they were unharmed.

First man: We were the subjects, not the person getting the pain.

Second man: We were taking the punishment.

Milgram: In a way, that's true. But how do you feel about the— do you think an experiment of this sort should—just forgetting that it's Yale behind it, do you think that one should do an experiment of this sort, assuming that you do learn something? We learned something about human nature and that's what the aim is, and yet is it proper to call a person in and to bribe him with $4.50 and the promising of an interesting experiment? . . . Do you think you've been abused by having been sucked into this?

First man: If I thought so, I wouldn't be here now.

Second man: I think asking us over here—

Third man: I think it's sort of a reward, but, I mean, we're still in on it, so that—if we just never heard anything about it maybe then we would have been a little bit annoyed after a while.[30]

Yet sometimes Milgram was defensive. In the following exchange, after Errera had left for the evening, Milgram argued vehemently with a man who challenged his statement that only subjects were qualified to judge whether such experiments should be allowed.

Milgram: One of the problems is that some of the most interesting questions of human nature do touch on moral dimensions.

Now, ordinarily as a scientist you're interested in creating situations that increase behavior or decrease it along this particular dimension. This means, in a sense, on the one hand, that you're inducing people to do things that from many standpoints may be considered immoral. That's probable, but how do you deal with it? Those significant aspects of behavior which we call morally—morally relevant—I must—it's a dilemma . . .

Man: This question may be out of line or not fruitful to even discuss now, but may I just ask it? Can you get any guidance at all from other psychologists, or other psychiatrists, who are more objective?

Milgram: I haven't found it very helpful, particularly people who haven't seen the experiment. They tend to express the same kind of concern that you've expressed for others, but the only concern that's truly important is what one—how you feel in person? And if you've gone through it and you're glad you've gone through it, if you are . . . that's the only answer. Why deny to another person what you regard as a positive experience?

Man: Well, I would like to ask Dr. Errera if he was here . . . are you saying that no psychiatrist reading this thing or looking at it could really understand what went on unless he were a subject?

Milgram: Well, he has to be a psychiatrist who has had contact with the subjects who've been in it and that's one of the reasons why Dr. Errera was here.

Man: Oh, I see.

Milgram: I think it's a difficult question. I don't think one should make it more difficult than it is because, after all, people have been through—let's say people have been through concentration camps, and you ask them, "Are you glad you were in—if you had the choice would you do it again?" There's no question, you see. No, I wouldn't have done it again if I had the choice and the—

Man: 'Course this is kind of an iffy question.

Milgram: The kind of manipulations to which you're subjected in the real world by all sorts of people who have no interest in values that you cherish, like scientific advance, is extraordinary, and—

Man: But of course they're not taking advantage of your—I don't know. We've been over this and I see your point without being able to—

Milgram: Well, I don't think there's that answer. . . . It has the quality of a dilemma, at least to me.[31]

In this exchange, it seems that Milgram wanted the same endorsement in person that he got from the majority of people who answered his questionnaire who said they felt experiments like his should be conducted and they were glad to have taken part. But despite his philosophical musings on whether it was justified, and despite the anguish he had heard expressed in the meetings he had watched, later in the interview Milgram made it clear that he would repeat the experience gladly.

Man: I've got a question for you. If you had to do it over again, would you do it?

Milgram: Would I do it? Yes, easily.

Man: It's caused—you know, there are a lot of much less difficult projects that perhaps you might have chosen.

Milgram: There's no question in my mind that I would do it over again. I mean, I may have done it a little better, but I would definitely do it over. I think I learned a tremendous amount in this project. I think I got insights into behavior that I just couldn't have gotten any other way, and unless—it's really my job to probe what I can identify as an important aspect of behavior, and I think that's terribly important. . . . That's an easy—it's simple—it's such an easy question for me to answer. There's no question that I'd do it over, even if I were—let's just say I'm very curious about such things.[32]

In one meeting, Milgram came out from behind the mirror after a man told Errera that he didn't think the learner was being shocked: "I continued more or less because I couldn't conceive of anybody allowing me to continue on with an experiment knowing somebody was going to be hurt." Milgram was dismissive when the man repeated his belief.

Milgram: So when you say, for example, that you didn't conceive the possibility that Yale would kill a man, they would never—

Man: [Inflict] pain to another man.

Milgram: But, look, this man *[gesturing to another subject]* said this is one of the most distressing experiences of his life.

Man: But, still, like I say—

Milgram: *[interrupting]* Is it inconceivable that Yale would in fact put a man through such a procedure?

Man: It might—

Milgram: *[interrupting]* Well, they did.

Man: Well, I think if you—I think you'll find in there *[gesturing to the questionnaire]* in one of the things I answered was possibly that you were checking us—the people instilling the pain.

Milgram: *[addressing the rest of the group]* Right. Are there any other questions I can answer?[33]

Despite the wording of the letter inviting them to "discuss frankly and intelligently their reactions to the experiment," some discussions were clearly unwelcome.

While Milgram saw his experiment as a moral test and applauded people who disobeyed during it, he nonetheless demanded obedience in the debriefing and discussions afterward. And when subjects challenged him or the experiment, he was critical, even combative. As in his writings, he alternated between sympathy and scorn for the subjects.

Milgram's volunteers had a hard time knowing what was real when they arrived at his lab, even for their interviews with Errera. Meanwhile, Milgram himself had a similar struggle with his changing feelings about the reasons for their behavior.

In 1962, when the experiments were over, Milgram would probably have argued with those subjects who blamed themselves for their behavior. He spelled out why in the report he had mailed them:

> Situations control Behavior
> . . . There is a tendency to think that everything a person does is due to the feelings or ideas within the person. However, scientists know that actions depend equally on the situation in which a man finds himself. In the studies in which you took part, we were interested in seeing how changes in the situation would affect the degree to which people obey the requests of the experimenter.[34]

Milgram told several subjects that going to the maximum said more about the power of the situation than the personality of the person pressing the switches. It would be wrong, he suggested, to explain what happened in terms of character traits. He reminded subjects of their politeness, desire to help, sense of having made a commitment, and fear of being disrespectful—some of the "binding factors" that had trapped them into obedience. Above all, he stressed the normality of their behavior: anyone in the same situation would have felt the same pressures, he argued.

Yet it is clear that, at the same time, Milgram didn't really believe that. Privately he felt no such reservations about where to place the blame: during the same period in which he was soothing and reassuring his subjects, he was describing their behavior to others as "terrifying" and calling those who obeyed "moral imbeciles" capable of staffing "death camps."[35] By framing the experiment as a moral conflict—a choice between not harming a man and abiding by an authority's commands—he passed judgment on those he perceived had failed the test. His desire to portray his subjects as Nazis in his writings meant that he could not accept Errera's view that subjects' reactions were dictated by their life experiences.

Regardless of his ambivalence toward Errera's theory, it is likely that Milgram, hoping for further funding, would have been awaiting with a mixture of dread and anticipation Errera's assessment of whether there had been psychological damage. He didn't have to wait long: Errera offered his impressions at the fifth meeting. He assured Milgram that, of the nineteen people he'd spoken to so far, he had found no evidence of people suffering harm. Perhaps Errera saw an uncertain and worried young man whose career was on the line and felt the need to ease his anxiety.

Milgram must have been relieved with this verdict. But, with the issue of a theory on his mind, he immediately changed tack, asking Errera's opinion on what had motivated the obedience. "Do you feel on the basis of interviewing these subjects that—is aggression feeding their compliance or is the situation so invitingly compliant that you don't even have to think about aggression?"

"I don't know the answer to that," Errera replied. Milgram's study didn't examine the reasons for people's behavior; it measured only the behavior itself. To answer that question, he said, Milgram would have to do another experiment.

Errera's son Claude told me that Errera was "pretty disappointed (maybe even disgusted) by the study itself."[36] Errera's role was to assess the impact of the experiments on the people who had taken part. And, like Williams, he was left with the difficult task of confronting these people's distress and accounting for what had happened. Milgram's interjections, and his desire to sound out his ideas on Errera, wouldn't have made Errera's job any easier.

Yet it wasn't until it came time for Errera to finalize his report that major tension between the two men arose. The report was published with the title "Statement Based on Interviews with 'Forty Worst

Cases'"—a title that Milgram wanted but Errera was unhappy with, because it implied that he had interviewed the forty people who had been most troubled by the experiment when in fact he'd simply interviewed the thirty-two who had shown up. Errera referred to the mismatch between the title and his understanding in its opening: as if distancing himself from it, he stated that he had no information on how those he interviewed had been selected, how they compared with the total sample, or why many invited didn't attend.[37]

Nevertheless, Errera's involvement and eventual declaration of a clean bill of health regarding the impact on his subjects gave Milgram great ammunition in his future dealings with critics. With Errera's interviews complete in May 1963, his new job about to start at Harvard, and his daring research about to make his reputation, Milgram must have felt that a new chapter in his life was about to begin. He couldn't have foreseen that after the publication of his article, life would never be the same.

9

THE ETHICAL CONTROVERSY

I was on my way to Fordham University to meet Harold Takooshian, who had been a student of Milgram's at the City University of New York (CUNY). I was looking forward to it. I knew from my own teaching experience that your students can come to know you in a way few others can. It's hard to hide your moods from a group who watches your every gesture.

Harold Takooshian, all in black—with black hair and a pencil-thin black mustache to complete the look—had borrowed the president's boardroom for our meeting. It was an imposing wood-paneled room, at the end of which was a vast table presided over by a portrait of Fordham's founder, Archbishop "Dagger John" Hughes, who famously wore a crucifix sharpened to knife point dangling over his somber robes. Harold had prepared a folder of clippings in advance and sent an e-mail to the "Milgram alumni," inviting them to meet us for lunch. The alumni were a loose collection of people—Milgram's colleagues, friends, students, and relatives—who first came together for a memorial service after Milgram's death in 1984 to share their memories. They have been meeting every five or so years since.

"I feel lucky my life intersected with his," Harold told me, his eyes shining. "He was a brilliant teacher," he added, flinging his hands theatrically for emphasis.

Harold could still remember his first class vividly. Milgram gave the thirteen graduate students the job of moving the tables and chairs into a suitable arrangement. First, they tried an octagonal shape, and

Milgram asked them what they thought of it, encouraging suggestions and giving instructions. Next, they tried a rectangle. No good, so they tried a circle. "For two hours we were rearranging the tables and chairs, and nobody said, 'This is ridiculous' or 'Let's sit down'—nobody did. Instead, Milgram was able to do it in such a way that people tried to please him. Somebody would say, 'I've got an idea,' and Milgram would say, 'Well then, people,' and we'd start all over. At that point we did think he was crazy because it was just over the top. And the next class, there was no talk about chairs at all." Harold shook his head.

What was he doing, the class puzzled afterward. Testing them? Teasing them? Was there some mysterious scientific purpose to his behavior? "This is my interpretation twenty-nine years later," Harold said. "He was testing us to see what type of people we were, individually and as a group." But it sounded to me as if he were still uncertain.

It was a characteristic introduction to Milgram's teaching style, which was often puzzling and confrontational, although never boring. Sometimes his students had a hard time knowing where his teaching ended and his research began.

Still, Milgram's students have a particular bond, Harold told me. "Very few people studied with Stanley Milgram. We feel special because we studied with this genius."

Milgram's reputation had preceded him when he arrived at CUNY, but it had also affected people's perceptions of his trustworthiness. At Harvard, where he had worked from 1963 until 1967, students and staff had become wise to his tricks. On November 22, 1963, the day President Kennedy was shot, Milgram ran into a lecture theater yelling out the news—and none of the students took him seriously, putting it down instead to one of his experiments.[1] His obedience research had just been published, and already it was shaping people's reactions to him.

Just two months before this incident, in September 1963, the Milgrams had moved to Cambridge for the beginning of the new academic year. It must have felt like a new chapter in Milgram's life. He was newly married, back at Harvard but as a member of faculty, rather than a student, and being courted by publishers. His daring research was quickly making him a reputation, despite disquiet in some quarters.

His next project would be literary, rather than scientific. That month, Milgram set out to find himself a literary agent, saying that he planned to "devote more and more time" to writing fiction, and he aimed to publish in "quality" magazines such as *The Atlantic*, the *New Yorker*, *Harper's*, and *The Reporter*.[2] He found an agent, but a month later all plans for the literary life had to be temporarily shelved.

Milgram's first article was published in October 1963, and he had clearly underestimated the interest that it would generate. Although he had been hoping to confine publicity to the academic world, just three days after it appeared in the *Journal of Abnormal and Social Psychology* it burst onto the pages of the *New York Times* under the headline "Sixty-five Percent in Test Blindly Obey Order to Inflict Pain." "What sort of people, slavishly doing what they are told, would send millions of fellow humans into gas chambers?" the paper asked its readers.[3]

In the following two months, Milgram was inundated with media requests, fielding calls from ABC; United Press International; London's *The Times* and *Daily Mail*; and the magazines *Life*, *Esquire*, and *Popular Science*. And once the story hit the UPI wire service, several more media outlets wanted to cover it. Milgram, it seemed, had held up a mirror that reflected something deeply compelling about contemporary American life.[4]

It's no wonder that the media leapt on the article: it met all the criteria for a highly newsworthy story. In the pages of a rather dry academic journal, Milgram appeared to have reported on something extraordinary. According to him, he had replicated the same processes of blind obedience that turned the wheels of destruction and murder in Nazi Germany but with ordinary Americans. He also made much of the surprising and shocking nature of the obedient subjects' behavior and how observers were astounded by the results.

But, curiously, Milgram seemed desperate to limit the publicity. He turned down several offers, telling ABC broadcaster Ted Koppel that he did not want the experiment publicized "at this time." He even went so far as to phone and telegram Walter Sullivan, a *New York Times* reporter, to discourage him from publishing a story.[5]

Just why he was so intent on keeping the research under wraps is unclear. It could have been because he was still hoping to conduct more research—although, six months earlier, he had assured the NSF that no further experiments were planned.[6] It might simply have been that he was worried that premature news of his research would make his book old news by the time it was published.

The flurry of press reports tended to emulate the emphasis of the *New York Times* story, focusing on the sensational aspects of the results. Newspaper reports reproduced and strengthened Milgram's claims about human nature. Journalists translated Milgram's scientific prose for lay readers and frequently used the second person, inviting readers to identify with the subjects and to view themselves as "potential Nazis."[7] It tells us something about the power of science that reporters disseminating news of the experiment, which was beamed worldwide, had failed to report or failed to notice that the condition that Milgram wrote about in his article was the first one he had conducted and involved just forty men.

Only a handful of pieces questioned the morality of Milgram's methods. An editorial in the *St. Louis Post-Dispatch*, published on November 2, 1963, concluded that "the more genuine gauge of human cruelty was not the subjects but the experimenters; that the showing was not one of blind obedience but of open-eyed torture" and questioned whether "there was anything in the performance worthy of a great university."

Milgram responded quickly, arguing that the responsibility for the experiment was his and that Yale had in fact "advised caution." But he had gone ahead with his "test of humanity" because he felt that it was important to "teach men to be free from destructive obedience." He wrote that he couldn't have foreseen either the high rates of obedience or the high levels of stress and "unexpected tension and conflict" among his subjects ("an experimenter does not have a crystal ball in his pocket"). As for the accusation of cruelty, this was not a view shared by subjects, who "overwhelmingly endorsed" the experiment. Finally, a doctor, Paul Errera, had conducted follow-up interviews with subjects and pronounced the experiment "safe."[8] These points, along with his later assurances about the careful debriefing he offered, would become his standard response to accusations of cruelty.

Milgram *was* tempted by media interest in February 1964, even going so far as meeting with Dick Siemanowski, the executive producer of CBS's *Chronicle* news program. Siemanowski described the proposed program in a follow-up letter:

> The first half of the show would be devoted to your description of the nature and conditions of the experiment. I think what we could accomplish here is what you suggested in our conversation, namely, we could build up in our audience the kind of anticipation of results which the experiment and the film would counter.

Clearly, Siemanowski had realized that one of the compelling features of the research was the pitting of expectations about how people would behave against the reality of what they did. The second half, Siemanowski went on, would include a moderated discussion between Milgram, Hannah Arendt, and social psychologist Erich Fromm.[9] Milgram would, by implication, join the ranks of leading Jewish American intellectuals. But Milgram backed away. Two days later, he had his literary agent, Joan Daves, tell CBS to "hold off any TV commitments [for] . . . a year or 18 months." It was a decision she agreed with: "I believe the decision to hold off is the right one. I will be in a stronger position to negotiate and the exposure and publicity will be of great benefit to the book."[10]

While reaction from the media was immediate, reactions from Milgram's peers took longer to make themselves known. Journal articles could take months before they made their way into print, so the first published response from a fellow psychologist, Diana Baumrind, did not appear until June 1964, eight months after Milgram's article. Unlike most of the media reports, Baumrind's focus was on Milgram's methods rather than his results.

For many American psychologists, Baumrind's highly critical

article—published in *American Psychologist*, a high-profile journal distributed to all the members of the APA—would have been their first introduction to Milgram's research. Baumrind described her misgivings forcefully. His obedience experiment, she argued, raised the ethical issue of the duty of care that researchers owed to participants. She was bothered by what she saw as his "posture of indifference" toward his subjects. She questioned how, given the trauma that his subjects went through, his cursory debriefing could have prevented long-term damage to their self-esteem or faith in authority. After all, she argued, many people must have left the lab with new and perhaps unwelcome knowledge of what they were capable of, and the "friendly" debriefing that Milgram described offered them little chance to express any anger. Milgram, Baumrind argued, had underestimated the potential for long-term psychological harm, and his "casual assurances" that no one was harmed were "unconvincing."

Second, Baumrind argued that Milgram was less concerned with his subjects' welfare because he felt the gain in knowledge outweighed their distress—but she doubted that Milgram could justify any risk of harm to subjects on the grounds that the results offered "concrete benefit to humanity." She challenged the link that Milgram sought to make to Nazism. The social psychologist's laboratory, she argued, could hardly replicate a "real-life experience" such as Nazi Germany. His subjects had little in common with SS subordinates: the SS man was likely to regard his victims as subhuman and believe both he and his superior officer were working together for a "great cause." The guilt and conflict of Milgram's subjects were further evidence that the parallel between the Yale laboratory and concentration camps was weak. She implied that experiments such as Milgram's brought the profession into disrepute and should not be condoned.[11]

While the appearance of Baumrind's article was unexpected— Milgram later said that he had had no warning of it—the content wouldn't have been a surprise. He had already had plenty of evidence of others' uneasiness and distaste for his research. As he put it in a letter to Leon Mann, "There have [*sic*] been foreboding from the timorous, the concerned, and the stupid for many years now."[12] And even before the article, Milgram seems to have been marshaling arguments in his defense. In a document dated April 1964, Milgram anticipated just the sort of points that Baumrind would make. He described "several well known studies" in which "considerable degrees of stress were considered acceptable for the attainment of particular research goals." One study of the effects of sensory deprivation had handcuffed and blindfolded subjects, making them spend twenty to forty hours exposed to constant noise. As a result, they hallucinated and felt "extreme anxiety and severe malfunctioning of the psychic system." He cited another study in which subjects were drugged without their knowledge and "provoked into states of extreme emotional arousal." He also included Asch's experiment in this litany of predecessors, of which he said that subjects were "likely to feel great stress and conflict" because they were forced to lie and could "feel ashamed and devalued." If other psychologists got away with pressuring subjects to lie, giving them electric shocks, and terrifying them by pouring smoke into a room, he argued, why was he any different? He was merely continuing an experimental tradition.[13]

However, his private reaction to Baumrind's article was not nearly as full of bravado. She had obviously touched a nerve. Among his papers at Yale, there's a drawing of a dog with a human head, captioned, "After reading Dr. Baumrind's article, I feel bad."[14] It's dated June 1964, and Milgram must have drawn it just after he got his copy of the APA journal.

Milgram obviously felt aggrieved at being singled out for criticism, especially in such a high-profile publication. He told one interviewer that he "wasn't prepared for criticism of that sort, being rather thin-skinned."[15] He had some justification in this: ethically questionable psychology research had existed long before his, but published criticism of it was rare. Yet he may have failed to understand the social context surrounding Baumrind's article. The civil rights movement, the women's movement, and antiwar demonstrations—which Milgram would probably have been sympathetic to, given his apparently liberal political views—meant a change in what was seen as acceptable treat-

ment of subjects in scientific research.[16] What had been par for the
course was now under scrutiny.

Even though Baumrind's criticisms echoed many of the doubts he
had struggled with during his research, Milgram made no mention
of this in his published reply. Nor did he reveal that for more than
three-quarters of his subjects, the "dehoaxing" didn't take place for
months, and, when it did, it was by letter. His reply was a variation on the same arguments he had given in his letter to the *St.
Louis Post-Dispatch*: he claimed that the stress his subjects experienced wasn't intentional and that he hadn't expected either the high
levels of obedience or the degree of distress. While a lab was certainly not the same as a death camp in Nazi Germany—it was a
"background metaphor"—it was important that he had been able to
illuminate the power of authority. He also argued that he did treat
his subjects with dignity and in fact assumed that they were capable
of making choices about how to behave, in contrast to Baumrind's
view that they were passive recipients of orders. While he agreed
that their distress was intense, he argued that it was only temporary
because he had conducted a "careful post-experimental treatment,"
which included a "dehoax." Most found it "instructive and enriching," and 84 percent said they were glad to have taken part. Milgram
also mentioned that the follow-up questionnaire and interviews had
found no evidence of long-term harm. He promised that the detailed
results of the questionnaire and Errera's report would be published
in a "forthcoming monograph," but he would never make good on
this promise.[17]

But if he thought he had laid the ethical controversy to rest, Milgram
was wrong. The public disagreement sparked what has been called
"the most intense debate on research ethics in the history of psychology," contributing to a crisis of confidence among social psychologists
that would continue until the late 1970s.[18] Baumrind's dissatisfaction
with experiments such as Milgram's was echoed and amplified by a
chorus of critics, who engaged in a public reexamination of the role of
the discipline, its motives, and its methods in journal articles and book
chapters during the next decade.

Some felt strongly that this form of social science dehumanized participants, subjecting them to embarrassing and traumatic experiences in the name of science. They argued that the lab had become "a theater where experimenters get to stage-manage their creative fantasies" with little thought of the emotional cost for those involved. Experimentation had become an intellectual game for many of the psychologists who used deception; they competed with one another in a kind of macho one-upmanship to see who could come up with the most ingenious scenarios. The goal of social psychological research, an increasing number of critics complained, seemed to be to provide intellectual amusement for experimenters, who confused "notoriety with achievement" and engaged in gimmicky manipulations that offered little serious contribution to the understanding of human behavior.[19]

Others argued that creating such believable and vivid experiments was an art, and those creating them should be treated as artists. Shelley Patnoe noted:

> The procedures became little dramas with the subject as both the star and the audience. . . . Giving form to emotional experience is one central function of art. These men were creating art and then testing it. Seen in this light, it is possible to understand some of the frustration expressed by experimental psychologists when the ethics of their enterprise came into question. They reacted as painters would if deprived of the nude for study, simply on the grounds of moral outrage.[20]

Psychologists of this ilk, Milgram among them, saw their work as a validation of the discipline—their experiments were grand revelations of the depths of the human soul, in the same manner as art. For such psychologists, the end justified the means, and many no doubt felt that the subjects should be honored to have been included in such a triumphant scientific exercise at all.

As a result of this furious debate, the APA tightened professional ethical standards for its members in 1973. Researchers would be required to obtain informed consent from potential subjects, which meant they would have to tell potential subjects the purpose of the experiment and what was involved, so that volunteers could weigh the risks before deciding whether to participate. Even then, subjects would have the right to decline or withdraw after an experiment had started. Milgram's style of research, with its potential to cause harm to subjects and its use of misinformation and deception that prevented informed consent, would effectively be outlawed. Some, such as Philip Zimbardo, would mourn the passing of the era of daring and inventive research, brought to an end by "a cabal of some cognitive psychologists, human subjects research committees, Protestants, and female social psychologists."[21] Others would see it as the beginning of a new, more enlightened approach to psychological research.

Meanwhile, over time Milgram would become increasingly dismissive of criticisms about the deception, stress, and mistreatment of his subjects. His tactics in handling criticism would always be to attack and deflect: he would use psychology against his critics. He would suggest that it was not his research or his results that were the problem but the uncomfortable feelings they aroused, and that people who attacked the research did so in order to avoid acknowledging these uncomfortable feelings. He would come to view ethical criticisms as a case of shooting the messenger. It was an argument that both deflected criticism and bolstered his status, casting him as a purveyor of unpalatable truths who was being punished for the unflattering light he cast on human nature. By 1977, he would be downplaying Baumrind's influence on the field. In an unpublished interview, he would go as far as to refer to her criticisms as little more than a domestic squabble, "a tempest in a teapot," despite the fact that this tempest changed the APA's guidelines forever.[22]

However, for the most part the ethical concerns about Milgram's research would be contained to academia.[23] Neither Baumrind's response nor the other sustained critiques of Milgram's research could make a dent in the public's interest. In people's imagination, Milgram had simply discovered something shocking about human nature. Through mass media, Milgram's research had been absorbed into popular culture.

It seemed that the ethical furor made Milgram more cautious. While he had taken the shock machine with him when he left Yale in 1963, his research at Harvard avoided direct contact with subjects. However, it was still bold and imaginative. In 1964, he developed a more elaborate version of the Lost Letter study. This time, he used a plane to distribute pro-Democrat and pro-Republican letters favoring presidential candidates Lyndon Johnson and Barry Goldwater. But letters got caught in trees and on rooftops or landed in creeks and rivers, as well as on the plane's wings, and the study had to be aborted. In another study, Milgram tested the "small world" phenomenon—known today as six degrees of separation—by testing how many acquaintances it took to connect two strangers. A parcel had to be mailed from one stranger to another; how many people did it take to reach the target person? Milgram's answer: six.[24]

While Milgram's fame was growing, his colleagues continued to make their mixed feelings about him known. Milgram had arrived at Harvard with one article about the obedience research in print. By the time he left in 1967, he had published three additional articles, each bringing fresh academic attention. During his time at Harvard, Milgram weathered both increasing fame and criticism; while there were those who dismissed the research, there were just as many who defended it. American psychology developed a deep ambivalence toward him, as reflected by the Harvard committee responsible for assessing his application for a tenured position. After months of debate, the committee, whose decision had to be unanimous, could not agree on Milgram, offering the job to someone else. Milgram told an interviewer that it was "a trauma" and "an exceptional blow." He blamed it on the fact that he didn't pay enough attention to the "social context" ("I suppose I was never very good, nor very interested, in the politics of the profession"), but it probably had less to do with his inability to play politics than his seeming inability to quell people's concerns about criticisms of his research. In addition, his manner tended to be dismissive, if not arrogant, which wouldn't have helped his cause. Some among the committee thought he was "manipulative."[25]

By 1967, Milgram's job prospects were grim. Few "prestigious research departments" would hire him. Fortunately, a colleague and friend, Howard Leventhal, was negotiating for a job at CUNY and made it a condition that if they took him, they would take Milgram, too. Moving from an Ivy League institution to CUNY would have been a comedown for Milgram.[26] Nevertheless, in the summer of 1967 Milgram joined the CUNY faculty, where he would work until his death in 1984.

The tide of criticism over the experiments continued in his new role. In 1968, an article by Martin Orne and Charles Holland published in the *International Journal of Psychiatry* questioned the validity of Milgram's results and the meaning of his research. Milgram's subjects, they argued, viewed the experimental situation differently from him—they made assumptions about what was happening that shaped their responses, and this had to be taken into consideration in interpreting the results. How could Milgram have measured destructive obedience, the authors asked, if his subjects saw the experimenter as a benign authority? Didn't they naturally perceive the lab as a safe place, and the experimenter's imperviousness to the learner's cries as evidence that they weren't really inflicting pain?

In questioning how believable the subjects found the situation, Orne and Holland queried "the entire foundation of the obedience research."[27] Like Baumrind, they challenged the parallel between the trusted environment of a respected university laboratory and the concentration camps of Nazi Germany and raised issues with which Milgram had privately struggled.

Milgram's reply to Orne and Holland would not be published until 1972, four years after their article appeared. The reasons for the delay are unclear, but it's possible that he needed the time to draft a response that satisfied him. With Baumrind, he could argue that whatever he put his subjects through was worth it for the result, but Orne and Holland had queried that result. His response to the latter did little to quell the controversy.

Harold Takooshian met Stanley Milgram a year before his published response, in 1971, when he applied for graduate school at CUNY. He told me that he had been nervous about his application. Like Milgram had done, Harold was applying for graduate study in social psychology without having a background in psychology, although he didn't know of this similarity at the time. He had applied to a number of graduate schools, but CUNY was the top of his list because it had Milgram. They first met when Harold dropped by CUNY to deliver some paperwork in support of his application. Harold explained who he was, and he found Milgram "very encouraging."

Harold was delighted to be accepted, and even more delighted to be studying with the famous Milgram. "But when classes started, things were a little bit different." Milgram had clear rules for the classroom—as in the obedience experiments, he was in control. He was explicit that there was to be no eating, drinking, or smoking, and no sunglasses to hide behind. He wanted to see the students' eyes. The hierarchy was clear: while he addressed all students as "Mister" or "Miss," they always referred to him as Professor Milgram. "I never called him Stanley when he was alive," Harold said sheepishly, as if the very idea of being so familiar was slightly risqué.

In contrast to the rarefied atmosphere of Harvard, at CUNY Milgram was in the thick of city life—his office at the Graduate Center was in the heart of Manhattan, with a view of Bryant Park—and the surroundings influenced his teaching. Milgram encouraged his students to share his interest in the psychology of city life. His classes were almost *Seinfeld*-esque in taking the city of New York as their laboratory and its citizens as their subjects. Among other things, students conducted research on how helpful city dwellers were, compared to rural people; why New Yorkers were reluctant to give up their seat on the subway; and how many passersby would stop to help a lost child.

Classes, for Harold, were often heated and noisy, but always engaging. "We weren't just talking about articles; we were really debating and challenging each other, and it became very exciting." But one gesture from Milgram would stop the conversation. "He knitted his brows in a kind of upside-down V. And we knew that when he did that, we should be quiet and listen. The other thing he did was put his hand up and shake it a little bit." Harold waved his hand like a conductor wielding a baton. He frowned as best he could and adopted a stutter: "Ah, I really don't think we understand what is happening here." He smiled and shook his head. "He could restore order just like that."

These days Harold calls Milgram "maestro," a term that conjures an image of a conductor directing, goading, and inspiring his classes to outperform themselves. Harold felt that part of the excitement generated in classes was due to the students' sense that anything, anything at all, could happen in their scheduled class time; the only predictable thing about Milgram was his unpredictability. He would often do things that left his students puzzling over them years later.

Suddenly, Harold leaned forward. "I want to ask your help. I want to mention an example of one of the things that Milgram did. Now, I'm going to mention this to you, and you tell me what you think about it, okay?" I nodded. "Toward the end of semester, ten minutes before the end of one social psychology class, Milgram said he needed the class's help. 'You people know each other better than I know you, don't you? You speak with each other all the time. I have to give out grades at the end of the semester, and I'd really appreciate your help.'"

He told them to take out a piece of paper and write down everyone's names. Then, to write down the grade they would give each person beside their name. "People looked at each other and began writing, but I didn't write anything."

After five minutes, Milgram collected and counted the papers, asking the class why he was one short. "Sheepishly, I raised my hand and said, 'I didn't give in a paper,' and he said, 'Why not?' And I said, 'I don't know, I just felt uncomfortable,' and he said 'Okay.' So what do you think he did once he collected the papers? He opened each one and he read it out. He said, 'Let's see, this is Jerry Cohen. Sabini, A. Silver, B minus.' And he read the grades! And some people gave As to everybody, and some people gave Bs and Cs. I got a couple of Bs and Cs from people, and because he read out their names I knew who'd given them to me. And after he read them, he said, 'Well, does anybody have any comments?' Nobody said anything, so he said, 'Well, I'll see you next week.' And that was it. We disbanded, and next Tuesday we met again."

Harold asked me to speculate on why I thought Milgram did it.

Well, I said cautiously, he was probably testing how far people would go in following an instruction to do something that might make them uncomfortable. But if I were one of the students, I'd feel pretty angry if other students had given me low grades.

"You can imagine how much we thought about it that week, and that year. And he never explained it. He did this in class constantly. You really had to think about it afterward. I think he was a brilliant teacher."

He had offered this anecdote as proof of Milgram's brilliance. But to me, it had all the hallmarks of his most famous research. It was clever but careless about consequences, ingenious but insensitive to the feelings of the people involved. And it remained enigmatic, with people wondering what it meant.

Didn't Milgram just seem . . . a bit strange? I asked.

Harold laughed. "There's a psychological term called 'idiosyncrasy credit' that distinguishes a weirdo from a genius. The more brilliant someone is, the more odd things they can do and still be accepted. If someone didn't have enough idiosyncrasy credit, they are seen as a weirdo. He had loads of credit. One of the more outlandish things he did—he did not like the idea of dogs defecating on the street. He felt that that was uncivilized. He actually made a film with the steam coming up off the dog poop. And he showed that film in class. He said he wanted to convince people that this was uncivilized and New York should do something about it."

Milgram *was* unusual for a social psychologist, Harold said, because he regularly co-authored articles with his students. In addition, his research style made him one of a kind. "He was in the 5 percent who do the research to find the answer, as opposed to the 95 percent who do it to test a theory. That's why he was a maverick. He didn't really have a theory—theories to him were not that important."

But Harold acknowledged that Milgram was more mercurial than most of his teachers at CUNY. At times he could be playful, witty, and endearing. One day he replaced his speech with song, serenading instead of speaking, and refusing to respond to anyone who wouldn't sing back. He could also be warm and gracious. "I asked him if he would be my mentor, for example, and he acted like he had been just waiting for me to ask," Harold said. At other times, he was harsh and critical. He could be sarcastic, dismissive, and intolerant of ideas he'd heard before. "He was always interested in new ideas. And if he heard the same idea, he would just pooh-pooh it, even if it was a new idea for the student. He was somewhat selfish that way; he wanted to learn from the students." For as many students who loved Milgram, there were just as many who loathed him. "Even the students who were happy with him kept their distance sometimes. . . . He challenged people. He did not feel an obligation to be nice to people. He could be caustic, and some students found his combative style off-putting. . . . He could be St. Nick one minute, Ivan the Terrible the next."

This sounded familiar to me: Milgram as sympathetic but cruel; both warm and cold; encouraging and, a breath later, dismissive. I had encountered these same attitudes in the archives, in particular in his writings about his subjects. But although Milgram could be abrasive, Harold had no memory of any student standing up to him.

Milgram's alternately gracious and rude manner extended to colleagues, too. According to Tom Blass, Milgram was "controlling and domineering" and behaved like a "prima donna" at CUNY. Tom suggested that Milgram's mood swings—between dictatorial and democratic, between charming and scathing—could have been fueled by his use of amphetamines, cocaine, and marijuana, a practice that began in his student years at Harvard.

I asked Harold if he thought that his teacher's behavior might have been influenced by his drug use, and he said he had "no firsthand knowledge" of this. Instead, he thought that one explanation for Milgram's erratic behavior at CUNY could have been the stress of unwelcome and continual critical attention. He characterized Milgram as a "very sensitive man" whom criticism "hurt deeply." He recalled that Milgram viewed criticisms of his research as a "trial by fire" and that responding to it "wore him down."

It seemed that Milgram was particularly touchy about people who said that his results were predictable or little more than common sense. Harold told me, "One thing that really got to him was when he was giving a talk on obedience, and someone in the audience would inevitably question Milgram's claim that he was astonished by the extent of people's obedience. Someone would ask, 'Didn't you know at some level that this would happen? You must have anticipated it.' And he would get really angry. He felt it undermined the importance of his research, that the person was saying that it didn't make a contribution. I remember one time he was really furious with a lady—we had to restrain him."

No wonder he got so mad. The notion that he had made a profound discovery was a central justification for what he had done.

But Milgram also disliked being associated with only one piece of research. "He got tired of it. He saw it as only part of his career. He said in one article that he felt typecast in the same way the actor James Arness was typecast with *Gunsmoke*. He had been typecast with obedience. And yet most of his work was not obedience. He was such a creative researcher—his other research was so diverse, it had no relation to obedience."[28]

And the criticism was totally unfair, Harold said. "There's just no question about it: they were attacking what he found, rather than how he studied it." People tuned out the research because the results made them uncomfortable. Was this what I was doing, I wondered, conscious of how hard I found it to pay attention as Harold went on to defend the research? "The worst you could say about it is that 12 percent of people wished they hadn't participated. Eighty-four didn't care or benefited. People attacked him as a boogeyman who did something unethical. Which wasn't the case; he was never reprimanded by the APA—in fact, he was elected a fellow. Even his critics acknowledge that you can't teach a course in social psychology or introductory psych without mentioning his work. It's frozen in time."

Harold believed that the fame of Milgram's obedience research was proof of its value. "If people thought his work was unethical, they wouldn't cite it. The fact that they do cite it means he won the day. They wouldn't cite Nazi research on twins or things like that because they are unethical. And I would challenge anyone to find an introductory psych textbook that doesn't cite his work."

* * *

Carla Lewis, another of Milgram's former students, was waiting for me and Harold when we got to the Indian restaurant on Broadway. Harold had asked her to meet us and share her reflections of the CUNY lecturer who had dazzled her back when she was a graduate student.

The restaurant was blessedly cool after the intense heat outside. Despite having caught the express from 125th Street in Harlem— which I imagined would have been hot and crowded—Carla looked cool and fresh. On our way up to the buffet, she told me that she always felt "so fortunate to have been taught by such a genius."

Carla told me that she had kept all of her notes from Milgram's classes for a long time after she had finished her degree.

Harold interrupted. "Don't tell me you threw them out!" he exclaimed, aghast.

She looked sheepish. "I live in an apartment," she said. "You always have to make room."

Harold told us how a visiting Russian Milgram scholar had rummaged delightedly through Harold's thirty-year-old lecture notes as if he'd struck gold.

I didn't feel like eating; it was too hot. So I picked at my food while Carla told me that her class had worked with Milgram on his cyranoid study, named after Cyrano de Bergerac, the title character in a play who supplies his friend with just the right words to woo a lover. Milgram's cyranoids repeated, word for word, what Milgram relayed to them through an earpiece from his hiding place behind a one-way mirror while the cyranoid was engaged in a supposedly natural conversation with a third person. Milgram was the ventriloquist, and the cyranoid was the dummy. The research was designed to explore how people form judgments of others. In one variation, Milgram sent two boys—one of whom was a cyranoid—to a selection panel of six teachers who would assess them for placement in their school. The panel recommended that the cyranoid boy be placed two years above the non-cyranoid boy. Carla said it was fascinating to watch other variations from behind the mirror—for example, as a shoeshine boy spoke animatedly to a young woman about Greek philosophy and existentialism, being fed the lines by Milgram.

The cyranoid idea was just one of "a thousand ideas" that Milgram had at that time, according to psychologist and author Carol Tavris, who interviewed Milgram at CUNY in 1974 for *Psychology Today*. In her article, she summed him up tellingly: "I have never met anyone quite so serious about his whimsy or quite so logical about his imagination."[29]

When I spoke to her on the phone from California, Carol told me that she had no trouble recalling the interview, even thirty-six years and countless interviews later. Milgram apparently sang her songs, read her stories, and showed her drawings. "I found him funny, charming, and very smart," she said. "He was a dynamo, he was a flame, he was exuberant, he was exhilarated by ideas in psychology. Our conversation was freewheeling, very spontaneous. He loved social psychology—he loved coming up with ideas to show the influence of a situation. He was very committed, and full of passion for the work he was doing."

Carol told me that, compared to other psychologists, Milgram was different because he didn't follow the typical career path. "It was—and still is—usual to choose an area of research and stay there, and become expert in that, doing many different refinements of it. In contrast, Milgram did excellent research on a wide variety of topics, from obedience to cognitive maps to the 'familiar stranger,' but because he was such a good experimenter he got away with it. That is, his colleagues respected his work rather than seeing him as a dilettante."

Milgram certainly wasn't a stuffy academic. "His appeal was that he was interesting, lively, and passionate about his work and its importance to the 'real world.' He took social psychology out of the ivory tower and brought it straight into people's lives."

Perhaps it was this—his sense of fun, his playfulness, and his passion, which drove him from one research topic to another—as well as the notoriety of his obedience research, that hampered him professionally. During his time at CUNY, Milgram failed to get funding for his many project ideas. While he obviously had a lot of "idiosyncrasy credit" with his students, the same couldn't be said with professional funding bodies. Funding would have given him the capacity to turn ideas into measurable problems, but would also represent the endorsement of the psychology community. The obedience research and the continuing controversy it had sparked might have made him famous, but it had cast a shadow over his reputation.

But Milgram had something up his sleeve that he hoped would silence his critics and put any criticisms of his obedience research to rest. It was his book *Obedience to Authority*.

10

MILGRAM'S BOOK

It wasn't until I was through customs at Calgary International Airport that I realized I didn't know who to look for. I had never seen Hank Stam; I had only e-mailed him and read his articles. I glanced around anxiously.

Luckily, we found each other surprisingly quickly. He looked like a Hank: tall and tanned with thick, graying hair. Dependable-looking. I probably looked how I felt: startled and out of place.

I had come to Canada because it was home to a thriving community of scientists and historians who had a more critical view of North American social psychology. They were interested in the psychology of the psychological experiment.

Hank, a professor at the University of Calgary, had pinned black-and-white photographs of two of Milgram's subjects on the bulletin board behind his desk.[1] One was a plump, giggling woman in a pillbox hat and cat's-eye glasses. The other was a man with his head bowed, mouth open in a wide smile. These photographs are stills from the documentary film *Obedience*, which Milgram shot in May 1962. Hank and his colleagues Lorraine Radtke and Ian Lubek had been fascinated by the laughter of Milgram's subjects. They had also been fascinated over the years by the laughter of their students when they watched the film for the first time.

"Why do the students laugh?" Hank wondered aloud. "Is it nervous laughter? Is it because the film looks like a sixties period piece—is that what makes it funny? Or are they laughing because of what the film says about social psychological research? Is it because they can't take it seriously?"

No matter how often Milgram wrote about this laughter (and he did, on and off, for fifteen years), it was something that he never understood. Then again, he may never really have seriously tried to understand it—he saw it as symbolic and looked no further.

Hank sat opposite me behind his desk, the images of the two subjects just visible above his head. As he spoke, he stroked the ink blotter in front of him and, when he made a point, he made little chopping movements on the blotter with the edge of his hand. *Sssshh, ssshh; thump, thump.* It made a kind of music. Soothing and then unsettling.

Hank believed that Milgram's research told us more about 1950s social psychology than anything else. Experiments like Milgram's became important demonstrations of the power of the newly created discipline. "Look, we can show you in a laboratory the exact process by which the Holocaust occurred, and it applies to everybody—it's a universal process. No matter who comes into the lab, we can create the right conditions. The implicit analogy is between the cholera bacteria, which becomes an epidemic. Here you have in a lab a demonstration of obedience to authority that, let loose on the world, becomes the Holocaust. You have this neat analogy. But without that rhetorical framework, Milgram's experiments become no more than reality TV. It's clothed as science and, once clothed as science, you can sell it as science. The rhetorical framing is crucial to the survival of the obedience studies.

"Do we understand what went on in Milgram's lab? I think social psychologists have no idea what went on in there. They've called what someone does obedience, but if you change the context you could call it something else. Call it rule following, or trust."[2]

I looked at the gray clouds outside the window, threatening snow. Was it really as simple as that? In this warm office, in this moment, Hank's analysis was convincing, but if I agreed with him, didn't that mean that I had, somewhere along the way, accepted an alternative rhetorical frame through which to view the experiments? What about Milgram's results? What about the number of people who went to the maximum voltage? The hand on the switch, which had seemed to me so long ago a clear and unambiguous act, had become mysterious. I just wasn't sure what it represented.

I tuned back to Hank, who seemed to have sensed my distraction. "There's all sorts of ways of categorizing what Milgram's subjects did. You could put another label on Milgram's behavior, too. You could say he facilitated torture. He was asking those people to torture someone. He let them do it. They didn't know that they weren't. So wasn't he in some sense facilitating torture?"

The heater was sending up ripples of air, making the photos on the notice board quiver. The giggling lady had her hand to her mouth, mischievously. Hank smoothed his hands across the blotter. "What do the results really tell us? And why did he ignore those conditions in his research that showed people resisting authority? He had this other story in mind already. He knew what success would look like."

Take another look at Milgram's journal articles, Hank told me, and compare them to the film. He gestured at the photos behind him. "People are absent. There's no sense of actual people participating. He has established an experimental context that is abstract. Milgram refers to what happens in terms of functional categories: subjects, obedience, conformity, and conditions. You have no real sense of who people are and what they are doing." And neither, Hank implied, did Milgram.

So, I asked him, it all came down to what label you put on the subjects' behavior, on Milgram's? Hank shrugged. "You get a 65 percent aggregate response, but you know nothing about why they did it. People are defined by what they do or don't do in the lab. There's a kind of emptiness, as if psychologists are interested in just one small aspect of people. In fact, they were real people with real lives somewhere." To really understand what went on in the experiment, Hank said, one had to understand people "not just as those things that appear briefly in the lab and interact with the equipment," but to look at the world in which they lived. For an experiment that claimed to be about social psychology, to Hank it had a "very limited perception of the social world."

But surely, I argued—perhaps partly to play devil's advocate—the fact that the experiments are so famous was proof that they pointed to something enduring. Yes, Hank said, there was no question that experiments like Milgram's had an impact. But "social psychologists frame them as illustrating profound issues. It's only once you take them out of the context that social psychology gives them that you can ask questions."

Listening to Hank, I had the strangest sense of déjà vu. It was only later that I realized why. Just about everything he had raised were things that Milgram had confided doubts about in his private papers. The torment he was putting people through; whether his ambition, rather than altruism, was his driving force; the label he had given subjects' behavior; the tenuousness of the link to the Holocaust; even the meaninglessness of the results—Milgram had grappled with them all during his research. But none of it appeared in print, least of all in his book *Obedience to Authority*, published in 1974, twelve years after the experiments were completed. Over that time, his doubts had seemed to vanish and certainty had taken their place.

This was possible, of course. Opinions can change, and Milgram had been immersed in the research and its aftermath for more than a decade. But this explanation seemed a little too neat. How could such extreme doubts—doubts that went to the very foundation of the research—have been so effectively quelled?

The more likely explanation seemed to be that once the public criticism had erupted, Milgram couldn't afford self-doubt. His reputation and career were at stake. With his response to Baumrind, he began rewriting the story to portray himself and the results in a particular light. By the time his book was published, his doubts that the experiments might be no more than art seemed to have hardened into a conviction that they were serious science. In his book, the Holocaust became not just a metaphor but the inevitable outcome of what he found in his lab.

Milgram chose to cast the story of his research in dramatic terms, as a moral struggle revealing a profound truth and obedient subjects as flawed and troubled figures. It seemed consistent with what I had learned about him: his ambitious personality, his love for art and literature, and his intuitive sense of performance. In addition, he needed the book to make a splash—he had a lot to prove. *Obedience to Authority* would be the first full account of his research program. It was also the first piece of writing in which he would provide an overarching theory to explain his subjects' behavior. It was a chance to make a comeback, to put his derailed career back on track. He would have put himself under pressure to produce something that would establish him as a serious scholar. It had to silence critics of his ethics and methodology. In addition, he wanted it to appeal to the masses.

Milgram was well aware of the power of writing, and particularly scientific writing, to establish power and authority. Judith Waters, who had been his research assistant at CUNY, said that the two of them used to play a game in which they would transform everyday words or expressions into "psychologese." One of them would suggest a phrase such as "I guess," and the other would have to come up with its academic equivalent—"Based on the previous assumptions as enumerated above, it is possible to hypothesize that the following outcomes will obtain under certain limited conditions." While Milgram may have played this game to poke fun at the inflated language of academic discourse, he understood its importance. In 1964, he had written to Leon Mann from Harvard that he was writing up the data they had collected in the Yale Lost Letter study: "What I am trying to do is [a] theoretico-methodological introduction to give it intellectual underpinning and to remove it from the realm of gimmicks."[3] He was conscious that the creativity and playfulness that often inspired his experiments could also cause them to be perceived as lightweight and used academic lingo to bolster their credentials. He clearly understood the persuasive power of some well-aimed words in the right context.

In his articles, Milgram had revealed a negative and judgmental view of his obedient subjects, an attitude that would become even more pronounced over time. In his book, any sympathy for the obedient subjects had disappeared. Although he argued, somewhat disingenuously, that the people who obeyed were not "monsters" or "sadistic types," he did suggest that they were like Eichmann, "an uninspired bureaucrat who simply sat at his desk and did his job."[4] In the pages of his book, Milgram's obedient "ordinary men and women"—several of whom I met years later—became America's incarnation of Nazis.

Obedience to Authority isn't the the most gripping read. It begins with a chunk lifted from Milgram's first published article, and then sets obedience against a philosophical and historical backdrop that references Plato, Sophocles's *Antigone*, and the Third Reich. His experiment, Milgram wrote, sprang from his need as "an empirically grounded scientist" to "move from abstract discourse to the careful observation of concrete instances," but he stressed that his study was "simple."[5] Then, to establish the authenticity and believability of the experiment, Milgram devoted twenty-eight pages to descriptions of the preparations involved.

In fact, nine out of the book's fifteen chapters are devoted to descriptions of preparations and the various permutations of the experiments. Only after that, in the following forty pages, did Milgram present his theory. Why did his subjects behave the way they did? It was neither personality nor background, according to him, but an inborn tendency to obey, and particular situations brought out this tendency. While our conscience keeps destructive obedience in check most of the time, put us in a hierarchy and strange things happen. When individuals are submerged in an authority system, he argued, they enter an "agentic state" in which they become the passive recipients of others' orders. In this state, the person "no longer views himself as responsible for his own actions but defines himself as an instrument for carrying out the wishes of others." It's a kind of sleepwalking state. For subordinates in Hitler's Germany and Stalin's Russia, it was more a "profound slumber," compared to the "light doze" of the subjects in his lab, but the process was the same. Once people merge with an authority who gives the orders, entering the twilight zone of the agentic state, they feel "virtually guiltless"—even though they might be doing inhumane things that they would never normally consider.[6]

Was it just me, or did it sound like sci-fi, a reworking of *Invasion*

of the Body Snatchers or something invoking the mysterious powers of mind control supposedly wielded by the Chinese during the
Korean War?

It wasn't a very convincing explanation. The zombie-like behavior he described was at odds with the frequent protests and agoniz-
ing that he had earlier reported in journal articles. In fact, in some
passages, the theory seems downright bizarre. The "agentic state"
didn't explain why some people disobeyed, nor why there was so
much variation in degrees of obedience across different conditions.
If it was the power of the situation that brought out destructive
obedience and prompted the agentic state, why didn't Milgram get
100 percent obedience in his research? Even Tom Blass, an admirer
of Milgram's work, agreed that his theorizing was "the weakest part
of the book."[7]

What could explain this apparently halfhearted attempt at a theory
that, even to the lay reader, seemed to be filled with holes? What accounted for the uneven structure? Was it evidence that Milgram never
really developed a satisfactory theory and tried to disguise this with
academic jargon, or did it show that the task of writing the book had
been too daunting and, ultimately, too difficult for him? Perhaps he
had enjoyed writing only the early parts of the book, and, by the time
he got to the theory, he simply ran out of steam.

He certainly found the writing process difficult. While the first two
chapters were relatively easy, because they were based on previously
written material, the others were more demanding.[8] Given all the con-
siderations he had to address, the mass of data he had collected, and
his interest in practicalities rather than theories, it's little wonder that
he found writing so difficult.

But it wasn't only these challenges that slowed his writing—he
frequently got distracted by envisioning the look and feel of the finished product. In his papers are early sketches of the cover, complete
with taglines, which indicate that he was aiming for popular appeal:
"Obedience to authority. Here is the controversy. You decide." Or,
written in German blackletter: "Perhaps there is something in their
national character that makes them follow orders unquestioningly.
Perhaps this is what makes them . . . Americans. The most con-

troversial book of the decade." In total, Milgram drafted over fifty taglines, such as, "Is your neighbor a potential Eichmann? This brilliant and controversial book pursues the truth to its core." He played heavily with the Eichmann theme, trying out blurbs that focused on the individual, the community, and the nation: "Where's Adolph [*sic*] Eichmann. Check your mirror, friend"; "Read this book, so you don't have to change your name to Eichmann"; "a BRILLIANT, FASCINATING and CONTROVERSIAL exploration of what people do when ordered by authority to act inhumanely against an innocent victim"; "If Eichmann had read this book, he would not have become an Eichmann"; "I'm a psychologist and I need your help. Buy this book. Obey this one command and You may be free of authority for evermore"; "the Brilliant Book that ignited a controversy on the Eichmann potential in America—obedience to orders, as American as cherry pie. A brilliant probe into how Americans respond to inhumane orders"; and "'I WAS JUST FOLLOWING ORDERS.' The five most controversial words of the century provoke the most controversial book of the decade."[9] Aware of the power of controversy to generate interest and sales, Milgram embraced the sensationalist aspect of his research, regarding it as a powerful selling point.

To get over his writer's block, Milgram used drugs. In drafts, there are occasional notes in the margins about the effect that a drug was having on his thinking and writing. For example, "NOTE: at 10:00 pm or more exact 9:57 the effects of M are quite strong, and I hope they do not become stronger, because this seems to be about the right level for rather free thinking at the scientific level."[10] I laughed when I saw this note. I had been taught, as Milgram had been in the 1950s, that scientific writing is marked by rigor, objectivity, and clarity. But here he was, getting high in order to let his mind roam freely—looking, perhaps, for some kind of mystical insight into his own work. The idea that Milgram, after carefully controlling for variables in his experiment, tried to write it up while high was absurd.

Perhaps this pointed to the real problem behind Milgram's lackluster theory: he didn't take it seriously enough. He was more focused on presenting his subjects as potential Nazis—a desire that was in evidence early in the writing process. In an unpublished paper, he noted to himself:

> Let us stop trying to kid ourselves; what we are trying to understand is obedience of the Nazi guards in the prsinon [*sic*] camps, and that any other thing we may understand about obedience is pretty much of a windfall, an accidental bonus. So we might as well write the book as if this were our purpose, and then apologize to being a hopeful poet who finds metaphoric illumination between what subjects do at Yale University and what happened in Germany.[11]

Milgram had strengthened the Holocaust connection over the years, and he milked it in the book. In an early draft that he sent to Alan Elms for feedback, Milgram wrote that "every man who gives himself to authority is a psychopath. He kills without shame or guilt if ordered to do so." Although he changed the wording on the advice of Elms, who said that such comments were too extreme and "easily refuted," his sentiment remained the same.[12]

In the published version, he began the first chapter by drawing a parallel between Eichmann and the obedient subjects, reinforcing Hannah Arendt's concept of the "banality of evil," as he would throughout the book.[13] The pressure to write something that would appeal to the public, combined with his desire to contribute to an understanding of the Holocaust, meant that Milgram focused his attention on presenting his subjects as American Eichmanns, only afterward piecing together a theory to support this representation.

As if to emphasize just how small a role personality played in obedience, early in the book Milgram argued that the kind of "destructive obedience" he studied in the lab could be traced not to an individual's personality but to the situation they found themselves in. In a three-page chapter, he highlighted it as the reason why so many people underestimated the levels of obedience he would find: "Most people . . . focus on the character of the autonomous individual rather than on the situation in which he finds himself. With this view, they are likely to expect few subjects to go along with the experimenter's orders."[14] He relegated to an appendix descriptions of unsuccessful efforts by himself and his staff to find personality traits or particular attitudes that would predict obedience levels. As proof of the unexpected nature of his results, he described how he asked a group of thirty-nine psychiatrists to predict how many people would go to 450 volts. Their verdict? Only about one in a thousand, or 0.001 percent—"a pathological fringe"—would go all the way. He noted, "Their estimates were completely out of line with what happened in the laboratory. This suggests that we have not simply demonstrated the obvious, but have learned something that goes beyond intelligent conjecture."[15] Milgram would use the results of this exercise time and again to demonstrate that he had discovered something counterintuitive, something that even psychiatrists could not have predicted.

Milgram provided lengthy case studies of individual subjects in his book. However, he warned that even though each person's experience gave us "clues" as to why they behaved as they did, we shouldn't rely on such accounts:

> While we must take seriously everything the subject says, we need not necessarily think that he fully understands the causes of his own behavior. A line must be drawn between listening carefully to what the subject says and mistaking it for the full story. The subject is controlled by many forces in the situation beyond his awareness, implicit structures that regulate his behavior without signaling this fact to him.[16]

This disclaimer had the effect of reinforcing negative stereotypes and casting doubt on the notion that subjects were reliable narrators—particularly the sort of people who obeyed orders from authority.

Milgram's descriptions of ten subjects reveal that he associated obedient behavior with lower intelligence, less education, and the working classes.[17] In contrast, his defiant subjects are depicted as intelligent, educated, and middle to upper class. For example, here is a description of Jan Rensaleer:

The subject is a thirty-two-year-old industrial engineer, sporting blond hair and a mustache. He is self-contained and speaks with the trace of a foreign accent. He is neatly dressed. In the interview he tells us that he emigrated from Holland after the Second World War and that he is a member of the Dutch Reformed Church. He is mild-mannered and intelligent.

In Milgram's eyes, Jan Rensaleer was cultured, well turned out, polite, and smart. Although he defied the experimenter at 225 volts, "he still feels responsible for administering any shocks beyond the victim's first protests. He is hard on himself and does not allow the structure of authority in which he is functioning to absolve him of any responsibility."

Contrast that with the description of Bruno Batta, a working-class man who was simply dressed:

Mr. Batta is a thirty-seven-year-old welder. He was born in New Haven, his parents in Italy. He has a rough-hewn face that conveys a conspicuous lack of alertness. His over-all appearance is somewhat brutish. An observer described him as a "crude mesomorph of obviously limited intelligence" . . . [yet] he relates to the experimenter with a submissive and deferential sweetness.

Implying that Batta was slow, Milgram noted, "He has some difficulty in mastering the experimental procedure and needs to be corrected by the experimenter several times." Batta, who was required to push the learner's hand onto the electric plate to receive the shock, at first ignored the learner's complaints and continued. Milgram's description of his behavior was far from flattering:

He maintains the same rigid mask. The learner, seated beside him, begs him to stop, but with robotic impassivity he continues the procedure. What is extraordinary is his apparent total indifference to the learner; he hardly takes cognizance of him as a human being. . . . The scene is brutal and depressing: his hard, impassive face showing total indifference as he subdues the screaming learner and gives him shocks. He seems to derive no pleasure from the act itself, only quiet satisfaction at doing his job properly.[18]

As scholar Omer Bartov pointed out, these portraits reflected Milgram's assumptions, rather than facts, about Nazis.[19] Milgram seemed to have held a belief that the morally weak were more likely to be less educated and of lower class. Unlike Jan Rensaleer, whose behavior Milgram excused sympathetically, Batta was an object of disgust. Rensaleer expressed his remorse; Batta, it was implied, felt none.

But it was Milgram's portrait of housewife Elinor Rosenblum that made me consider whether his dislike of some subjects went beyond their education level and class. This passage, unlike the others, did not begin with her age or a physical description—instead, it was her personality that was the focus. Milgram's sarcasm was palpable as he related her achievements to the readers:

> Mrs. Rosenblum takes pleasure in describing her background: she graduated from the University of Wisconsin more than twenty years ago, and her husband, a film distributor, attended Dartmouth. She does volunteer work with juvenile delinquents once a week and has been active in the local Girl Scout organization and the PTA. She is fluent and garrulous and projects herself strongly, with many references to her social achievements.

This uncharitable portrait continued as Mrs. Rosenblum proceeded with the experiment: "She attempts to project an image of competence and social grace. . . . She maintains a pretentiously correct, almost authoritative tone in reading the word pairs to the learner, which contrast with the weak, girlish comments she directs to the experimenter."

Afterward, in discussing her reactions with the experimenter, Elinor explained that she was "nervous because I was hurting him" and still shaking. Milgram concluded, "She was nervous not because the man was being hurt but because she was performing the action. . . . A self-centered quality permeates her remarks."[20]

I was fascinated by this searing portrait of Elinor Rosenblum. I wanted to know why Milgram disliked her so intensely, apart from her obedience. What had she done that had so antagonized him? I went looking for her in the archives and found her. As Milgram's pseudonym suggested, she was Jewish. She was also a forty-four-year-old whose parents had been born in Poland and Germany. When I listened to the tape, I could see why she had antagonized Milgram, who appeared to have been watching from behind the mirror, and Williams. She wasn't a willing or passive recipient of Williams's orders—she was firm and sassy. After Williams gave her a sample shock, he asked her to estimate the voltage that she'd just been given.

Elinor: 255?

Williams: No—

Elinor: [interrupts] That was terrible.

Williams: That was 45 volts.

Elinor: Oh, don't give him that, he'll have a heart attack, cross my heart. You don't have to do that with an adult. It's ridiculous! Give him the very littlest! Give him that.

As Williams embarked on his rapid spiel, she corrected him when he made a mistake, then stopped him to ask if he could repeat the instructions.

At only 120 volts, when McDonough said that his heart was bothering him, she started to falter. When she read the word pairs, she deliberately emphasized the right answer. She sounded positively elated when McDonough got one right and said loudly, "Correct!" What was going through her mind, I wondered, when Williams, who could clearly hear her prompting McDonough with the right answer, said nothing to stop her? She got bolder. Her emphasis became more pronounced, but even so, McDonough got the next one wrong. She kept up a running commentary to Williams: "I'm worried, I'm shaking, I'm shaking here." But he would only tell her to keep going.

Within minutes, she was challenging the experiment's rationale, telling Williams that the idea of shocking a person to help them learn was "ridiculous." She worked with high school dropouts, she said, and punishing them was not the answer. The way to help people to learn was praise, encouragement, and love.

Milgram related this in his book, too, but he used it to highlight what he saw as her hypocrisy—she was a "loving" leader to the boys but willingly shocked McDonough. He did not say that she told Williams repeatedly how much she was shaking, or how horrified she sounded when Williams kept telling her to continue, or how at times she almost shouted the correct answer to McDonough as the voltage climbed.

When it was over, and she had gone to the maximum voltage, Williams gave her a form to complete while he unstrapped McDonough. She was shaking so hard she couldn't write. As the debriefing began, she turned on Williams.

Elinor: Well, you asked me and I told you it was ridiculous, the whole thing!

Williams: It isn't, really; it isn't, really. From a scientific viewpoint, we are actually—

Elinor: [talking over him] Why should you, why should you? You wanted to see how I feel in punishing someone.

Williams: Well, not—well, something like that. We're interested in—

Elinor: [to McDonough] I didn't want to do it to you. I didn't know what to say to you when you came out here. Forgive me, please.

Later, Williams told her that she had behaved normally—just as a nurse would in giving an injection to a protesting patient because the doctor had ordered her to.

Elinor: There's a difference. A complete difference.

Williams: *[sounds irritated]* Well, sure.

Elinor: A complete difference. Being the oldest, there were many times I had to put iodine on my little brother or sister, let's put it that way. I knew I was inflicting pain, but I didn't get nervous—you know why?

Williams: Because it was to help them.

Elinor: That's right.

Williams: Well, we know there are differences, but it's, er, the situations do have some similarities.

Elinor: I don't think so.

Williams: Well, the fact that they are inflicting pain and are reluctant to do so—

Elinor: But they're helping them!

Williams: This is the similarity.

Elinor: No.

Williams: Well—

Elinor: No.

Williams: Well, okay.[21]

Elinor Rosenblum might have been an obedient subject, but that wasn't her only crime in Milgram's eyes. She turned on Williams and refused to accept his explanation. There was a kind of horror and outrage in her voice. Milgram's portrait of her was suffused with loathing not just because of her obedience during the experiment but also because of her disobedience afterward.

The book also describes Fred Prozi, the man who starred in Milgram's documentary *Obedience*. He was fifty years old, unemployed, and dressed "in a jacket but no tie": "He has a good-natured, if slightly dissolute, appearance. He employs working-class grammar and strikes one as a rather ordinary fellow." It went without saying from this description that Prozi would eventually continue to the maximum voltage. Milgram described how he became agitated and argued with the experimenter, at one point pleading to check on the learner. The transcript that Milgram included bore witness to Prozi's confusion and distress. Despite this, Milgram concluded:

> The language employed by the participant is revealing. Despite the considerable tension of the situation, a tone of courtesy and deference is meticulously maintained. The subject's objections strike us as inordinately weak and inappropriate in view of the events in which he is immersed. He thinks he is killing someone, yet he uses the language of the tea table.[22]

It was hard to believe, reading Milgram's description, that this was the same man who, in the film, so attracted my sympathy. In the book, Milgram instructed readers to have no sympathy with him at all.

Pasqual Gino, or Subject 1817, was portrayed as a typical obedient subject. But Milgram did not mention something that he and Errera had discussed—Gino was under psychiatric care for a "nervous condition," which we would nowadays call post-traumatic stress disorder. Without this information, Gino's description of what he said to his wife when he got home seemed shocking and callous.

"I said to my wife, 'Well, here we are, and I think I did a good job.'"
"She said, 'Suppose the man was dead?'"
"'So he's dead—I did my job.'"[23]

Milgram couldn't have asked for a better line, given his thesis about Eichmann, but it was merely another example of the way he selected and manipulated information to lead the reader toward a conclusion. The portraits of obedient subjects were shot through with what Omer Bartov labeled "contempt and disgust."[24] This depiction of his obedient subjects as proxies for Nazi perpetrators was evident in early drafts of the book. Here is a passage of imaginary dialogue in which the subject addresses the experimenter that Milgram wrote while the book was in its early stages:

> Now we have given him the maximum current; is there anything more we can do to him. He was only a fat, flabby old man, garbage who deserves what he gets. This was an exhilarating moment for me; let me work by your side. I have always wanted a leader; the Germans have a word for it: Fuehrer. [Subject stands and raises his right arm.][25]

He may well have written this in a spell of idle doodling but it is revealing. The individual has disappeared and an evil archetype has taken its place.

And yet, for all his manipulations, Milgram appeared to have a genuine fondness for some of his subjects. The book's acknowledgments simply read: "I owe a profound debt to the many people in New Haven and Bridgeport who served as subjects." But the draft version reflected at length on his gratitude:

> Finally, but perhaps most important, grateful thanks to our 900 subjects, individual men and women who made this study possible. I remember many of them so vividly, fine men and women who, caught up in an altogether human conflict, and trying to resolving it according to their best sights. [sic] While we cannot mention all these contributors by name, perhaps I may take the liberty of mentioning a few.

He goes on to mention six, including Herb Winer, and concludes: "These few names symbolize the 900 individual men and women, who came to our laboratory and displayed their humanity for the benefit of human understanding."[26]

I knew that at least two of the six men he named had taken up their complaints directly with Milgram. If Herb was anything to go by, Milgram would likely have taken each man into his confidence, making them feel like co-researchers engaged in a study of terrific import.

This idea was supported by his private papers. He wrote:

> I have been on the friendliest terms with several of the subjects. . . . Sometimes, after I encounter a professional psychologist who [criticizes] the experiment's "brutality" and cruelty (these qualities being attributed to the investigator) and I am suitably depressed for the day, I sometimes come across a subject in the Post Office or on the street, and such subjects seem invariably delighted to meet me, pump my hand with warmth and may even say: "That was one of the most fascinating experiences I ever had; I want to thank you for that; and don't forget to include me in your next study." Only then do I remember that the . . . criticism has no foundation in reality—the only reality of importance here . . . is—the subjects themselves, the people who were in the experiments.[27]

But it was an odd statement from a man so unsympathetic in some of his character portraits. It's one of the curious inconsistencies of the experiments, and indicative of Milgram's ambivalence toward his subjects, that he demonstrated an almost sentimental view of some subjects while lambasting others in print. It is ironic that, on the one hand, he gave his subjects the ultimate authority for judging whether the experiments were acceptable, and yet on the other he discounted their experiences, thoughts, and feelings in his book. He excluded almost all of the vast material from their point of view. And when he did include some, it was with a warning to the reader about its reliability.

Far from being a scientific monograph, *Obedience to Authority* includes photographs, anecdotes, case studies, transcripts from television news reports, and references to popular culture from *The Caine Mutiny* to

Dr. Strangelove. But amid the wide-ranging cultural references, the details of elaborate preparations, and the character portraits, Milgram's purpose was serious. He was determined to defend and bolster his results.

With *Obedience to Authority*, Milgram was anxious to rebut some of the academic criticism that had dogged him for over a decade. Banished from the pages was any information that might give his critics ammunition. And just as Milgram's subject portraits were carefully crafted, so was his own. He presented himself as a thorough, careful, and neutral scientist who had discovered, not planned, the profound and disturbing results of his research. He had merely set the stage; it was his subjects who had behaved in a "shockingly immoral way."[28] The vast majority of the subjects were glad to have taken part, and the psychological insight gained dwarfed any trauma to subjects. Anything that might undermine this portrait of an unbiased man of science was gone. Condition 24 was not mentioned; subjects' skepticism or disbelief was dismissed in an appendix; and the laughter of his subjects, which he made so much of in his first paper, received only a passing mention.

A critical issue for scientific credibility is whether an experiment can be conducted in other laboratories and produce the same results. Milgram reported that his experimental results had been replicated in Australia, South Africa, Germany, and Italy, all finding even higher rates of obedience than he had. This was a key claim to support the universality and importance of his findings. However, it was misleading. Contrary to what he wrote, the Australian study found significantly lower levels of obedience than Milgram's; the authors of the Italian study had gone so far as to send him a newspaper report on their findings, which showed that they had also found lower levels. The German study appeared to find similar results, but had used university students and variations on Milgram's conditions. As for the South African replication, Milgram provided no reference details, but Tom Blass succeeded in tracking it down, finding an unpublished student report involving only sixteen subjects.[29]

Why the deliberate obfuscation? Milgram seemed irrationally intent on proving that he had identified something universal. This was in stark contrast to Solomon Asch, who, when a replication by two British researchers failed to mirror his results, commended the researchers for their "intriguing" finding and acknowledged that he had probably captured something transient about American culture, a fleeting mood inspired by the Cold War.[30] But Milgram, his experiment beset by criticism, could perhaps not afford such magnitude. Or perhaps he was unwilling to give it.

Apart from this misleading information, did he address the criticism successfully, and convince readers that his results were persuasive?

Milgram sent out sixty-nine copies of his book when it was published. At the top of the list was Hannah Arendt. His publisher sent review copies to over 170 newspapers in forty-two states and to sixty magazines around the United States.[31] The reaction from the mass media was immediate. Milgram's book gave his research new power. His publisher made the most of the attention, organizing a range of high-profile interviews, including on national and international television, in newspapers, and on radio. Parts of the book were serialized in London's *Sunday Times*, and the BBC made a *Horizon* program about it that was broadcast in September 1974. Milgram's British publisher urged him to agree to the program:

> *Horizon* have very high standards and they do not devote programmes to individuals of merely transient importance. I should hesitate to say that an appearance on *Horizon* is a passport to immortality—but it certainly counts very very heavily with the intellectual community in this country. And it also has striking effects on the sales of books.[32]

But reviews were mixed. Many promoted the importance of his findings, some calling them groundbreaking, but several worried about the ethical dimension, bringing the moral issues under public scrutiny in a way that had not been done before. Unlike the more sensational reports of the research in the early 1960s, with their focus on the results, this time reviewers displayed more sensitivity to, and interrogation of, research that had exposed people to such stress.[33]

Many questioned the price paid for the knowledge that Milgram claimed.

His results and theory were not immune from criticism, either. Most noticed that Milgram had largely ignored the 35 percent who disobeyed and commented on his tendency to make statements about humankind by generalizing from a 65 percent (and, in some variations, even lower) obedience rate. Some focused on the shortcomings of Milgram's theory to account for obedience and bemoaned the fact that such a high-profile piece of research had yielded so little in terms of understanding.

Others criticized the book's literary merit. Milgram wasn't accomplished at character portraits. The chapters that describe the staff and the setup are vivid and lavish in detail, but the ten subjects remain wooden—one reviewer complained that they were "flatter than New England witches pressed beneath Puritan barn doors."[34] Nonetheless, the book was a National Book Award finalist.

I found forty-nine book reviews in Milgram's papers at Yale. But I didn't find the one with the highest profile among them. Stephen Marcus's review ran on January 13, 1974, as a double-page spread in the *New York Times Book Review*. In addition to teaching English at Columbia, Marcus had been a fellow of the Center for Advanced Study in the Behavioral Sciences at Stanford that year. While Milgram had expected controversy, Marcus's criticism went far beyond the ethics or the results. It examined Milgram's role itself.

The review began with a recap of the experiments, describing them as a "sinister combination of melodrama and visual excitement." Marcus deftly summarized the ethical debate that had erupted in the 1960s and wrote that it was hard to know if the "furore" was about the methods or the results. He found it difficult to know which position to take: on the one hand, the effect on Milgram's subjects was "incalculable," and, on the other, "it's important that we know or that we do not forget these things about ourselves."

Having lulled readers with a general outline of the issues, Marcus then twisted the knife. When it came to analysis, it was "hard to know where in this woeful and lamentable performance to begin." How could he choose, he wondered, among the "intellectual calamities that make up this book"?

Marcus focused on three points. First, he alleged that Milgram was far from impartial. By paying attention to the language, readers could see how Milgram's judgmental attitude revealed his "outright contempt" for some subjects. Second, Milgram's use of abstract and vague terminology such as "autonomous man" and "malevolent authority" reflected woolly thinking. Last, and worst of all, in using mechanistic terminology borrowed from general systems theory and cybernetics, where people are "automata," Milgram denied his subjects' individuality. "In short," Marcus concluded, "nothing has been explained. And a considerable part of that nothing has to do with the 35% or more who disobeyed in the experiments. About these, Milgram has nothing to say."[35]

Roger Brown, one of Milgram's mentors at Harvard, sprang to his defense. Brown's reply to Marcus was published in the same pages on February 24.[36] Alongside it was a letter from Saul Rosenzweig, a psychologist who supported Marcus's point of view.

On *The Dick Cavett Show* soon afterward, Milgram was asked what he thought of Marcus's review. He dismissed it as "not serious" and the reviewer as "not competent to review the book from a scientific standpoint, since he is a teacher of English."[37] Defenders made this point, too, the implication being that the book was best reviewed by a social psychologist. But I for one don't buy this: it was written for the mass market, so if only a social psychologist could appreciate it, Milgram had failed in his aim.

I also wasn't sure if Milgram had been as unaffected as he claimed. Harold Takooshian told me that, when the book was published, he and his classmates had ridden the emotional roller coaster of Milgram's reactions to the reviews. "It showed in class. He didn't conceal things about himself; he was open. He got very upset if it got negative reviews." But at a celebratory dinner party to mark the book's publication at Judith Waters's house (presumably before the reviews began to run), Milgram had been able to admit that the book had flaws. He asked Waters's twelve-year-old son, Mitchell, what he thought of it. Mitchell answered that "in the beginning of the book when Dr. Milgram was first describing the experiment it was excellent but that, in [his] estimation, the interpretation at the end went far beyond the actual data." Milgram took the boy's feedback good-naturedly, and told him that his editor "had said much the same thing."[38]

Two weeks after Marcus's review, on March 24, the *New York Times Book Review* took what it said was an unusual step of publishing another letter because they considered it of "exceptional interest." It was from Lawrence Kohlberg, a friend of Milgram's who had interviewed some of his subjects. Kohlberg felt that the experiment fell short because Milgram merely reassured subjects rather than engaging in "moral dialogue." Such a dialogue would have involved the experimenter reflecting on his behavior and recognizing his "moral vulnerability." Kohlberg described standing behind the one-way mirror with Milgram, watching the subjects' anguish as the experiment progressed. Just as the mirror acted as a buffer between them and the subjects, Milgram's belief in "objectivity" prevented him from understanding the impact of the experiment. "He was another victim, another banal perpetrator of evil. Serving the authority science under the banner of 'objectivity,' he himself inflicted pain on others for greater social welfare." Kohlberg admitted that he had been equally culpable by "turning it to my own intellectual advantage by researching it": "I, too, used a utilitarian logic to justify my action, blinded by the idols of scientific psychology." He regretted his passivity: "At the time I did not have what I now have, a conviction that I could have intervened, not by force but by moral reason to aid my friend Milgram in clarifying and developing his own moral reasoning about what he was doing."[39]

I didn't find this letter in the Yale archives either. It must have stung. Milgram would have felt betrayed because they had been friends, and he shared a particular bond with people he invited to stand with him behind the mirror.

Kohlberg's description of the one-way mirror obscuring Milgram's vision reminded me of what Hank Stam had said about the ethical debate obscuring the much bigger issue of whether the results meant anything at all. Judith Waters wrote that she didn't think Milgram ever expected the degree of notoriety or the passionate, often personal, criticism he got, and I think she was right.[40] He seemed to maintain a curious attachment to the idea of scientific entitlement that he expected others to share.

Still, it seems that, if popularity is the ultimate test, Milgram was vindicated. *Obedience to Authority* is still in print today, thirty-nine years later. It has sold consistently and has been translated into at least eleven languages.[41]

I would never be able to read *Obedience to Authority* again without a sense of all the material that Milgram had left out, the stories he had edited, and the people he had depicted unfairly. I wondered how many of those people he'd reassured had read his harsh portrayals. After leaving Hank Stam's office, I went back to my hotel and decided to leave Milgram's book there, in that anonymous hotel room. Snow had begun to fall, and in the square below, the shapes of park benches and trees were being erased. Tomorrow the snow would be gone, but for the moment I enjoyed the obliteration of everything dark and sharp-edged, the blurring, the white.

11

REPRESENTING OBEDIENCE

The black-and-white film opens with a slow pan of Yale's familiar sandstone buildings, their shadowy archways and studded doors. We hear Hitler shouting and a crowd roaring "Sieg Heil!" in response. Yale dissolves, replaced by images of the führer, Nazi soldiers shoving prisoners onto trains, a mushroom cloud, and the atomic bomb. It dissolves again, and we are in a classroom. From this opening scene onward, Professor Stephen Turner's interest in obedience is portrayed as a sinister obsession—one that he will pursue with reckless disregard for the consequences.

In August 1976, the TV movie *The Tenth Level*, inspired by Milgram's obedience research, screened to around 30 million viewers as part of CBS's *Playhouse 90* series. William Shatner played Stephen Turner, a handsome, solid, normal-looking guy. But two minutes into the film, viewers get the sense that Turner is far from normal. Spooky music plays each time he gazes at secret drawings of a lab and a machine or listens to interviews with SS men.

Yet while he's sinister and driven, he's not a monster. For all its flaws, the film attempts to explore and understand the scientist. Turner is single-minded, ruthless, and hell-bent on scientific knowledge, but he has his vulnerabilities. He yearns for the affection of fellow scientist Barbara (only ever identified by her first name) and seems fragile and unsure of himself when she fends him off. His friend Benjamin Franklin Reed, an African American fellow academic, attributes Turner's obsession with Nazi behavior to a WASP-like "guilt in reverse" because "you've never been a victim of a pogrom or lynching." But Turner is driven: despite his friend's advice and the protests of Barbara (who calls the research "a fiendish concept"), he plunges on with his plans.

The inevitable confrontation between Turner and Barbara takes place once it has all gone wrong for Turner—a hearing has been held, subjects have revealed how traumatic the experiments were, and Turner's evidence (that his research has been replicated internationally and subjects confessed that they knew themselves better as a result of participating) has failed to persuade his colleagues. Barbara finds him wandering disconsolately through his lab. He is desperate for her approval but also accusing: "You hate my results! My ethics!"

Barbara tells him that he has failed his own test. "You watched them pushing those switches every day and you can't admit to yourself that they were tortured! . . . Admit it! That's all I ask of you," she pleads. "You had a choice. You could have stopped them. But you chose to go on."

Turner finally breaks down. "I don't deny the pain they felt!"

"Deny it? You measured it!"

He loosens his tie. Gulps.

"Stephen! Stephen! Stephen!" she cries in close-up, as if calling him back from the edge of an abyss.

Turner's face crumples. They hug, and he sobs. We see a close-up of her face over his shoulder, saying quietly, "Enough pain. Enough. This place has seen too much." Turner's shoulders shake, and he continues to sob as the credits roll.

While some of it seems pure soap opera—one unkind online commentator called the film "*The Andromeda Strain* meets *Days of Our Lives*"—parts of it seem eerily true to life.[1] The hearing that the "Federation" (read: APA) convenes to establish whether there was harm to subjects, for example, uses authentic details in the evidence that's given, and the casting of a thin, ascetic-looking experimenter and a rotund, friendly victim is appropriate, too.

What I found interesting is that the film, while it dramatizes the experiments, has as its major focus the role of the scientist. We see Turner in the lab, coldly instructing the first subject to continue. We see the excitement in his eyes as the man, despite protests and stress, continues to the maximum voltage. We catch glimpses of other subjects—one who calmly puts on his jacket midway and leaves; another who laughs maniacally and has to be helped out of his chair; and a third, a young man who throws the Williams character to the ground, smashes the machine, and runs across the university campus, chased by Turner. But the focus is on Turner and his struggle to reconcile scientific endeavor with the morals of those around him. It marks a shift away from the sensationalization of the results to a fascination with the man behind them.

The film was made during Milgram's lifetime, with his participation and consent. It's intriguing because it explores many of the problems with which Milgram had privately struggled, as well as elements of the drama that was unfolding in his professional life. This led me to wonder if Milgram had confided in the screenwriter, George Bellak, or whether Bellak, having met Milgram and interviewed him, had intuited much of the story that became *The Tenth Level*.

I wondered if any of its reported 30 million viewers were former subjects, and what they thought of it, seeing themselves and Milgram as Bellak did. For others, it would have been the first introduction to the experiments—apart, perhaps, from the snippets on *60 Minutes* when Milgram's book came out. What would those viewers have thought of the experiments and of the determined scientist behind them? And Milgram, depicted as eccentric, proud, brilliant, and sensitive—I wondered how he felt about being portrayed in that way.

Depictions of Milgram's experiments have morphed and evolved over time, and the representations map society's changing view of the research. Since news of the experiments was first published, they have been cited and repurposed to demonstrate the human propensity to obey orders, explore ideas of ethics and science, and provide popular entertainment.

Early newspaper articles delivered the shocking results first, following them with factual reports of the details of the experiment, with little or no attention on the man who conducted them. Fast forward ten years, to the mid-1970s, and the dramatic potential of the events was being explored onstage and on the small screen, with Milgram's motivation as much the focus as the seeming transformation of his subjects. Things went quiet in the 1980s and 1990s, but another surge of representations in the past decade has shown that society's interest in, and ambivalence toward, the experiments has not abated. In 2006, Derren Brown, a British psychological illusionist, drew on the experiment for his television program *The Heist*. Recruiting participants with a newspaper advertisement much like Milgram's, Brown used techniques such as suggestion, hypnosis, and manipulation—as well as plain showmanship—to convince four ordinary people who had volunteered for what they thought was a "motivational seminar" to rob a security van in broad daylight. In 2010, the experiment surfaced on international screens as a form of documentary-cum-reality-television program. French documentary filmmaker Christophe Nick devised a modern version of Milgram's setup with *The Game of Death*, a pretend game show. Contestants thought they were taking part in a real show, complete with a cheering audience and cash prizes. The game? You guessed it—shock another contestant to 450 volts and win a prize.

Watching these television shows and reading the changing depiction of the experiments reminded me of a note that Don Mixon had sent me after our last meeting. He had written: "What people believe about Milgram's experiments comes from *descriptions* of the experiment." Don was speaking from experience: he had replicated Milgram's "prediction study," describing the experiment to a group of psychiatrists and asking them to predict how many people would obey. He found that psychiatrists predicted much lower rates of obedience when he told them the story from Milgram's point of view, one in which the situation seemed clearly and unambiguously defined. But if he told the story from the subjects' point of view, with all of its ambiguity and contradictions—the details of the gradual foot-in-the-door process of entrapment—they predicted that many more people would go to the maximum voltage. Don found that they predicted obedience rates between 0 and 100 percent, depending on how he described the experiment. He wrote, "Something as complex as Milgram's experiment can be described in many, many ways. What the public believes about the experiments comes from Milgram's very compelling descriptions or from descriptions based on Milgram's descriptions."

We have been dependent on Milgram's descriptions, too, because it would be almost impossible today to gain university approval to conduct such research. Unless, of course, you could find some way of quelling their concern—some way of pulling off a version that was close to the original but lacked the ethical ambiguity.

Professor Jerry Burger managed to do just that.

Burger has been a professor of psychology at Santa Clara University for twenty-eight years. He leapt to national attention in 2007, when he repeated the Milgram experiment for American television.

In July 2005, the producer of ABC's *Primetime* contacted Burger. "The first thing she said was that they were interested in Milgram and they wanted to replicate the study." The idea had occurred to the show's producers because of recent media attention on the torture of detainees at Abu Ghraib. "They wanted to see if we were more independent thinkers now because that was back in the sixties, when people were more obedient, more robotic." The producer had contacted the APA, who had given them Burger's name. He laughed. "And I'm pretty sure my first words to her were, 'Can't be done. Period. Discussion is over. It's just not possible.'"

Burger told them he wouldn't be part of a full replication, even if ABC had somehow figured out how to conduct one, so they came up with a compromise. Revisiting Milgram's book, Burger noticed that in condition 5, when the learner mentioned that he had a heart problem, there was a critical point at 150 volts. "When they hear the man on the other side of the wall yelling, 'Let me out,' if people are going to stop, that's the most likely place they are going to stop. And, in fact, if they don't stop, there's a 79 percent chance that they will continue all the way." After consulting widely, including with the APA, he proposed an experiment in which subjects would be taken to 150 volts to see how they responded. Burger believed that this was a responsible place to stop, because it was beyond 150 volts that Milgram's subjects began to experience signs of trauma.

After a lengthy approval process with his university's institutional review board, in 2006 he began. Using Milgram's descriptions, film, and transcripts from the experiment, and with Tom Blass's help, Burger set about reproducing the obedience experiment as closely as he could.

Burger, like Milgram, was responsible for every last detail. And he had the added pressure of having to keep the project secret so that ABC would not be scooped by a rival station. He was allowed to tell his wife and son but no one else, unless they had a need to know. That meant keeping it from his colleagues and doing everything clandestinely, on evenings and weekends, on his own.

The preparations took months. "And every day there was another challenge: finding the right kind of chair, table, the right kind of contact paste for the electrodes—and the lab coat, even the lab coat. Milgram didn't want a white lab coat because it suggested something medical, so I had to get a gray one, but they don't make gray lab coats, so I had to make do with a blue one. This is the kind of thing I had to wrestle with. I bought these tables that would work with the machine, and I brought my saw from home and cut off the legs so they would be the right height. Then I had to figure out how to get the learner to escape. Milgram never explained the Houdini part of it. He straps this guy in—how does he get out?"

Burger also organized the building of a shock machine. When he saw the original, he realized he would have to make one that looked more contemporary if his experiment was going to be believable. "It looked like something out of Frankenstein's lab, really old-looking. I told the guy building it to make it modern, but keep it as close as possible. The dimensions are the same, the levers are in same place, the words are the same."

As Milgram had done, he put ads in the local paper to recruit volunteers. "The first morning, I ran out when the paper was delivered, and the ad was perfect except for two mistakes—the phone number was wrong and the e-mail address was wrong. I could have shrugged it off, but I had people on planes flying out here from New York."

Unlike Milgram, Burger had a clinical psychologist screen out any people who might be particularly vulnerable to stress, which meant he lost almost 40 percent of his subjects. He was "horrified," having expected that he would lose no more than 5 percent. "I had to scramble around then and find more because we were starting the next week." In the end, he had a total of seventy-six subjects.

This screening process would also expose Burger to criticism. In an article in *American Psychologist*, Alan Elms called it "obedience lite," the connotation being that it had all the substance taken out of it. He argued that this psychological assessment had the effect of screening out the potentially disobedient.[2]

After the preparations were complete, there was a tight two-and-a-half-week window in which to get the filming done. Burger lost eight pounds during it because he "didn't have time to eat."

Burger's involvement in organizing the experiment led him to be impressed with the "genius" of Milgram's research design. He had clearly had a good understanding of what it would take to get people to follow instructions. "Milgram claims he was surprised as anybody at the results, and he said this in answer to ethical charges that he hadn't intended for people to have these experiences. But I think he also had an idea it wasn't going to be a failure because obviously it wasn't going to be very interesting if people stopped at the first scream. I think he had an intuition—he knew that if you started at 100 volts it wouldn't work, so [he devised] things like using the 15-volt increments, telling the experimenter to say, 'I'm responsible if anyone asks.'"

But he found that Milgram's story of the experiment wasn't as straightforward as he made it seem. The process of administering the memory test, for example, was more complicated and confusing than he had expected. "It's much more difficult than it seems from the subject's point of view. You have to keep track of what the response is, what that aligns with in terms of which item you're on, you have to give the right answer, you have to press the right button—there's a lot to do in a long sequence, so for a lot of our participants, they needed help for the first few times. . . . I am sure that when Milgram said, 'These are the only things my experimenter said,' that that's not correct. It really isn't. There are all kinds of questions that people asked. I'm sure his experimenter had to do a lot of off-the-cuff comments that deal with confusion and questions and problems that surface, which of course adds a lot of variance to the whole process. So even though we tried to follow as tightly as possible exactly what his person did, I realized that's probably not possible."

While Burger could see how brilliantly Milgram had set up the dilemma for subjects, he hadn't appreciated how difficult a struggle it was until he watched it firsthand. "It's not as clear-cut as it seems from the outside. When you're in that situation, wondering should I continue or should I not, there are reasons to do both. What you do have is an expert in the room who knows all about this study, and presumably has been through this many times before with many participants, and he's telling you here's nothing wrong. The reasonable, rational thing to do is to listen to the guy who's the expert when you're not sure what to do."

Burger had been worried from the start about the levels of distress his subjects might experience. "I can say honestly that I was prepared to pull the plug if, after the first few subjects, the reaction was stronger than I'd anticipated. I was going to tell the ABC, 'I'm sorry, but I'm not going to participate in this if people are going to have a bad reaction.'" But after that anxious first day, it was clear to him that the people he had recruited weren't showing signs of extreme stress. As soon as a subject refused to continue or reached 150 volts, the experiment was stopped, and Burger debriefed each subject immediately. He was amazed at how positive most people were. He could think of "one or two" who weren't happy afterward, but 90 percent of people, when asked, said they would be happy for their parts to be shown on television and "nowhere did I pick up anywhere that anyone had a problem." "I think our people had the benefit of being able to say they were about to stop. And I did a debriefing that gave them credit for that. I did my best to make them feel they weren't monsters, that they didn't do anything wrong. They'll never know what they would have done. They were able to tell themselves they would have stopped. There's comfort in that."

The replication was successful, and the program aired on January 3,

2007. Burger wasn't surprised to find he got similar results to Milgram and believed it shows that it was about the situation, rather than personality.

It took two years for his results to be published, finally appearing in the January 2009 issue of *American Psychologist*. As they had with Milgram, the media were all over the story. "The reaction was huge. I did nothing but interviews for days afterward. Everybody everywhere was calling." He couldn't get over the professional boost he had gotten since. He was invited to give talks on the research both inside and outside academia. A self-described shy person, Burger told me, "It seemed that when I went to conferences, people who wouldn't normally come up and talk to me were coming up and talking to me. Some of the big shots in the field, whom I'd never met, acted like we were old friends, and they knew me. I was going to say, you know, 'We've never actually been introduced, but that's fine with me if you want to schmooze.' So I think it's really been a plus professionally."

I thought about Don Mixon telling me how actually conducting the experiment had revealed the full cruelty of it to him. Did it challenge Burger's thinking about the Milgram experiment? "I used to give the usual spiel about how it tells us a lot about Abu Ghraib and the Holocaust, but what I've come to understand is that in some ways Milgram was thinking too big, and in some ways he wasn't thinking big enough. With a complex phenomenon like the Holocaust, you need to be cautious in drawing that parallel. On the other hand, I don't think it's unrelated. It helps us understand the Holocaust experience, but it's a little piece of it. But I don't think he was thinking big enough. I may not commit Nazi atrocities, but I'm certainly capable of doing things that surprise me and disappoint me, so I think that's the bigger message."

And there's no arguing with the importance of Milgram's study, Burger said. "Everybody understands the ethical questions. Fifty years later, who else in social psychology are people still talking about? It's got a place in the history of social psychology and psychology that's well respected." He paused, perhaps waiting for me to agree. "All of us [psychologists] have criticisms of his interpretations and the way he describes things, but we all recognize the importance of his study."

Do we? I wondered as I followed him out of his office. He was taking me to see his shock machine. We went down a flight of stairs and into the basement, then through a door and into a windowless waiting area facing two rooms. Burger took me into the larger of the rooms where under a heavy plastic cover was the machine.

"Here," Burger said, pulling back the chair. "Take a seat."

I sat down. From this position, it seemed bigger. It looked slick, almost industrial, with its red lights, levers, and dials. It looked authoritative and powerful, certainly not fake.

"Go ahead," he said, as if sensing that I needed his permission.

I pulled the chair closer to the desk. I pressed the first switch and a light came on, a low buzz sounding. Even though I knew what to expect, I could feel my shoulders tensing. I pressed the second switch, and then the third. I knew the drill—it wouldn't be until the fifth switch that I would hear the first noise, a grunt of pain. But when I reached the fourth, a voice suddenly screamed, "Let me out of here! My heart's bothering me—let me out, let me out, let me out!" I jumped and let go of the switch, but the voice kept going, on a continuous loop. "I told you, let me out. [*Screams*] I can't stand . . ." The cries ran into one another, a jumbled mishmash. Burger darted over. "The computer's playing up again," he said, flipping the next switch so that the voice stopped.

Even though I knew it was just a recording, I felt startled. My heart was beating faster. In the sudden silence, I did something, in what should have been a solemn moment, that I still can't explain. I don't know what drove me—a mix of fear, surprise, foolishness, relief, or sheepishness at my gullibility. Whatever it was, I couldn't help myself. I laughed.

Thirty-three years before Burger's replication, Milgram's documentary *Obedience* had brought his research to the attention of audiences when it screened on *60 Minutes*. It was the first visual representation of the experiment and set the benchmark for subsequent films, TV movies, and plays.

Milgram shot the film over the final three days of his experiments, on May 25, 26, and 27, 1962, with staff from Yale's AV center as cameramen and a freelance sound engineer. He shot five reels of eleven men, including one pair of friends who took part in condition 24, over that weekend. But it took another three years before the editing would be complete.

Milgram knew when he shot the film that further research funding was unlikely; the NSF had made that clear. But it's probable that he wanted to capture a record of his work, as well as gather proof of the procedure and his subjects' behavior. Perhaps it was three years before he got around to finishing the edit because his job at Harvard kept him particularly busy, or perhaps Baumrind's article in 1964 and the ensuing controversy gave him fresh impetus. Milgram hired aspiring filmmaker Christopher Johnson to edit the footage and record a voice-over to accompany it. He had been given some funding by the NSF in June 1963 to analyze his results and report his research, and he may have used the last of this in July 1965 to cover editing costs.

Milgram had already noticed that explaining the experiment was not the same as seeing it. He told one interviewer that no matter how many times he tried to explain it to colleagues, most of them looked "puzzled."[3] From his early applications to the NSF onward, he had used photographs to illustrate and offer evidence of what he was trying to describe. Privately, he guessed that his experiments were more successful as drama than as science:

> Several men of intelligence, having observed the experiments, felt that the procedures bared for them profound and disturbing truths of human nature . . . three young Yale professors, after witnessing an evening session, declared that the experience was a brilliant revelation of human nature, and left the laboratory in a state of exhilaration. Similar reactions were forthcoming from other observers. Whether all of this ballyhoo points to significant science or merely effective theater is an open question. I am inclined to accept the latter interpretation. One reason is that almost all witnesses say to their friends: "You have to see it to understand it," or

"You can't imagine what happens unless you see it yourself; words simply won't do." This is precisely the kind of talk one would expect to hear in connection with a play or some other artistic performance. In genuine science a mathematical or verbal description of the phenomenon is good enough. But the truth or significance of music, or a theatrical performance, or a painting, depends on direct confrontation and experiencing of the event. So the drawing power of the experiments stem in part from their artistic, non-scientific component. This makes them more interesting; it does not necessarily make them more valuable for a developing science of man.[4]

He wanted the film to be arresting. In Milgram's film folder, there are detailed notes analyzing Hitchcock's technique in *Strangers on a Train*. He noted that the intrigue of Hitchcock's film took place "on two planes—the physical and the moral," giving insight into his thoughts about the purpose of the film.[5]

Before passing the footage to Johnson, Milgram did his own edit. He chose seven of the eleven men, cutting the other four. The film, like his book, had to function as proof of his scientific credentials, to show that subjects believed the setup and that the results were real. His handwritten notes on the unedited footage read like a screen test. He noted that the first man on the first reel "reeks of obedience" and "is not bad at all." The second, Milgram wrote, had potential: he was "animated and alive." But the subject said, "I didn't believe the experiment was real. The groans and moans were not real." It was these doubts that let his performance down, in Milgram's view: "At one point he said he didn't believe it—at another he said he believed completely." Unreliable subjects might cast doubt on the experiment's believability. The next one was "fair"; the next, Milgram noted glumly, was "not very convincing," although the next man showed promise, demonstrating "considerable tension throughout."

By the fourth reel, Milgram's excitement was palpable. It was an "excellent" reel. One man was "excellent on tension," and another was "brilliantly anti-authority" and "a good laugher." The next man, who was in fact Jim McDonough's neighbor, the one who would later try to revive him after his fatal heart attack, received an "IN," indicating he had made it to the final cut.

The man that Milgram would call Fred Prozi came next and was termed "brilliant" not just once but three times because of his "complete abdication and excellent tension." Milgram had found his star: "He should be used in the final film as a demonstration of our obedient subjects."[6]

Milgram's excited comments about Prozi reminded me of the notes he had made when he first met Jim McDonough: "Excellent as victim. A+ victim." Only Prozi hadn't been acting.

Among those left on the cutting-room floor were a pair of friends, one of whom was still agitated after the debriefing. He said to Williams, "I was sweating bullets. I'm still jumping!" while his friend, who seemed much younger, stood in the background, looking uncomfortable.

Chris Johnson edited the film to depict one run-through of the experiment in its entirety, splicing together clips of different male subjects from different conditions. We see one man listening to Williams's instructions and then watching as the learner is strapped in, another receiving a sample shock, another refusing to go on at 150 volts, another laughing, another telling Williams to take the money back, and another reaching 345 volts before refusing to continue. Then we get to Fred Prozi. The only one who goes to 450 volts, he dominates the narrative: he is allocated more time than the other subjects combined. And it's a riveting performance.

Prozi's segment begins when he's about to give the ninth shock. For thirteen minutes, or almost a third of the film, we watch Prozi's excruciating attempts to convince the experimenter to stop. His tension is both physical and verbal: he gets up, walks around, pleads with the experimenter, and calls out to the learner.

A couple of times I've screened the film in classes, showing a snippet of Prozi to give students a sense of what the experience was like from the subject's point of view. Each time, a cry has gone up when I've tried to switch it off before Prozi's segment is over. It's hard not to become engaged with Fred, with his kindness and conflict, his deference and confusion. Our sympathies, and a kind of horrible fascination with how far he'll go, make it impossible to turn off. Johnson noted this in his first test run of the edited version. In July 1965, he reported to Milgram:

> I ran it in Holt, Rinehart and Winston's small screen-
> ing room. A number of other employees from the Foreign
> Language Dept. were also present . . . no one was fooled by the
> "punishment-learning" front, and all found it incredible that
> subjects could have been deceived. They thought the subjects
> protests phoney. . . . They also felt their lunch hour had been
> ruined and their faith in mankind shaken. Yet for a week now
> several of the women have been pestering me to rerun the film
> on a Saturday for them and their husbands.[7]

Fred Prozi's role in *Obedience* reveals a moral ambiguity that has been obscured in most subsequent popular depictions. Milgram wanted us to believe that his experiment was a stage on which a strug-gle between morality and immorality, victim and torturer, and good and evil was played out. But the footage of subjects, even despite the editing, is not nearly so clear-cut. Who was the victim and who was the torturer? What was good and what was evil? Milgram's choice of Prozi as star reveals Milgram the artist, with his sensitivity to dramatic potential, at work. What he missed was how Prozi's performance il-luminated many of the complex and troubling inconsistencies of the experiment.

Part of the cutting-room footage shows Milgram asking each man if he would agree to the film being shown to psychologists. Fred Prozi hesitated, then asked whether his face would be shown "nationwide or something?" but Milgram assured him it would be for psychologists only and Fred, reassured, agreed. This wasn't true. In December 1965, Milgram registered copyright on the film, and by 1969 it was avail-able for sale or hire for university teaching programs. However, televi-sion producers recognized the potential in the material, and Milgram was approached repeatedly for permission to broadcast it. He initially turned down such requests, honoring the agreements he had made with those who had been filmed. But in the late 1960s, he granted permission to broadcast it on Italian and German television.[8] And in

1974, Milgram allowed CBS's *60 Minutes* to screen part of it to coincide with the publication of his book.

On Sunday, March 31, 1974, a story about Milgram's research titled "I Was Only Following Orders" appeared on the show, sandwiched between "Apricot Seeds: Cure or Quackery?" and an interview with Helen Gurley Brown, editor of *Cosmopolitan*, who had been quoted in the promo saying, "No one ever went broke underestimating the intelligence of the American public."

This feature report on the experiments, the first to be aired in prime time, capitalized on the sensationalism surrounding Milgram's claims that his experiment cast a light on the reasons behind wartime atrocities. It began with a montage of marching soldiers, Eichmann on trial, and footage from concentration camps, showing bodies piled on top of one another. Then Vietnam: people running from bombings, napalm attacks, more bodies. Reporter Morley Safer interviewed Milgram about his research, and Milgram, sitting rigidly, half-turned from Safer, looked wooden and self-conscious. Instead of looking at Safer when he replied, Milgram kept glancing down at his lap. (Tom Blass told me it was because he was looking at his notes.)

The eighteen-minute segment about Milgram's research featured ten minutes of *Obedience*. I wonder if Prozi ever saw it and, if so, how he felt about his actions being contextualized against images of genocide and torture.

As the *Obedience* footage played, Milgram described what was happening in solemn voice-over. The black-and-white film looked curiously dated in what was by then a world of color television.

Safer remarked that he wouldn't have gone past the third switch. "Well, Mr. Safer, I'd have to say that's an illusion," Milgram intoned. "If a system of death camps were set up in the United States of the sort we have seen in Nazi Germany, one would be able to find sufficient personnel for those camps in any medium-sized American town." His hesitancy, his lack of eye contact, and his reliance on notes undermined the bravura of his words. He did not look like a man confident about the claims that he was making. Perhaps he was just nervous being on such a high-profile television show, especially in light of the recent criticism his book had received. Or perhaps he sensed that he was going too far. I like to think that Milgram looked uncomfortable because he had a twinge of remorse—that he hesitated because he was conscious that, while few of his subjects might read his book, many might be watching *60 Minutes* that night and that his responsibility to them extended to how they were depicted in the media.

The *60 Minutes* story was the first in a series of current affairs reports during the 1970s that explored the link between Milgram's subjects and Nazism. The run sheet for BBC's *Horizon*, for example, began, "The barbed wire of Auschwitz. Officials loading Jews into railway wagons. A long tracking shot past railway lines in Holland from which the Jews set out on their last journey."[9] It was hardly surprising that in the public mind, despite Milgram's insistence that it was not personality that shaped behavior, his subjects became synonymous with murderous brutality and ingrained evil.

While prime-time television depicted Milgram's subjects as New Haven Nazis, other portrayals were concerned about the ethical dimension of the research. Milgram's use of deception was the inspiration for several imaginative representations, including plays, films, and screen dramas.

The Dogs of Pavlov, written by Welsh playwright and doctor Dannie Abse, appeared on the London stage in 1971. A fictionalized account of the experiments, it explored the ethics from the subjects' point of view. In his introduction, Abse argued that research such as Milgram's divested subjects of their human dignity because they were cheated and lied to (or, as he put it, they were "taken in" by a "bullshit cover story"). Abse addressed the subjects of the experiment directly: "You were conned, and in my view, you have a right to feel angry." He also called Milgram's role into question. "In order to demonstrate that subjects may behave like so many Eichmanns the experimenter [referring to Milgram] had to act the part . . . of a Himmler." He argued that while Milgram was motivated by noble intentions, his subjects were treated like "guinea pigs" and that Milgram had continued when he had a choice to stop.[10]

Abse sent Milgram his introduction to the play. Milgram replied that he felt Abse had been "harsh." He regarded it as hypocritical that

Abse, who relied on illusion as a playwright, was critical of the same quality in Milgram's experiment. In fact, he pointed out the similarities between their projects:

> I will not say that you cheated, tricked and defrauded your audience [in the play]. But I would hold the same claim for the experiment. Misinformation is employed in the experiment; illusion is used when necessary to set the stage for the revelation of certain difficult-to-get-at truths. . . . As a dramatist you surely understand that illusion may serve a revelatory function. . . . The participant, rather than the external critic, must be the ultimate source of judgement; otherwise the criticism is akin to denouncing the misinformation fed to the guest of honor at a surprise party without taking into account his reaction to it.

Soon after this letter, he sent another, as if he couldn't get Abse's criticism out of his mind. Abse seems to have infuriated him. In the second letter, Milgram was on the attack. He pointed out that Abse, a playwright and a physician, experienced "contradictions" in both roles—"a reliance on illusion and a hatred of it, a need to treat people as individuals but a need to objectify them"—and yet attacked Milgram for doing the same. While writing a play with the theme of victimization, Abse had "created a victim of [his] own" in Milgram: "You benefit artistically by involving an audience in my experiment, but you keep yourself untainted by denouncing it." It's an extraordinarily angry letter, and Milgram admits in the final lines that he "might have gone too far" but hopes that by being frank Abse will understand him better.[11]

I wondered why Abse's introduction had made Milgram so mad. It certainly wasn't the first time he'd been criticized; he'd had years of it by then. Perhaps it was that he wanted Abse's approval more than that of his fellow scientists. Perhaps Milgram identified with Abse, who successfully combined his medical career with playwriting and poetry. And even though Milgram did privately admit doubts about the experiment's status as science, he never doubted its status as a work of art.

Abse's play reflected a more skeptical view of science and scientists that had gathered momentum since the 1960s. By the mid-1970s, depictions of the experiment in popular culture increasingly focused not only on the ethics of the research but also on the man behind it.

I wondered if it was the experience with Abse that led Milgram to work more closely with the next playwright who approached him. In the mid-1960s, George Bellak had unsuccessfully tried to interest two television networks in the idea of a drama based on the experiments, one of which rejected it as "anti-God." But, in the following years, the My Lai massacre, the photograph of Phan Thi Kim Phúc (the "napalm girl"), and the Watergate scandal dominated the headlines and captured the public's interest in the issue of obedience to authority. On his next approach, this time to CBS, the idea of a drama based on the experiments was "snapped up."[12]

Bellak wrote to Milgram in September 1974, stating that he'd carried a clipping about the experiments around with him for eleven years with the idea of writing about them, and news of Milgram's book had prompted him to revisit the idea. CBS had commissioned a script. Would Milgram meet with him or call him to talk about his research? They met, and two months later Bellak sent Milgram his script for *The Tenth Level.*

Clearly, Milgram didn't like what he read, because he immediately sought legal advice on copyright infringement (presumably of the machine and the experiment) and defamation. But the legal advice stated that they were unlikely to win because the character was fictional.[13] Perhaps resigning himself to the inevitable, about a week after he received the script Milgram asked for a fee for helping Bellak to develop the story and 25 percent of any royalties if the play made its way onto stage or screen.[14]

Milgram served as a "technical adviser" during the filming and was paid $5,000 by CBS.[15] His name doesn't appear in the credits, which former student Sharon Presley said was because he "wasn't too happy with it and wouldn't let his name be associated with it": "It misrepresents several crucial aspects of the experiment. NO ONE ever went berserk in the real experiment and Milgram never regretted what he had done as the Shatner character does."[16]

But that wasn't quite the case. In the year between first seeing the script and its finalization, Milgram seemed to have warmed to the idea of it. Perhaps he took heart from the fact that it was fiction. Two months before the first screening, he approached *TV Guide* and the *New York Times Magazine* to see if they would do an article about him, linked to the upcoming show.[17] And Milgram's notes as he watched the program indicate that, overall, he was happy with what he saw. He recognized one character, a woman instrumental in arranging the hearing, as Diana Baumrind. He thought the scenes of the hearing were "excellent" and, despite some "tv hokum," the show was "quite good." He was pleased enough, in fact, to draft new ads for his book, tying it to the production:

> You saw and were stunned by the *Playhouse 90*
> drama
> **THE TENTH LEVEL**
> Starring William Shatner
> Now read the book behind the play:
> **OBEDIENCE TO AUTHORITY**
> An Experimental View
> By S. Milgram
> Published by Harper and Row
> Hardcover $10.00 Paperback $3.45
> A National Book Award Nominee 1974[18]

Milgram dominated the interviews and representations of the obedience research throughout the remainder of his life. Following his death in 1984, Milgram's associates were sought out whenever the experiments hit the news again. At least one program interviewed Williams for comment, and the story focused on his behavior in ordering subjects to continue.

In a 1997 episode of the news program *Dateline NBC*, the story opened with a clip from the original *Candid Camera*, featuring Allen Funt's voice-over and a laughter track. Referring to a replication of Solomon Asch's conformity experiment, the journalist asked, "But what are the outer limits of conformity?" and then warned that the footage to follow "had rarely been seen on network television." Film from *Obedience* was shown. This time, instead of Fred Prozi, it was another man. Why not Prozi? I wondered. I like to imagine that he was approached and refused permission. Yet the face of a second subject, who looked on as McDonough was strapped into the chair, was blurred, suggesting that the man or his family had also refused permission. The man would eventually be classed as disobedient, but the viewer didn't know this yet. *Dateline*'s voice-over instructed people to pay attention to the man's struggle—how he repeatedly turned to Williams as the learner cried out, and Williams's cold voice, off-camera, instructed him to go on. It was a marked departure from the *60 Minutes* story more than twenty years earlier.

Dateline tracked down Jack Williams in what may have been his only public interview about the research. His shoulders seemed broader; the thin young man had filled out. It suited him. He also looked more distinguished, dressed in a dark suit and tie.

"That's disturbing," the journalist, Dawn Fratangelo, said of the footage they'd just seen.

"We thought so. I thought so," Williams answered.

"When you first saw that machine, did it ever occur to you that people would go to the very end?"

"No." Williams was emphatic.

Was it cruel? Was it possibly damaging? Interestingly, Fratangelo posed this rhetorically, speaking to the camera rather than Williams. Maybe she asked him questions that he refused to answer. Keith Williams told me his father "was very annoyed with their line of questioning. . . . He almost got up and walked out on them because of their manipulation of the interview. They tried to make it dramatic." The program clearly put much more emphasis on Williams's role and less on the ethical controversy that had repeatedly dogged Milgram.

In recent times, television depictions of the experiment have proliferated, unfettered by the restraints of ethics committees or review boards. On YouTube, *South Park*–type cartoons, *Gumby*-style Claymations, and student reenactments proliferate.

In the clamor of representations, Milgram's message has been con-
taminated, simplified, and milked for its entertainment value. In May
2009, BBC's *Horizon*—which had made a program about Milgram's
book in 1974—revisited the topic with a program as part of its *Violence*
season called "How Violent Are You?" The show reproduced the
Milgram experiment, interspersed with interviews with a Sudanese
former child soldier who had tortured and slaughtered those who had
killed his parents, among others. Described as "thought-provoking"
and "uncomfortable," the program was promoted as taking viewers on
a journey to the disturbing side of human nature, asking "if anyone
can be driven to deliberately kill."

In March 2010, *Dateline NBC* screened what they called a "*Dateline*
experiment," in which the experiment as performance was taken to
extremes. The subjects were aspiring actors who arrived for what they
thought was an audition for a television show called *What a Pain*.
They were told that, as part of the audition, they must give shocks
to a contestant that would hurt but wouldn't do permanent damage. Each actor "auditioned" while hidden cameras recorded their reactions. In the promo, there was Latifa, a young African American
woman, grimacing and wincing as the man's cries increased with the
voltage. Over her shoulder, we could see the handsome host behind
an antique desk, looking at the camera with an eyebrow raised. "Our
brains are hardwired to obey authority," a voice-over told the viewer.
But the worried-looking presenter asked in a deep voice, "What were
they thinking?"

What were they thinking indeed? Viewer reactions reflected the full
gamut of praise and criticism that have been directed at the experiments over the last half century. Comments posted on the program
blog called it everything from "awesome" to "exploitative," "unethical"
to "terrifying."

Most recently, horror director Eli Roth hosted the television show
How Evil Are You?, which aired in the United States on October 30,
2011. The program was billed as carrying out a series of experiments
"that will shed light on the capacity for evil that lurks within ordinary men and women." A reviewer in *Variety* commended the
production, noting that it was hard to argue that the "temporary

discomfort" of those involved outweighed what it told us about human nature.[19]

But what about us, the ones watching these programs? Are we better than people who used to watch the Christians being thrown to the lions in ancient Rome? Or does the fact that such programs tout themselves as probing the inner recesses of our psyches make it okay, a rationalization for the kind of sadistic voyeurism that has us watching with fascination at home? Network executives offer all sorts of justifications for why they make such programs, but I can't help feeling that viewers are complicit in something more shameful than the experiment itself. Perhaps, for some, they explain contemporary events in a way that makes sense. But for me, the uncritical mirroring of the original and the simplistic take-home message puts a new spin on the term "banality of evil." It's certainly banal if we can watch and marvel at torture from our living rooms.

For better or worse, whether you believe his work had more in common with performance art than psychology, Milgram lives on—in art, in culture, and in our imagination. Milgram sensed this: he knew it in his early, worried notes about the experiment being more like art than science in 1962, and he knew it twelve years later when he was writing his book. Anticipating criticism, he described himself as "a hopeful poet who finds metaphoric illumination between what subjects do at Yale University and what happened in Germany."[20]

Artistic representations of the obedience experiments seem to provide an insight into our darkest natures. As with a horror movie, in which we enjoy the thrill of a good fright, they allow us to return, gratified, to the safety and comfort of the familiar when they end. In addition, the experiment and its replications continue to shock, thrill, and be evoked as a powerful moral lesson. Fresh news of torture or incomprehensible violence by those under authority still brings new comparisons with Milgram's work. It taps into a fascination that humans have with knowing more about ourselves. It is the same curiosity that has us watching reality-television shows or doing quizzes and questionnaires that claim to tell us who we "really" are, which we believe because they are produced by "experts." Perhaps we seek answers like these because we are more exposed than ever to violence and mindless brutality in modern society. Perhaps, in a strange way, Milgram's obedience experiment reassures us not only of our predictability, our frailty, and our weakness but also that science can continue to explain us to ourselves.

CONCLUSION

What you think of the Milgram obedience experiments depends on which story you are told and who is telling it. The standard version that has been reproduced in the media and handed down to generations of students through lectures and textbooks tells it in the third person. We are invited to take the perspective of an omniscient observer and to imagine subjects like Fred Prozi arriving for their appointments. Some details are delayed to make the story more engaging, to heighten tension. Crucially, we're often not told that the experiment is a hoax until later, after the horror of discovering how many seemingly normal people like Prozi went on to electrocute another man.

But what if I told the story in the second person, asking you to identify with one of Milgram's volunteers and imagine yourself arriving for an experiment at the lab? Maybe I'd get your attention for a few lines, but soon I would lose you. Maybe it would be when you had to imagine yourself agreeing to give electric shocks to someone; perhaps it would happen later, when I asked you to imagine hearing the man cry out after you had pressed a switch. It's hard for anyone to imagine themselves as anything other than a defiant subject. We just can't imagine doing what they did.

Milgram understood that his research was a powerful piece of theater, that the seeming transformation of ordinary men and women into Eichmann figures was a compelling story. It was startling, counterintuitive, and it reinforced the notion that we might like to think we know ourselves but social psychologists know better: inside all of us is a concentration-camp guard just waiting to be called into service.

Milgram's experiment can be viewed as a form of performance art.[1] Jeffrey Shandler points out that Susan Sontag made the same observation about the Eichmann trial. "No longer confined to the virtual world of the theater," she argued, tragedy has become

> a form of history. Dramatists no longer write tragedies. But we do possess works of art (not always recognized as such) which reflect or attempt to resolve the great historical tragedies of our time. . . . As the supreme tragic event of modern times is the murder of the six million European Jews, one of the most interesting and moving works of art of the past ten years is the trial of Adolf Eichmann in Jerusalem in 1961.[2]

But while the influence of Milgram's research has waned in the field of Holocaust studies, the two are still inextricably linked in the public imagination, reinforced in the past fifty years by the accompanying visual images—of Hitler, concentration camps, and the horrors of genocide—that introduce the research to new generations.

One of the reasons that Milgram's obedience research remains powerful is because it seems to provide an answer to something we still don't understand, François Rochat told me by phone from Switzerland, where he is a psychology lecturer at the University of Fribourg. "We are still looking for ways to understand what went on in Nazi Germany, and although it's a bit too easy, Milgram's obedience research seems to provide an answer."

François's research interest focused on those who had rescued others from the Nazis in World War II and what drove them "to make a choice between closing their eyes or doing something." He admired the fact that "Milgram wanted to take part in the discussion about Nazism and felt he had an answer to it." François felt that the research does tell us about the dynamics of face-to-face interaction between ordinary people and an authority figure because, as I too had come to feel, "there's more, much more going on in history than goes on in the lab": "You have to take from the lab what you can take from the lab, not more."

Should we call what Milgram measured "obedience"? "Obedience is a general term; it's not precise enough to tell us about what was going on," said François. What *was* going on, he thought, was the inexorable subordination of the less powerful by the powerful. He believed that Milgram, in his focus on outcomes, missed the social interaction between Williams and each subject. He overlooked a powerful and unacknowledged variable: the relationship between the subject and the authority figure.

François analyzed the interaction between Williams and the subjects and concluded that people arrived at the lab in a spirit of cooperation, pleased to be taking part in an experiment "for the advancement of science." Once it began, subjects were faced with either giving electric shocks or ruining the experiment they came to assist. Few people appreciated how difficult it was for subjects to call a halt once the experiment had started. "It's like being on a highway—if you go fast you miss the exit. There is a rhythm to the experiment that goes faster and faster." If you were cued in, François said, you could watch the subordination unfolding in a sequence. By analyzing the tapes, he and his colleague Andre Modigliani identified a sequence of steps by which people, after first feeling cooperative, began to hesitate, question, object, and sometimes disobey. "Both obedient and disobedient subjects had a hard time inflicting pain on their fellow participants. It was obvious they were all looking for a way to get out of the experiments."

When I thought about this later, I could see how Milgram had accounted for Williams's influence as an aspect of the environment, a feature that could be controlled in much the same way he controlled how far away or how audible the learner was. Milgram captured behavior at only one moment in a person's life, François said. A week, a month, or a year later, the same people could have behaved differently. He contrasted Milgram with a friend of his who had worked for twenty-six years with the same fifteen Holocaust survivors, interviewing each person repeatedly, "because his or her story is always changing." Milgram had tried to fix subjects' behavior like points on a map:

"He describes his subjects as if they would be like that forever, like statues. They are alive, these people."

I thought of some of the people I had spoken to, still blaming themselves after so many years for what they saw as an enduring flaw, fixing themselves as static and unchanging in exactly the same way.

The one fixed feature in the obedience experiments was the shock machine. Between August 1961 and May 1962, as subjects flowed in and out of the lab, it was the constant. Later, the machine was occasionally taken out of its home at the Archives of the History of American Psychology at the University of Akron in Ohio for traveling exhibitions—most recently for the hundredth anniversary of the APA in 1992. Titled "Psychology: Understanding Ourselves, Understanding Each Other," the exhibition toured fourteen science museums across the United States from 1992 to 1996, then spent five years at the Arizona Science Center in Phoenix.

The exhibition's goal was to present three-dimensional exhibits of psychology experiments. Curator Caryl Marsh wrote that her first reaction when she was told the shock machine was in the archives was that "the APA would never let us display it." It was such a controversial piece of equipment. But a colleague persisted. For the exhibition to work, it needed controversy: the machine would be a draw. When Marsh took the idea to a dinner meeting with APA officials, "I might as well have dropped a bomb." But she eventually got her way.

Some psychologists were outraged by its inclusion. Others felt just as strongly in favor of it, arguing that it had earned a place in an exhibition about the history of psychology and promoted the profession.

The exhibit for the shock machine, Marsh wrote, was inspired by *Candid Camera*. Visitors arrived at an enclosed passageway with a black-and-white checkerboard floor. A sign read, "Attention! Please walk on the black squares ONLY!" Ninety percent of visitors obeyed, hopscotching down the walkway to the end of the corridor, where Milgram's machine sat in a Plexiglas case with a description of how it was used to measure our propensity to follow orders. In visitor surveys, the shock machine was the most mentioned exhibit, but people were polarized by it. They reacted either with amusement or with anger at being duped. They were disgusted, admiring, curious.[3] Milgram's experiment had lost none of its power to provoke.

David Baker, director of the Akron archives, enthused about the countless untold stories in the archives as we made our way through its labyrinth of rooms. We passed a shelf housing Skinner's glass-sided box, in which he had studied animal behavior; the uniforms of the guards in Zimbardo's Stanford prison experiment; and seven thousand reels of film spanning the entire twentieth century in psychology. But I gave all this just a quick glance. I had come here to see one thing. Finally, we reached the reading room, and David pushed open the door and stepped to one side to reveal Milgram's machine.

My first impression was how big it was, and how real it looked. It was 3 feet long, 15.5 inches high, and 16 inches deep. There was an array of switches, labels, and other buttons and dials—a main power switch, an attenuator, a voltage energizer, a voltage meter—to add to its authenticity. Even switched off and inside a glass case, it was a sinister-looking piece of equipment.

Milgram was inordinately proud of his creation, and intensely proprietary about it. He described it as "more than a stage prop" because "no subject in the experiment, including a score of electrical engineers, ever suspected that the device was a simulated generator."[4] In *Obedience*, the camera lingers over it in close-up, and it is depicted in photographs and drawings in *Obedience to Authority*. If he could have patented the design, he would have.[5] For Milgram, it was an instrument of measurement, classifying people as defiant or obedient, leaders or followers. It had the potential to turn men and women into monsters.

But the shock machine was also what connected the experimenter and the subject, the subject and the victim. It was a symbol, a metaphor. It was proof of scientific credentials, a buffer, a prop.

For many of the subjects, it was an instrument of torture.

I thought of the hundreds of trembling hands that had pushed those levers and of the stuttering voices, the sweating palms, the uncanny laughter. These were the symptoms of distress and agitation that Milgram and others had observed from behind the mirror as they watched each person who sat in front of the long line of switches.

I was disappointed that it was behind glass. I had hoped to touch it—to push the levers, hear its low buzz, watch the lights flash and the needles swing as the machine came to life. Instead, I moved around taking photos, trying to get one where my image was not reflected. After a while David left, and I moved closer and put my hands flat against the glass. I'm not sure what I expected. Perhaps I was hoping that it would hum, that I would feel the power of the machine through my fingers, as in a 1950s science-fiction film.

After I had finished, I sat at one of the tables in the reading room, looking through Solomon Asch's papers. Among them was a letter from Milgram, dated September 1974. Milgram wrote that he hadn't heard from Asch since December 1973, when he had sent him an advance copy of his book and asked if he would appear in Milgram's next documentary.[6] I sat there thinking about what Asch's silence must have meant and how in later years Asch refused to be associated with the research. I realized with a start that I was staring into space at a dusty mass of faded wires—the back of the shock machine. In contrast to the front, which looked so solid and real, the back was simply an empty box, filled with a jumble of wires. It was like the experiment itself: the closer I looked at the inner workings of the experiment, the more contrived and unconvincing the results seemed.

Even the experts have moments of doubt about what the research really meant. Ian Parker wrote that it was disconcerting to hear the then-leading expert on Milgram, Arthur Miller, wonder "if the experiments meant anything at all."[7] Milgram himself had expressed similar doubts soon after the experiments were over: "Sometimes the research does not seem to have advanced my understanding in any important way. And perhaps the way we went about it was the fault."[8] He wrote of a fictional thirteenth-century man called Sylvanus, who wanted to "build a system of knowledge about flames" and decided to study the height of a candle's flame under various conditions, "just as we chose those conditions we thought we alter [sic] the level of obedience." Sylvanus measured the flame at sea level, then halfway up a mountain, then at the mountain's peak. He measured it when there was wind, then when there was none, then with different wicks and at different temperatures, recording it all in his book. Finally, he wrote a treatise, "The Height of a Candle's Flame as It Is Altered by Various Conditions":

> And while he knew he had contributed little, he had the feeling that there was at least something there, something he did not know before. He took his treatise to the wisest man in the realm and asked for his judgement. The wisest man read it carefully, and noted the diligence with which Sylvanus had collected his information, and the exactness with which he worked—more exact perhaps, than any other person in his time. But he said to Sylvanus: "I have read your treatise with interest, and I find your efforts admirable. However, there is a very important question that you did not answer: What is the nature of burning?"
>
> Sylvanus then said: "I am sure that is an important question, but the height of the flame is all I could measure, so that is all I could know."
>
> Then the wise man adjoined: "Pehraps [sic] Sylvanus, if you had climbed fewer mountains, and explored more ideas, you would have found the right method; for in choosing the easy method, you have lost the question."[9]

In Milgram's parable, he is of course the hapless and myopic Sylvanus. It suggests that, even before his findings were published, he sensed that his preoccupation with technique had blinded him to bigger issues of meaning. As François noted, "He was an experimenter looking for results—findings—and it became like an enterprise, a machine, and findings were the products."

The obedience experiments might not be good science, but they are a powerful metaphor, an artistic if not scientific triumph. Through them, Milgram created a dramatic and sinister performance perhaps worthy of Hitchcock with his subjects as actors, Williams in the lead and McDonough offstage in a supporting role.[10] He was a scientist and an artist yearning to take his place among the intellectuals of his time, to contribute something profound to our understanding of such an overwhelming and impenetrable event.

I left Yale's Sterling Memorial Library on the last day of my trip just on closing. Outside, the trees cast deep, inviting shade over the benches in the quadrangle, and I took a seat beneath one. I looked across to Linsly-Chittenden Hall. It was hard to imagine that I'd been surprised that there was no plaque to commemorate Milgram's work. Or to remember a time when I had had so few doubts about the most famous psychological research of the twentieth century.

On the other side of the quadrangle wall, I could hear the faint buzz of New Haven traffic. The leaves of the trees moved, stirred by a faint breeze that soon died again. A cyclist did a lazy figure eight and disappeared through an archway. In that stillness, I tried to recall what I had thought I would find when I first arrived here. I had come in search of those who had taken part in the obedience experiments, and I had found some. Every person had a different story, a particular take on the event and its aftermath.

In the course of my research I had wondered sometimes if it was just that I was easily influenced: swayed by the next person I met, the next opinion I heard, the next article I read. I didn't know if that was true. But I had become certain that, in the journey across the United States, Canada, and Australia, I had traded my admiration of Milgram for a better view of people.

In telling this story, I've probably been just as guilty of shaping, selecting, highlighting, and discounting things that don't fit the narrative I'm trying to tell. Some might say I've worn my own set of blinkers. Psychologists even have a phrase for it: "confirmation bias," which describes the habit of paying attention to those things that confirm our worldview.

Suddenly, the courtyard seemed stifling. I got up quickly and crossed the grass, toward the fresh air, movement—the ebb and flow of life on the footpath. When I had arrived here, I had expected to tell a particular sort of story: a kind of retelling of Milgram's version with a contemporary twist. I hadn't expected that I'd end up with the story you've read and that my view of the profession I'd trained in would be shaken. Just like many of Milgram's subjects, I emerged from the grassy quadrangle and onto the street sensing that a spell had been broken. I blinked in the sudden light and noise. Cars tooted, a bus roared past, and a group of teenagers hooted with laughter on the edge of New Haven Green. People flowed past on their way home from work, and I joined them.

APPENDIX:

LIST OF CONDITIONS

The conditions were conducted in chronological order between August 1961 and May 1962, except for condition 22, which was conducted at various periods during 1961 and 1962.

1. No feedback

This variation tests how an almost silent learner may affect obedience. The learner, in the adjoining room, does not cry out. Nothing is heard from him until the twentieth shock (300 volts), when he pounds on the wall. He pounds again at 315 volts, and then is silent.

Number of subjects: 40
Number who went to 450 volts: 65 percent

2. Voice feedback

Perhaps the best-known variation, this tests the effect of a vocal learner as the teacher hears his cries and shouts from the adjoining room. The first sound from the learner is a grunt at the fifth shock (75 volts). At the tenth shock (150 volts), he demands to be let out. His protests and cries increase in intensity with each subsequent shock.

Number of subjects: 40
Number who went to 450 volts: 62 percent

3. Proximity

Follows the same script as above, except that the learner is in the same room as the teacher, seated 50 centimeters behind him.

Number of subjects: 40
Number who went to 450 volts: 40 percent

4. Touch

To test the effect of physical contact, the learner and the teacher are in the same room. In order to receive the shock, the learner must put his hand on a metal plate. At the tenth shock (150 volts), he refuses. The experimenter instructs the teacher to continue the shocks and hold the learner's hand to the plate each time.
Number of subjects: 40
Number who went to 450 volts: 30 percent

5. Coronary trouble

In this variation, the learner mentions heart trouble at the beginning of the experiment and, seated in the adjoining room, protests about his heart during the process. The script is the same as in condition 2.
Number of subjects: 40
Number who went to 450 volts: 65 percent

6. Different actors

This variation is the same as condition 5, except that different actors are used for roles of the learner and the experimenter. Emil Elgiss plays the experimenter and Bob Tracy plays the learner.
Number of subjects: 40
Number who went to 450 volts: 50 percent

7. Group pressure to disobey

Three teachers are chosen, two of whom are actors. Teacher one reads the word-pair questions, teacher two (the subject) reads the voltage and administers punishment, and teacher three reads the correct answer after punishment. After the eleventh shock (165 volts), the first teacher refuses to continue. The experimenter fails to convince him to go on but instructs the other two to continue. At the fourteenth shock (210 volts), the third teacher also refuses, leaving the subject to conduct the experiment while the others look on.

Number of subjects: 40
Number who went to 450 volts: 10 percent

8. The learner's proviso

To test the effect of the learner's preferences, the learner states at the outset that he will only agree to participate if he can leave when he wants. When he demands to be let out at the tenth shock (150 volts), the experimenter tells the teacher to continue regardless of the learner's wishes.

Number of subjects: 40
Number who went to 450 volts: 40 percent

9. Group pressure to obey

This variation is the same as condition 7 in the division of tasks between three teachers, except that two teachers (both actors) obey the experimenter's instructions and mutter their disapproval if the third teacher, the unwitting subject, hesitates or refuses to continue.

Number of subjects: 40
Number who went to 450 volts: 72 percent

10. Conflicting instructions*

The learner receives one message from a benign experimenter and another from an enthusiastic learner. In Part A, when the experimenter hears the learner's complaints about his heart at the tenth shock (150 volts), he tells the teacher to stop, but the learner wants to keep going. In Part B, the experimenter leaves the room on a pretense, and the learner implores the teacher to continue.

Number of subjects: 20
Number who went to 450 volts: 100 percent (Part A); 66 percent (Part B). Milgram's notes read: "Note special meaning of defiant and obedient in this condition. To obey is to stop giving shocks after the exptr. calls halt to expt. Defiant means to give shocks after exptr. stops expt."

11. Group choice

Milgram noted that this was an experiment in conformity, rather than obedience. Three teachers, two of whom are actors, are told that they can determine what level of shock to give the learner with each wrong answer. Each teacher puts in a bid for voltage level, with the lowest-voltage shock to be given. The two actors give their bids first, with the subject the last to suggest a shock level. The actors increase the suggested amount each time and pressure the unwitting teacher to follow their lead.

Number of subjects: 40
Number who went to 450 volts: 16 percent

12. Role reversal*

This variation tests the experimenter's authority as the victim. The learner states that he will only take on the role if the experimenter tries it first. The experimenter agrees and is strapped into the chair and given the shocks while the learner takes on the role of the experimenter, urging the teacher to continue.

Number of subjects: 20
Number who went to 450 volts: 100 percent. Milgram's notes read: "An obedient subject is one who obeys the exptr. and does not go on, after the experimenter demands to be let out."

13. Non-trigger position

This is identical to condition 7 in the allocation of tasks to three teachers, except that the subject simply reads the word pairs instead of administering the shocks. The shocks are given by one of the two actors.

Number of subjects: 40
Number who went to 450 volts: 92 percent

14. Carte blanche

In this variation, the teacher can choose any shock level he wishes in order to test how far a person would go without the experimenter's commands. It is akin to a control condition, designed to test the "sadistic and bestial in man."

Number of subjects: 40
Number who went to 450 volts: 2 percent

15. Good experimenter, bad experimenter*

In Part A, two experimenters conduct the experiment, and each gives the teacher conflicting orders—one tells him to stop, while the other tells him he must continue. In Part B, the "good" experimenter, who urged the subject to stop, leaves the room and the "bad" experimenter insists that the teacher continue.

Number of subjects: 20

Number who went to 450 volts: 0 percent (Part A); 20 percent (Part B)

16. Experimenter becomes learner

Again, two experimenters conduct the experiment, but one answers a rigged phone call announcing that the learner won't be coming. One experimenter volunteers to become the learner. The second experimenter conducts the experiment as per the script in condition two, urging the teacher to continue giving shocks despite the learner's protests.

Number of subjects: 20

Number who went to 450 volts: 65 percent

17. Teacher in charge*

This variation involves two teachers, one of whom is an actor. The experimenter is called away, but before leaving he asks one teacher (the actor) to plan the number and voltage of shocks to be given at each incorrect answer, which the second teacher must follow. In Part A, the actor instructs the subject to increase the voltage with each wrong answer. In Part B, the experimenter returns soon after leaving and urges the subject to follow the actor's plan.

Number of subjects: 20

Number who went to 450 volts: 55 percent (Part A); 15 percent (Part B)

18. No experimenter*

The experimenter is called away from the lab by a rigged phone call. Before leaving, he tells the teacher to conduct the experiment alone and leaves a phone number on which he can be reached. In Part A, if the teacher calls him, the experimenter says that he must continue. In Part B, the experimenter returns soon after leaving and urges the teacher to continue.

Number of subjects: 40

Number who went to 450 volts: 25 percent (Part A); 33 percent (Part B)

19. Authority from afar

To test the relationship between authority and proximity, the teacher arrives and has the experiment explained to him, after which the experimenter tells him that he has to leave but the teacher should follow the instructions prerecorded on tape. A phone in the room allows the teacher to call the experimenter if needed.

Number of subjects: 40
Number who went to 450 volts: 37 percent

20. Women

The only variation to use female subjects, this is the same as condition 5 except for the gender of participants.

Number of subjects: 40
Number who went to 450 volts: 65 percent

21. Educated opinion

In this variation, no questions or shocks are administered. Rather, a group of psychiatrists and students have condition 2 described to them and are asked to predict the overall levels of obedience.

Number of subjects: 110 (Yale psychiatrists, graduate students, and undergraduates and North Carolina high school students)

Obedience rate predicted: The groups combined predicted that only 1 or 2 percent of people would reach the maximum voltage. The psychiatrists predicted that most would not go beyond the tenth shock (150 volts), the point at which the learner first demands to be let out. They thought that only 4 percent would reach the twentieth shock (300 volts), and one in a thousand would go to the maximum voltage.

22. Peer authority*

This variation involves two teachers, one of whom is an actor. In Part A, the experimenter is called away by a rigged phone call and asks the actor to take over his role. Part B occurs if the subject refuses to continue; the actor then takes over at the shock machine, and the experiment concludes when the subject performs a physical action, such as switching off the machine or restraining the actor.

Number of subjects: 20

Number who went to 450 volts: 20 percent (Part A); 50 percent (Part B)

23. Bridgeport

To test the influence of the Yale setting on subjects, this variation was conducted in the nearby town of Bridgeport, an industrial area. The condition is otherwise the same as condition 5.

Number of subjects: 40

Number who went to 450 volts: 47 percent

24. Intimate relationships

In this highly controversial and little-known variation, subjects are asked to bring a friend or relative. One is allocated the role of the teacher, while the other is the learner. In the adjoining room, after being strapped in, the learner is clued in to the situation by Milgram and coached on what noises and shouts to give at which points.

Number of subjects: 20

Number who went to 450 volts: 15 percent

* A particularly complicated variation. For example, a variation in which the experiment is divided into Parts A and B or definitions of obedience and defiance are reversed.

ACKNOWLEDGMENTS

I'd like to thank Dr. Thomas Blass, whose enthusiasm sparked the idea for this book, and New Zealand scholar Nestar Russell, whose friendship and encouragement kept me going. Both generously shared their research with me and offered sound advice and practical help at many critical points in the research and writing of this book.

I'm very grateful to Mrs. Alexandra Milgram for permission to quote from material held in the Stanley Milgram Papers. I'm also indebted to the people who shared their experiences of the experiment and allowed me to tell their stories. Some, such as Bob McDonough and Keith Williams, helped by tracking down information for me between trips and tapping their own networks to locate people for me to interview.

I'd also like to thank the people whose experiences did not make it into these pages but whose memories added so much to my research: Lenore Mendes, Alex Bozzi III, Sharon Presley, and Professor Leon Mann.

Others who have shared their expertise and helped my thinking include Don Mixon, whose continued conversations with me by letter prompted me to consider things from a different perspective; Justin Oakley of Monash University; Rod Buchanan of the University of Melbourne; Ian Nicholson of St. Thomas University in New Brunswick; Stephen Gibson of York St. John University; Sue Hampel of Monash University; and Hank Stam of the University of Calgary.

David Baker and the staff at the Archives of the History of American

Psychology in Akron ensured my visits were both productive and enjoyable. Diane Kaplan, Cynthia Ostroff, Stephen Ross, and the rest of the staff at the Manuscripts and Archives Collection at Yale provided a wonderful service to me, both face-to-face and long distance.

Thanks to Dr. Tony Birch and Jenny Lee at the University of Melbourne, who saw the germ of a good book in my academic research, and to others who provided insightful comments on early drafts: Ming Ding, Vin Maskell, and Bob Gregory from Victoria University in Wellington, New Zealand. Thanks also to Sharon Davis and Sydelle Kramer, who in different ways helped me to sharpen my focus.

I'm grateful to those scholars and historians whose books and articles I have read in the course of my research. Without their scholarship it would have been impossible for me to write this book.

My American cousins made me feel at home with their hospitality and friendship. Melissa and Carl Shultz were extremely generous and responded each of the many times I asked for help with research details and my Weideman cousins went out of their way to welcome me. Closer to home, I am fortunate to have a bevy of friends and colleagues who kept me motivated; those in particular who helped me in the writing include Sherryl Clark, Chris Beck, and Deb Withers. My good friend Janey Runci provided invaluable feedback on later drafts, as well as encouragement during those times when I felt dejected or overwhelmed.

Henry Rosenbloom and the staff at Scribe welcomed me to their stable and took a great deal of care and thought with the Australian edition of this book. My editor at Scribe, Julia Carlomagno, offered inspired suggestions for improving the shape and pace of this story and patiently guided me through the process of redrafting and editing.

I'm very pleased to have worked with editor Sarah Fan and assistant editor Ben Woodward at The New Press. Their insightful feedback helped me shape the book for an American audience and their enthusiasm for this book made the editing process a pleasure. Thanks also to George Lucas of Inkwell Management and my Australian agent Clare Forster of Curtis Brown whose advice throughout this process was invaluable.

Lastly, I could never have finished this book without my loving family. Thanks to my sister, Jane, and my daughter, Georgia, for all their help with the fine detail, and to my husband, Dan, for his unflagging support, for putting up with my frequent absences, and for living with things Milgram for so long and with such good grace and humor.

NOTES

SMP = Stanley Milgram Papers, Manuscripts and Archives, Yale University
Library

INTRODUCTION

1. *Obedience to Authority: An Experimental View* (London: Tavistock, 1974), 26.

2. SMP, box 46, folder 163.

3. See Hannah Arendt, "Eichmann in Jerusalem," *New Yorker*, serialized in five issues, February 16, 1963–March 16, 1963; and *Eichmann in Jerusalem: A Report into the Banality of Evil* (New York: Penguin, 1963).

4. Milgram, *Obedience to Authority*, 6, 188–89.

5. Milgram argued that his results gave an insight into Nazi behavior and the My Lai massacre (ibid., 176). Thomas Blass made the link to events at Abu Ghraib prison in *The Man Who Shocked the World: The Life and Legacy of Stanley Milgram* (New York: Basic, 2004), 296.

6. See James H. Korn, *Illusions of Reality: A History of Deception in Social Psychology* (Albany: State University of New York Press, 1997).

7. Caryl Marsh reported that Roger Brown described the experiments as among the most important psychological research in the twentieth century in "A Science Museum Exhibit on Milgram's Obedience Research," in *Obedience to Authority: Current Perspectives on the Milgram Paradigm*, ed. Thomas Blass (Mahwah, NJ: Lawrence Erlbaum Associates, 2000),

147. Hans Askenasy quoted Bruno Bettelheim's description of the experiments as "vile" and linked Milgram's research and Nazism in *Are We All Nazis?* (Secaucus, NJ: Lyle Stuart, 1978), 131.

8. SMP, box 44.

9. SMP, box 62, folder 162.

10. In the Stanford study, which took place in a mock prison, volunteers were randomly assigned the role of either prisoner or guard. Guards took their roles seriously, taunting, harassing, and abusing the prisoners in their charge.

11. Philip Zimbardo et al., "Reflections on the Stanford Prison Experiment: Genesis, Transformations, Consequences," in *Obedience to Authority*, 197.

12. Stanley Milgram, "*Candid Camera*," in *The Individual in a Social World: Essays and Experiments* (Reading, MA: Addison-Wesley, 1977), 324–32.

13. See David Chazan, "Row over 'Torture' on French TV," BBC News, March 18, 2010.

1. THE MAN BEHIND THE MIRROR

1. Biographical information about Milgram's childhood, schooling, travels, and time at Harvard based on information in Thomas Blass, *The Man Who Shocked the World: The Life and Legacy of Stanley Milgram* (New York: Basic, 2004), 2, 3, 4, 10–15, 33, 57–58, 232–34; and SMP, box 71, folder 293.

2. The experiment and findings are discussed in Solomon Asch, *Social Psychology* (New York: Prentice-Hall, 1952), 454–58.

3. Henry Gleitman cited in James H. Korn, *Illusions of Reality: A History of Deception in Social Psychology* (Albany: State University of New York Press, 1997), 73.

4. James Korn noted that Asch was troubled by the ethics of his experiments and devoted more analysis to them than many contemporaries did theirs. Ibid., 74–79.

5. Blass, *Man Who Shocked the World*, 33.

6.   Stanley Milgram, "Nationality and Conformity," *Scientific American* 205, no. 34 (1961): 45–51.

7.   Stanley Milgram, *The Individual in a Social World: Essays and Experiments* (Reading, MA: Addison-Wesley, 1977), 217.

8.   Blass, *Man Who Shocked the World*, 57–58.

9.   SMP, box 14, folder 201.

10.   SMP, box 1a, folder 1.

11.   Kurt Danziger explored how Wundt adapted his training in *Constructing the Subject: Historical Origins of Psychological Research* (Cambridge: Cambridge University Press, 1990), 17. Robert Farr noted students flocking to Europe in *The Roots of Modern Social Psychology, 1872–1954* (Oxford: Blackwell, 1996), 35.

12.   Wundt's views from Farr, *Roots of Modern Social Psychology*, 21.

13.   See Danziger, *Constructing the Subject*, 41.

14.   Ibid., 53.

15.   Ludy T. Benjamin, *A Brief History of Modern Psychology* (Oxford: Blackwell, 2006), 139.

16.   John Watson quoted in B.R. Hergenhahn, *An Introduction to the History of Psychology*, 6th ed. (Belmont, CA: Wadsworth Cengage Learning, 2009), 406.

17.   See John B. Watson, *Behaviorism* (New York: W.W. Norton, 1925).

18.   Clarence J. Karier noted this in *Scientists of the Mind: Intellectual Founders of Modern Psychology* (Urbana: University of Illinois Press, 1986), 130.

19.   Dorwin Cartwright quoted in Farr, *Roots of Modern Social Psychology*, 6.

20.   Benjamin, *Brief History of Modern Psychology*, 199.

21.   See Alfred Marrow, *Practical Theorist: The Life and Work of Kurt Lewin* (New York: Basic, 1969), 128. Marrow defined action research as "the experimental use of social sciences to advance the democratic process."

22.   Kenneth Ring, "Experimental Social Psychology: Some Sober Questions About Some Frivolous Values," *Journal of Experimental Social Psychology* 3 (1967): 114.

23. Korn, *Illusions of Reality*, 46.

24. Marrow, *Practical Theorist*, 140. Despite Lewin's frantic attempts over seven years to find a way of bringing his mother to the United States, he was unable to save her. She was sent to a Polish concentration camp and died there in 1944.

25. Korn, *Illusions of Reality*, 42.

26. Shelley Patnoe, *A Narrative History of Experimental Social Psychology: The Lewin Tradition* (New York: Springer, 1998), 262.

27. Ibid., 261.

28. Elliot Aronson, "Adventures in Experimental Social Psychology: Roots, Branches, and Sticky Leaves," in *Reflections on 100 Years of Experimental Social Psychology*, ed. Aroldo Rodrigues and Robert Levine (New York: Basic, 1999), 87. Successive quotations ibid., 88.

29. Vivien Burr, *Social Constructionism* (New York: Routledge, 2003), 14.

30. These experiments are cited in Herbert Kelman, "Human Use of Human Subjects: The Problem of Deception in Social Psychological Experiments," *Psychological Bulletin* 67 (1967): 5.

31. See Philip M. Taylor, *Munitions of the Mind: A History of Propaganda from the Ancient World to the Present Day*, 3rd ed. (Manchester: Manchester University Press, 2003), 260.

32. During the Cold War, the CIA covertly funded a range of research programs aimed at finding ways to manipulate behavior. Alfred W. McCoy claimed that Milgram's experiment was secretly funded by the CIA as part of its interest in research on effective torture techniques and, in particular, how to persuade ordinary people to take on the torturer's role. Thomas Blass and others dismissed this. See Alfred McCoy, *A Question of Torture: CIA Interrogation, from the Cold War to the War on Terror* (New York: Metropolitan Books, 2006), 47; and Thomas Blass, "Milgram and the CIA—Not!" StanleyMilgram.com, www.stanley milgram.com/rebuttal.php.

33. Korn surveyed social psychology articles published between 1930 and 1970 that reported using deception as a research technique and found that the degree and intensity of deception increased from less than 10 percent between 1930 and 1945 to 50 percent in the 1970s. See Korn, *Illusions of Reality*, 24.

34. See Elliot Aronson, *Methods of Research in Social Psychology* (New York: McGraw-Hill, 1990), 83.

35. The experiment involving insults is cited in Korn, *Illusions of Reality*, 132; that involving homosexual tendencies is cited in Kelman, "Human Use of Human Subjects," 4; and that which required the reading of sexually explicit material is cited in Ian Lubek and Henderikus J. Stam, "Ludicro-Experimentation in Social Psychology: Sober Scientific Versus Playful Prescriptions," in *Trends and Issues in Theoretical Psychology*, ed. Ian Lubek et al. (New York: Springer, 1995), 174.

36. Benjamin Harris, "Key Words: A History of Debriefing in Social Psychology," in *The Rise of Experimentation in American Psychology*, ed. Jill Morawski (New Haven, CT: Yale University Press, 1988), 190.

37. Philip Zimbardo, "Experimental Social Psychology: Behaviorism with Minds and Matters," in *Reflections on 100 Years of Experimental Social Psychology*, 138. Successive quotations ibid.

38. SMP, box 17, folder 246.

39. SMP, box 1a, folder 4.

40. SMP, box 43, folder 126.

41. Parker claimed that the experiments would "make his name and destroy his reputation." See Ian Parker, "Obedience," *Granta* 71, no. 4 (2000): 102. Subsequent quotation, "cited, celebrated—and reviled," in ibid., 101.

42. Ibid., 101.

43. Augustine Brannigan, "The Postmodern Experiment: Science and Ontology in Experimental Social Psychology," *British Journal of Sociology* 48, no. 4 (1997): 608.

2. GOING ALL THE WAY

1. SMP, box 46, folder 165. The book was Nathaniel Cantor, *The Teaching–Learning Process* (New York: Holt, Rinehart, and Winston, 1953).

2. SMP, box 45, folder 161.

3. "Simplicity is the key to effective scientific inquiry. . . . Complicated procedures only get in the way of clear scrutiny of the phenomenon

itself. To study obedience most simply, we must create a situation in which one person orders another person to perform an observable action and we must note when obedience to the imperative occurs and when it fails." Stanley Milgram, *Obedience to Authority: An Experimental View* (London: Tavistock, 1974), 13.

4.   Wendy McKenna and Suzanne Kessler, "Asking Taboo Questions and Doing Taboo Deeds," in *The Social Construction of the Person*, ed. K.J. Gergen and K.G. Davis (New York: Springer-Verlag, 1985), 253.

5.   Thomas Blass, *The Man Who Shocked the World: The Life and Legacy of Stanley Milgram* (New York: Basic, 2004), 63.

6.   Nestar Russell, "Stanley Milgram's Obedience to Authority Experiments: Towards an Understanding of Their Relevance in Explaining Aspects of the Nazi Holocaust," PhD thesis, Victoria University of Wellington, 2009, 43, 44.

7.   Milgram wrote to his mentor Gordon Allport about comparing obedience. His letter is cited in Blass, *Man Who Shocked the World*, 65. Ian Nicholson notes the content of his funding applications in "Shocking Masculinity: Stanley Milgram, *Obedience to Authority* and the 'Crisis of Manhood' in Cold War America," *Isis* 102, no. 2 (2011): 243.

8.   Russell, "Stanley Milgram's Obedience to Authority Experiments," 47.

9.   SMP, box 43, folder 126. Subsequent quotations ibid.

10.   SMP, box 45, folder 160.

11.   SMP, box 75, folder 435.

12.   Milgram cited in Blass, *Man Who Shocked the World*, 68.

13.   SMP, box 43, folder 126.

14.   SMP, box 1a, folder 3.

15.   SMP, box 23, folder 382.

16.   SMP, box 46, folder 163.

17.   SMP, box 1a, folder 5.

18.   Ibid.

19.   According to Milgram's figures, 37.6 percent were skilled and unskilled workers; 44 percent were sales, business, and white-collar workers; 16.8 percent were "professional" (by which he presumably meant

college-educated, although he did not explain this anywhere). Twenty-four percent of volunteers were twenty to twenty-nine, 33.6 percent were thirty to thirty-nine, and 42.4 percent were forty to fifty years old. SMP, box 46, folder 163.

20. SMP, box 46, folder 163.

21. SMP, box 47, folder 12.

22. Alan Elms, *Social Psychology and Social Relevance* (Boston: Little, Brown, 1972), 120.

23. SMP, box 61, folder 122.

24. Quotations about Williams and McDonough in SMP, box 61, folder 122. Milgram's comment to subject in long interviews, March 21, 1963, 50, in SMP, box 45, folder 162.

25. Milgram in Carol Tavris, "A Sketch of Stanley Milgram: A Man of 1,000 Ideas," *Psychology Today* 8 (1974): 75.

26. Alan Elms, "Obedience in Retrospect," *Journal of Social Issues* 51, no. 3 (1995): 21–31, available at www.ulmus.net/ace/library/obedience.html.

27. SMP, box 46, folder 163.

28. Ibid.

29. Improvements to laboratory in ibid. and in SMP box 19, folder 2. Grueling schedule in box 46, folder 163.

30. Kurt Danziger, *Constructing the Subject: Historical Origins of Psychological Research* (Cambridge: Cambridge University Press, 1990), 2.

31. Baumrind quoted in Arthur G. Miller, *The Obedience Experiments: A Case Study of Controversy in Social Science* (New York: Praeger, 1986), 103.

32. SMP, box 62, folder 126.

33. SMP, box 45, folder 158.

34. Subject numbers were allocated to each participant. They were three or four digits long, depending on the condition. The first digit(s) identified the number of the condition the subject was in, ranging from 1 to 24. The second two digits indicated which number they were. For example, Subject 623 was the twenty-third person in condition 6, Subject 801 was the first person in condition 8, and Subject 2421 was the twenty-first person in condition 24. Subject comments from SMP, box 44.

3. THE LIMITS OF DEBRIEFING

1. SMP, box 62, folder 126.

2. James Wilkinson, "They Were Only Obeying Orders," *Radio Times*, October 24, 1974, in SMP, box 22, folder 354.

3. Stanley Milgram, "Behavioral Study of Obedience," *Journal of Abnormal Psychology* 67, no. 4 (1963): 374.

4. Stanley Milgram, "Issues in the Study of Obedience: A Reply to Baumrind," *American Psychologist* 19, no. 11 (1964): 849.

5. SMP, box 46, folder 163.

6. SMP, box 46, folder 165.

7. If you are interested in reading Alan's article, see Alan Elms, "Twelve Ways to Say 'Lonesome': Assessing Error and Control in the Music of Elvis Presley," in *The Handbook of Psychobiography*, ed. William Schultz (New York: Oxford University Press, 2005), 142–57.

8. Benjamin Harris, "Key Words: A History of Debriefing in Social Psychology," in *The Rise of Experimentation in American Psychology*, ed. Jill Morawski (New Haven, CT: Yale University Press, 1988), 194.

9. SMP, box 45, folder 160.

10. SMP, box 46, folder 163.

11. SMP, box 45, folder 160.

12. On the second page of the report, the following sentence is bolded and underlined: "The other man did not receive any shocks." SMP, box 45, folder 159.

13. Questionnaires for subjects 629, 805, 716, 1817, 711, 216, 829, and 623 in SMP, box 44.

14. Subject 501's wife's comments and exchange between Milgram and Subject 501, in long interviews, March 21, 1963, 24, 50, 55, in SMP, box 45, folder 162. The March 21 interview included Dr. Paul Errera, Subject 501, his wife, and Subject 612. Both subjects had been in the "heart attack" condition and gone to 450 volts.

15. Tapes 301, 331, and 332, SMP, box 155.

16. Alan also described Milgram's debriefing process in his article "Keeping

Deception Honest," in *Ethical Issues in Social Science Research*, ed. Tom Beauchamp et al. (Baltimore: Johns Hopkins University Press, 1982), 232–45. Alan described the debriefing: "He told volunteers as soon as their participation was over that the victim hadn't gotten nearly as much shock as they'd thought. Then Milgram waited for several months, until the bulk of the studies was completed, to notify participants fully of the experiment's purpose, the extent of the deceptions, and the early results, as well as emphasizing the value of their participation. Volunteers who participated after the experimental series was further along were told immediately afterwards exactly what was going on."

17. Milgram said, "I watched many of the experiments—perhaps a third of them—but about two thirds I did not see." Long interviews, March 21, 1963, 59, in SMP box 45, folder 162.

18. SMP, box 1a, folder 3.

19. In a November 1961 letter to a former subject who had confessed his suspicions, Milgram wrote, "You are one of the very few people to know about the true purpose of the 'Memory and Learning Project.' We will be conducting experiments through the academic year 1961–2, and I would appreciate your maintaining secrecy until the experiments are over." Letter held in SMP, box 46, folder 169.

20. SMP, box 44.

21. Tape 2316, SMP, box 153.

22. Tape 2340, SMP, box 153.

23. SMP, box 70, folder 283.

24. SMP, box 46, folder 173.

25. SMP, box 45, folder 159.

26. SMP, box 46, folder 163.

4. SUBJECTS AS OBJECTS

1. Hannah Bergman is a pseudonym.

2. Irwin Silverman, *The Human Subject in the Psychological Laboratory* (New York: Pergamon Press, 1977), 8–9.

3. Thomas Blass wrote that Milgram took a colleague's criticism to heart: "After hearing Milgram describe his pilot studies and its findings, the

colleague dismissed it as having no relevance to the ordinary man in the street. Yale students, he asserted, were so aggressive and competitive that they would step on each other's necks with little provocation." Blass, *The Man Who Shocked the World: The Life and Legacy of Stanley Milgram* (New York: Basic, 2004), 70.

4.   Ian Nicholson noted this in "Shocking Masculinity: Stanley Milgram, *Obedience to Authority* and the 'Crisis of Manhood' in Cold War America," *Isis* 102, no. 2 (2011): 243.

5.   SMP, box 43, folder 128.

6.   Jerome Karabel detailed the Yale admissions process in *The Chosen: The Hidden History of Exclusion at Harvard, Yale, and Princeton* (New York: Mariner Books, 2006), 327. Ron Rosenbaum's article "The Great Ivy League Nude Posture Photo Scandal," *New York Times*, January 15, 1995, reported the discovery of a cache of photographs of naked Yale freshmen.

7.   Although Kirsten Fermaglich (*American Dreams and Nazi Nightmares: Early Holocaust Consciousness and Liberal America, 1957–65* [Waltham, MA: Brandeis University Press, 2006]) found no evidence of Milgram suffering in his formative years as a result of anti-Semitism, prejudice against Jews was an open secret in academic psychology between the 1920s and the 1950s. Andrew Winston recounted how prominent American psychologist E.G. Boring wrote hundreds of letters of reference for Jewish students and colleagues, and frequently referred to their Jewishness in his appraisal of their suitability for the position. See Andrew S. Winston, "The Defects of His Race: E.G. Boring and Anti-Semitism in American Psychology," *History of Psychology* 1, no. 1 (1998): 27–51. In addition, twenty years earlier leading psychologist Harry Harlow, born Harry Israel, was urged by his mentor Lewis Terman to change his surname in order to get a job in academia. See Deborah Blum, *Love at Goon Park: Harry Harlow and the Science of Affection* (New York: Basic, 2002), 29.

8.   The first record of female graduates is in *Yale Statistics and Timelines*, www.yale.edu/oir/book_numbers_updated. Information about the Yale School of Nursing at "*Lux et Veritas*: History and Contributions of the Yale University School of Nursing," www.med.yale.edu/library/nursing /historical. The first woman to receive tenure was Bessie Lee Gambrill, who was tenured in the education department. Information about women and libraries at "Women at Yale," www.yale.edu/womenatyale /LinoniaBrothers.html.

9. Comments from subject questionnaires and interviews reveal that subjects up to and including condition 18 and 19 had not been informed of the experiment's real purpose. For example, one man in condition 18 told Errera, "The actor came out and put on his coat and mentioned that 'I told you I had a bum heart and been in the Veterans Hospital'—he said he just wanted to leave and he did, put on his coat and he left. . . . I thought a lot about it and I wish that I could have gotten some indication that it was a hoax." Long interviews, April 18, 1963, 24, in SMP, box 155a, folder 162. In an interview with four women, Errera asked how they felt when they got the letter explaining the experiment. The women told him that they were told the same day, right after the experiment. Errera responded, "Apparently they changed their technique. I thought you didn't know for several weeks." Long interviews, April 25, 1963, 35, in SMP, box 155a, folder 162.

10. See Williams's comments to Subject 2001.

11. Philip Zimbardo noted that "when I asked about his research, Stanley chose not to share his ideas or emerging data with me (or anyone else, I gather). He said that he preferred to wait until his work was published." Quoted in Philip Zimbardo et al., "Reflections on the Stanford Prison Experiment: Genesis, Transformations, Consequences," in *Obedience to Authority: Current Perspectives on the Milgram Paradigm*, ed. Thomas Blass (Mahwah, NJ: Lawrence Erlbaum Associates, 2000), 195.

12. Solomon Asch, *Social Psychology* (New York: Prentice-Hall, 1952), 454.

13. SMP, box 122.

14. Ibid.

15. Ibid.

16. Long interviews, February 28, 1963, 34, in SMP, box 155a.

17. Long interviews, March 14, 1963, 16, in SMP, box 155a.

18. Long interviews, April 4, 1963, 14, in SMP, box 155a.

19. Long interviews, February 28, 1963, 4.

20. Long interviews, April 4, 1963, 16, 17.

21. Subject 2020, SMP, box 122.

22. Subject 2030, SMP, box 44.

23. Kirsten Fermaglich noted Milgram's reluctance to discuss his Jewish

background in *American Dreams and Nazi Nightmares*, 97. Milgram's quotation in SMP, box 70, folder 291.

24. SMP, box 46, folder 165.

25. Subject comments in SMP, box 44.

26. Long interviews, April 11, 1962, 31, in SMP, box 155a.

27. The alderman (Subject 919)'s letter is dated December 19, 1961. SMP, box 46, folder 169. He recounted the effects at Yale and on the Holocaust survivor in the long interviews, April 11, 1962, 10.

28. Milgram's notes on the phone call with the alderman in SMP, box 46, folder 169.

29. Long interviews, April 11, 1962, 14, 27.

30. Subjects 2032, 2034, and 2302 in SMP, box 44.

31. Long interviews, February 28, 1963, 19.

32. Long interviews, April 4, 1963, 40.

33. Stanley Milgram, *Obedience to Authority: An Experimental View* (London: Tavistock, 1974), 63.

34. Subjects 2005 and 2302 in SMP, box 44.

35. Subject 2020, SMP, box 122.

36. I couldn't compare condition 20 to any other conditions except 3 because the only sanitized recordings available at the time of my research were conditions 3, 20, 23, and 24.

37. Nestar Russell, "Stanley Milgram's Obedience to Authority Experiments: Towards an Understanding of Their Relevance in Explaining Aspects of the Nazi Holocaust," PhD thesis, Victoria University of Wellington, 2009, 182.

38. Subject 2013 was instructed to continue twenty-six times; subjects 2026 and 2005, fourteen times each; Subject 2032, eleven times; Subject 2003, nine times; and Subject 2009, eight times. Williams's interaction with Subject 2014 ended in an "argument," Subject 2028 paced and argued with Williams, and Subject 2040 argued with him fourteen times. SMP, box 122. The women described being "railroaded" by Williams in the long interviews, April 25, 1963, 38.

39. SMP, box 44.

40. Arthur G. Miller, *The Obedience Experiments: A Case Study of Controversy in Social Science* (New York: Praeger, 1986), 7.

41. Blass, *Man Who Shocked the World*, 85.

42. Russell, "Stanley Milgram's Obedience to Authority Experiments," 173.

43. Stanley Milgram, "Behavioral Study of Obedience," *Journal of Abnormal Psychology* 67, no. 4 (1963): 374.

44. Alan Elms, "Keeping Deception Honest: Justifying Conditions for Social Scientific Research Stratagems," in *Ethical Issues in Social Science Research*, ed. Tom Beauchamp et al. (Baltimore: Johns Hopkins University Press, 1982), 241.

45. Elliot Aronson noted the concept of "*bubbe* psychology" in "Adventures in Experimental Social Psychology: Roots, Branches, and Sticky Leaves," in *Reflections on 100 Years of Experimental Social Psychology*, ed. Aroldo Rodrigues and Robert Levine (New York: Basic, 1999), 91.

46. Subject 2026 and Subject 2004 in the long interviews, April 25, 1963, 22, 23, 25.

47. Subject 2003, SMP, box 44.

48. Long interviews, April 25, 1963, 12, 16, 19, 43, 44.

49. See Diana Baumrind, "Research Using Intentional Deception: Ethical Issues Revisited," *American Psychologist*, 40, no. 2 (February 1985): 165–74.

50. SMP, box 44.

5. DISOBEDIENCE

1. Milgram in fact tested a similar scenario in his lab: condition 7. For a full description, see "Condition 7, Groups for Disobedience," SMP, box 46, folder 163.

2. Stanley Milgram, *Obedience to Authority: An Experimental View* (London: Tavistock, 1974), 172.

3. The subject's letter and Milgram's response are in SMP, box 1a, folder 3.

4. Ibid.

5. Subjects 408, 502, 722, 1914, and 929 in SMP, box 44.

6. Unidentified subjects and Subject 508 in the long interviews, February 28, 1963, 30, 31, 12, in SMP, box 45, folder 162.

7. Long interviews, April 18, 1963, 2, 4, 13, 25, in SMP, box 45, folder 162.

8. The man who took part in the condition was Subject 1817, quoted in long interviews, February 28, 1963, 8. Letters in the archives also show that the experimenter took the doorknob off the door until Milgram managed to replace it with one that locked with a key; see SMP, box 1a, folder 3.

9. Unidentified subject, long interviews, March 21, 1963, 28, in SMP, box 45, folder 162; Subject 1831, long interviews, February 28, 1963, 14; and Subject 1434 in SMP, box 44.

10. Long interviews, April 11, 1963, 9, in SMP, box 45, folder 162.

11. Ian Parker, "Obedience," *Granta* 71, no. 4 (2000): 118.

12. Martin Orne and Charles Holland, "On the Ecological Validity of Laboratory Deceptions," *International Journal of Psychiatry* 6 (1968): 282–93.

13. Milgram wrote that "the experiment is a nerve shattering experience, a reaction that is highly improbable if the subject does not think he is hurting the learner . . . it is clear . . . that the vast majority of subjects accepted the experiment at face validity. A small proportion of subjects do deny that the learner was being hurt; on occasion this denial reflected technical inadequacies of the experimental procedure; other times . . . as denial functions as a primitive defense mechanism, for some." SMP, box 61, folder 118.

14. Taketo Murata's unpublished analysis is titled "Reported Belief in Shocks and Level of Obedience," in SMP, box 45, folder 158.

15. SMP, box 75, folder 430.

16. SMP, box 95, folder 7.

17. Milgram kept clippings about the protests, such as "400 Arrested at Johnson's Restaurant," *News and Observer*, May 20, 1963, in SMP, box 29, folder 61.

18. SMP, box 75, folder 430.

19. Unnamed subjects in conversation with Errera, March 21, 1963, 3; April 4, 1963, 30; March 21, 1963, 3; and March 14, 1963, 25, in SMP, box 45, folder 162.

20. Milgram, *Obedience to Authority*, 68.

21. Martin Orne, "On the Social Psychology of the Psychological Experiment: With Particular Reference to Demand Characteristics and Their Implications," *American Psychologist* 17 (1962): 189–200.

22. Subject 2006 in SMP, box 44.

23. Unidentified subjects, long interviews, April 4, 1963, 2, 21, 27, in SMP, box 45, folder 162.

24. Milgram, *Obedience to Authority*, 68.

25. Tapes 2321, 2331, and 2333, in SMP, box 153.

26. Quoted in Alan Astrow, "A Shocker: Milgram Dispute Survives," *Yale Daily News*, May 1, 1974, in SMP, box 21, folder 340.

6. THE SECRET EXPERIMENTS

1. I would subsequently find that three other scholars had found and written about this condition. The first to do so were Andre Modigliani and François Rochat in "The Role of Interaction Sequences and the Timing of Resistance in Shaping Obedience and Defiance to Authority," *Journal of Social Issues* 51, no. 3 (1995): 107–23.

2. Tape 2425, in SMP, box 147.

3. These were subjects 2428, 2422, and 2435. The uncle and father both played the role of teacher.

4. Transcript based on that in Nestar Russell, "Stanley Milgram's Obedience to Authority Experiments: Towards an Understanding of Their Relevance in Explaining Aspects of the Nazi Holocaust," PhD thesis, Victoria University of Wellington, 2009, 148, 149.

5. SMP, box 152.

6. Ibid.

7. Ibid.

8. Tape 2432, in SMP, box 153.

9. Exchange between Thomas, Williams, and Milgram, and Milgram's comments, in SMP, box 70, folder 289.

10. Exchange between Carl, Williams, and Milgram; Williams's comments; and Milgram's comments in ibid.

11. Exchange between Peter and Williams, and Williams and Milgram joking, in ibid.

12. Report to the NSF in SMP, box 45, folder 160; obedience notebook in box 46, folder 146; and draft description in SMP, box 70, folder 289. Quotations from Stanley Milgram, *The Individual and the Social World: Essays and Experiments* (Reading, MA: Addison-Wesley, 1977), 153.

13. SMP, box 70, folder 289.

7. MILGRAM'S STAFF

1. Thomas Blass, *The Man Who Shocked the World: The Life and Legacy of Stanley Milgram* (New York: Basic, 2004), 325.

2. Nestar Russell, "Stanley Milgram's Obedience to Authority Experiments: Towards an Understanding of Their Relevance in Explaining Aspects of the Nazi Holocaust," PhD thesis, Victoria University of Wellington, 2009, 183.

3. Ibid, 183.

4. Williams's response and Milgram's notes in SMP, box 46, folder 163.

5. Stanley Milgram, *Obedience to Authority: An Experimental View* (London: Tavistock, 1974), 97.

6. SMP, box 152.

7. Bob McDonough, "Shocking!" *Derailed*, March 24, 2006, hbobby derailed.blogspot.com/2006/03/shocking.html

8. SMP, box 46, folder 174.

9. Nestar Russell noted this in "Stanley Milgram's Obedience to Authority Experiments."

10. Long interviews, March 21, 1963, 59–60, in SMP, box 155a.

11. Subject 603, long interviews, February 28, 1963, 6, 25–26, in SMP, box 155a.

12. Tape 2321, in SMP, box 53.

13. Alex Gibney, dir., *The Human Behavior Experiments*, Fearful Symmetry, 2006.

14. SMP, box 46, folder 163.

8. IN SEARCH OF A THEORY

1. Long interviews, April 18, 1963, 19–20, in SMP, box 155a.

2. Long interviews, April 4, 1963, 45, in SMP, box 155a.

3. Long interviews, March 28, 1963, 7, in SMP, box 155a.

4. Eichmann and trial preparations discussed in Jeffrey Shandler, *While America Watches: Televising the Holocaust* (New York: Oxford University Press, 1999), 83–132.

5. David Cesarani, *Becoming Eichmann: Rethinking the Life, Crimes, and Trial of a "Desk Murderer"* (New York: Da Capo Press, 2006), 257, 313.

6. Jeffrey Shandler noted the first use of the term "the Holocaust" on American television (83) and the American portrayal of Eichmann (108) in *While America Watches*.

7. SMP, box 43, folder 127.

8. Kirsten Fermaglich, *American Dreams and Nazi Nightmares: Early Holocaust Consciousness and Liberal America, 1957–65* (Waltham, MA: Brandeis University Press, 2006), 89.

9. SMP, box 1a, folder 3.

10. Stanley Milgram's article was "Behavioral Study of Obedience," *Journal of Abnormal Psychology* 67, no. 4 (1963): 371–78; quotations on this and preceding page, 371, 377, 375.

11. Susan Sontag quoted in Shandler, *While America Watches*, 121.

12. SMP, box 46, folder 164.

13. Thomas Blass, *The Man Who Shocked the World: The Life and Legacy of Stanley Milgram* (New York: Basic), 114.

14. SMP, box 1a, folder 3.

15. Letter from APA in SMP, box 231a, folder 4. Letter to Mann in SMP, box 1a, folder 4.

16. Milgram's Jewish background is discussed in Fermaglich, *American Dreams and Nazi Nightmares*, 97, 100. His bar mitzvah speech is described in Blass, *Man Who Shocked the World*, 8.

17. Philip M. Taylor, *Munitions of the Mind: A History of Propaganda from the Ancient World to the Present Day*, 3rd ed. (Manchester: Manchester University Press, 2003), 261. The Chinese, it was mistakenly believed,

had developed sophisticated techniques—derived in part from Pavlovian conditioning—to take over the mind, allowing them to replace one set of thoughts with another and convince people who had been enemies to become ardent followers.

18. Ian Nicholson discussed the effect of the Cold War on American masculinity in "Shocking Masculinity: Stanley Milgram, *Obedience to Authority* and the 'Crisis of Manhood' in Cold War America," *Isis* 102, no. 2 (2011): 238–68. He also pointed out that Marvel comics played a role in counteracting this anxiety—the depictions of conformist, suburban men tearing off their suits to reveal superhuman masculine powers were a form of wishful fantasy. The quotation appears on 251.

19. Milgram used the phrase "a kind of flobby moral character" to describe subjects' willingness to follow orders in long interviews, March 21, 1963, 37, in SMP, box 155a.

20. Milgram in an unpublished 1977 interview with Maury Silver, in SMP, box 23, folder 382.

21. SMP, box 46, folder 163.

22. Milgram had not made mention of any plans to conduct follow-up interviews to the NSF, likely because he didn't plan to conduct any until Yale insisted.

23. Long interviews, March 21, 1963, 56, 57.

24. SMP, box 45, folder 162.

25. Twenty-one of these were obedient subjects, and eleven were disobedient.

26. Long interviews, February 28, 1963, 16, 10, 19, in SMP, box 45, folder 162.

27. Long interviews, March 14, 1963, 21, in SMP, box 45, folder 162.

28. Errera's reassurances in long interviews, March 21, 1963, 3; March 28, 1963, 7. Exchange with man also in March 21 conversation, 29.

29. Long interviews, March 21, 1963, 60.

30. Long interviews, March 21, 1963, 48.

31. Long interviews, March 14, 1963, 52–55.

32. Long interviews, March 14, 1963, 57.

33.   Long interviews, March 21, 1963, 3, 38.

34.   SMP, box 45, folder 159.

35.   SMP, box 43, folder 128.

36.   Paul Errera's report was not published until 1972. See Errera's report in
      Jay Katz, *Experimentation with Human Beings* (New York: Russell Sage
      Foundation, 1972), 400.

37.   Claude Errera, by e-mail, October 17, 2011.

9. THE ETHICAL CONTROVERSY

1.   Thomas Blass, *The Man Who Shocked the World: The Life and Legacy of
      Stanley Milgram* (New York: Basic, 2004), 136.

2.   SMP, box 1a, folders 8 and 9.

3.   Quoted in Kirsten Fermaglich, *American Dreams and Nazi Nightmares:
      Early Holocaust Consciousness and Liberal America, 1957–65* (Waltham,
      MA: Brandeis University Press, 2006), 108.

4.   Information about media outlets in SMP, box 46, folder 165. Fermaglich
      notes the interest generated through the UPI wire service in *American
      Dreams and Nazi Nightmares*, 108.

5.   SMP, box 46, folder 165.

6.   SMP, box 45, folder 160.

7.   Fermaglich, *American Dreams and Nazi Nightmares*, 109.

8.   *St. Louis Post-Dispatch* editorial and Milgram's response in SMP, box 55,
      folder 9.

9.   SMP, box 1a, folder 10. Erich Fromm was a bestselling author, whose
      book *Escape from Freedom* (1941) "delved deeply into the psychology of
      Nazism," as author Andrew R. Heinze noted in *Jews and the American
      Soul: Human Nature in the Twentieth Century* (Princeton, NJ: Princeton
      University Press, 2004), 281. Fromm's later book *The Art of Loving*
      (1956) would sell half a million copies in English by the end of the 1960s.

10.   Ibid.

11.   Diana Baumrind, "Some Thoughts on the Ethics of Research: After
      Reading Milgram's 'Behavioral Study of Obedience,'" *American
      Psychologist* 19, no. 6 (1964): 421–23.

12. SMP, box 18, folder 263.

13. SMP, box 62, folder 126. This document could have been drafted to support his reapplication for APA membership. Alternatively, it could have been early notes for a draft of his book.

14. SMP, box 17, folder 246.

15. Milgram in an unpublished 1977 interview with Maury Silver, in SMP, box 23, folder 382.

16. Kirsten Fermaglich noted Milgram's left-leaning political views in *American Dreams and Nazi Nightmares*, 92. Annette McGaha and James H. Korn noted the increased scrutiny of the treatment of subjects in "The Emergence of Interest in the Ethics of Psychological Research with Humans," *Ethics and Behavior* 5, no. 2 (1995): 157.

17. See James H. Korn, *Illusions of Reality: A History of Deception in Social Psychology* (Albany: State University of New York Press, 1997), 108; and Blass, *Man Who Shocked the World*, 124.

18. McGaha and Korn, "Emergence of Interest," 147.

19. See Ian Lubek and Henderikus J. Stam, "Ludicro-Experimentation in Social Psychology: Sober Scientific Versus Playful Prescriptions," in *Trends and Issues in Theoretical Psychology*, ed. Ian Lubek et al. (New York: Springer, 1995), 179; and Kenneth Ring, "Experimental Social Psychology: Some Sober Questions About Some Frivolous Values," *Journal of Experimental Social Psychology* 3 (1967): 117.

20. Shelley Patnoe, *A Narrative History of Experimental Social Psychology: The Lewin Tradition* (New York: Springer, 1998), 270–71.

21. Philip Zimbardo, "Experimental Social Psychology: Behaviorism with Minds and Matters," in *Reflections on 100 Years of Experimental Social Psychology*, ed. Aroldo Rodrigues and Robert Levine (New York: Basic, 1999), 137–38.

22. SMP, box 23, folder 382.

23. Kirsten Fermaglich noted the contrast between reactions in the popular and academic press in *American Dreams and Nazi Nightmares*, 108.

24. Studies described in Blass, *Man Who Shocked the World*, 140, 145.

25. Milgram in an unpublished 1977 interview with Maury Silver. Committee's views in Blass, *Man Who Shocked the World*, 153.

26.   Milgram's job offer and likely feelings in Blass, *Man Who Shocked the World*, 152–59.

27.   Arthur G. Miller, *The Obedience Experiments: A Case Study of Controversy in Social Science* (New York: Praeger, 1986), 143.

28.   Arness played Matt Dillon, the brave, tough-talking marshal of Dodge City, Kansas, a Wild West town where lawlessness was rife.

29.   Carol Tavris, "A Sketch of Stanley Milgram: A Man of 1,000 Ideas," *Psychology Today* 8 (1974): 74.

10. MILGRAM'S BOOK

1.   Hank Stam is also the editor of *Theory and Psychology*, a journal whose focus is the history and context of psychology.

2.   Interestingly, in an unpublished musing Milgram too queried the use of the term
      "obedience," toying with the idea of calling it "cooperation": "Perhaps it is just as limiting and erroneous to say an obedient and a defiant subject as it is to say a cooperative and uncooperative subject. Cooperative and uncooperative about what? one must ask. Obedient and defiant with regard to whom?" He concluded that the labels didn't explain motives. In SMP, box 46, folder 165.

3.   Judith Waters's anecdote in her essay, "Professor Stanley Milgram— Supervisor, Mentor, Friend," published in *Obedience to Authority: Current Perspectives on the Milgram Paradigm*, ed. Thomas Blass (Mahwah, NJ: Lawrence Erlbaum Associates, 2000), 30; and letter to Mann in SMP, box 1a, folder 10.

4.   Stanley Milgram, *Obedience to Authority: An Experimental View* (London: Tavistock, 1974), 5.

5.   Ibid., 2.

6.   Ibid., 123–24.

7.   Thomas Blass, *The Man Who Shocked the World: The Life and Legacy of Stanley Milgram* (New York: Basic, 2004), 216.

8.   Ibid., 199.

9.   Sketches and notes on taglines and blurbs in SMP, box 63, folder 148.

10. SMP, box 70, folder 290. Blass also noted Milgram's use of drugs in *Man Who Shocked the World*, 213.

11. SMP, box 70, folder 289.

12. SMP, box 61, folder 110.

13. Milgram, *Obedience to Authority*, 5.

14. Ibid., 31.

15. The quotation "a pathological fringe" in ibid., 30. The description given to the psychiatrists in the audience included this: "If at any time in the procedure, from 15 volts onward, the teacher refuses to obey the commands of the experimenter, the experiment is at an end. No physical or other coercion other than the four standardized commands are used. If the subject refuses to continue after being given these commands, the experimenter calls a halt to the experiment." In SMP, box 45, folder 161.

16. Ibid., 45.

17. Omer Bartov pointed out that Milgram's prejudices about class, race, and gender influenced his portraits of subjects in *Obedience to Authority*. See Bartov, *Germany's War and the Holocaust: Disputed Histories* (Ithaca: Cornell University Press, 2003), 182–91.

18. Descriptions of Rensaleer on 50, 52 and Batta on 45, 46 of Milgram, *Obedience to Authority*.

19. Bartov, *Germany's War and the Holocaust*, 182–91.

20. Descriptions of Rosenblum on 79–80 of Milgram, *Obedience to Authority*.

21. Subject 2017 in SMP, box 122.

22. Descriptions of Prozi on 77 of Milgram, *Obedience to Authority*.

23. Descriptions of Gino and exchange on 88 of ibid.

24. Bartov, *Germany's War and the Holocaust*, 182–91.

25. SMP, box 61, folder 118.

26. Acknowledgments on xxii of Milgram, *Obedience to Authority*, and draft in SMP, box 70, folder 291.

27. SMP, box 62, folder 126.

28. Quotations from Milgram, *Obedience to Authority*, 194.

29. Milgram's claims in ibid., 171. The Australian study found an obedience rate of 28 percent; Wesley Kilham and Leon Mann, "Level of Destructive Obedience as a Function of Transmitter and Executant Roles in the Milgram Obedience Paradigm," *Journal of Personality and Social Psychology* 29 (1974): 696–702. The Italian report stated, "Compared to Milgram's results, we have 85% of complete Italian obedience against 100% of American obedience in the pilot-experiment"; Leonardo Ancona and Rosetta Pareyson, "Contribution to the Study of Aggression: Dynamics of Destructive Obedience," *Archivio di Psicologia, Neurologia e Psichiatria* 29 (1968): 340–72. The German replication was reported in David Mantell and Robert Panzarella, "Obedience and Responsibility," *British Journal of Social Psychology* 15, no. 3 (1976): 239–45. Blass reported on the South African replication in "The Milgram Paradigm After 35 Years: Some Things We Now Know About the Obedience Experiments" in *Obedience to Authority*, 59.

30. See Solomon Asch, "Independence or Conformity in the Asch Experiment as a Reflection of Cultural and Situational Factors: A Comment on Perin and Spencer," *British Journal of Social Psychology* 20 (1981): 223–25.

31. SMP, box 61, folder 114.

32. Letter from Patrick Taylor of Tavistock Publications, dated May 6, 1974, in SMP, box 61, folder 113. Thomas Blass also noted the *Horizon* program in *Man Who Shocked the World*, 220.

33. Kirsten Fermaglich noted this in *Nazi Dreams and American Nightmares: Early Holocaust Consciousness and Liberal America, 1957–65* (Waltham, MA: Brandeis University Press, 2006), 114.

34. Quoted in William Nichols, "The Burden of Imagination: Stanley Milgram's *Obedience to Authority*," in *Writing from Experience* (New York: Harcourt Brace Jovanovich, 1975), 173.

35. Stephen Marcus, "*Obedience to Authority*," *New York Times Book Review*, January 13, 1974, 24–25.

36. Brown was an assistant professor when Milgram was a graduate student at Harvard. Blass, *Man Who Shocked the World*, 20.

37. Ibid., 221.

38. Waters, "Professor Stanley Milgram," 32.

39. Lawrence Kohlberg, "More Authority," *New York Times Book Review*, March 24, 1978, 42–43.

40. Waters, "Professor Stanley Milgram," 31–32.

41. Blass, *Man Who Shocked the World*, 212.

11. REPRESENTING OBEDIENCE

1. Quoted in "The Tenth Level—A Toupological Analysis," *Shatner's Toupee*, January 3, 2010, shatnerstoupee.blogspot.com.au/2010/01/tenth-level-toupological-analysis.html.

2. See Alan Elms, "Obedience Lite," *American Psychologist* 64, no. 1 (2009): 32–36.

3. SMP, box 23, folder 382.

4. SMP, box 46, folder 16.

5. SMP, box 76, folder 44.

6. Ibid.

7. SMP, box 75, folder 435.

8. Register of copyright and availability in SMP, box 85, folder 448. The film cost $260 a copy. Even today, university libraries will loan the film only for viewing within the library. Anna McCarthy noted Milgram's permission to Italian and German stations in "Stanley Milgram, Allen Funt, and Me: Postwar Social Science and the 'First Wave' of Reality TV," in *Reality TV: Remaking Television Culture*, Susan Murray and Laurie Ouellette (New York: New York University Press, 2004), 35.

9. SMP, box 22, folder 534.

10. Dannie Abse, *The Dogs of Pavlov* (London: Valentine, Mitchell and Co., 1973), 22, 29.

11. Milgram's letters in SMP, box 61, folder 108.

12. Rejection and commission in Sharland Trotter, "CBS to Dramatize Milgram Studies," *APA Monitor* 6, no. 3 (1975): 4.

13. SMP, box 64, folder 164.

14. Letter from and meeting with Bellak described in SMP, box 64, folder 164.

15. Thomas Blass, *The Man Who Shocked the World: The Life and Legacy of Stanley Milgram* (New York: Basic, 2004), 229.

16. Sharon Presley commented in response to Vaughan Bell, "Stanley Milgram, the 70s TV Drama," *Mind Hacks*, July 23, 2010, mindhacks.com/2010/07/23/stanley-milgram-the-70s-tv-drama. Milgram may well have hoped to have some input into the film—he had already started his filmmaking career with a short documentary, *The City and the Self*, and had plans for more when he accepted the job with CBS. But he said in an interview with the *APA Monitor*, "They didn't really want a technical adviser . . . I could have helped them with the rendering of the lab scenes—but the most significant input I had was to suggest what kinds of journals might be on the professor's desk. I recommended the whole glorious APA list." In Trotter, "CBS to Dramatize Milgram Studies," 4.

17. SMP, box 64, folder 164.

18. Quotations and ad in ibid.

19. Quotation in Brian Lowry, "Eli Roth Probes Evil on Discovery's 'Curiosity,'" *Variety*, October 24, 2011, weblogs.variety.com/bltv/2011/10/roth-probes-nature-of-evil-on-discoverys-curiosity.html. See Michael Portillo, "How Violent Are You?" *Horizon*, BBC Two, 2009; Chris Hansen, "What Were You Thinking?" *Dateline*, NBC, 2010; and Eli Roth, *How Evil Are You?* Discovery Channel, 2011.

20. SMP, box 70, folder 289.

CONCLUSION

1. Ian Parker also made this point in his article "Obedience," *Granta* 71, no. 4 (2000): 99–125.

2. Quoted in Jeffrey Shandler, *While America Watches: Televising the Holocaust* (New York: Oxford University Press, 1999), 121.

3. Caryl Marsh, "A Science Museum Exhibit on Milgram's Obedience Research," in *Obedience to Authority: Current Perspectives on the Milgram Paradigm*, ed. Thomas Blass (Mahwah, NJ: Lawrence Erlbaum Associates, 2000), 145–59.

4. SMP, box 43, folder 128.

5. Milgram threatened psychologist David Mantell with legal action for

using his design, even though it was not patented. In SMP, box 18, folder 264.

6. Solomon Asch Papers, Archives of the History of American Psychology, University of Akron, box 2868, folder 15.

7. Parker, "Obedience," 121.

8. SMP, box 46, folder 164. Successive quotations in ibid.

9. SMP, box 46, folder 163.

10. Augustine Brannigan made this point in "The Postmodern Experiment: Science and Ontology in Experimental Social Psychology," *British Journal of Sociology* 48, no. 4 (1997): 594–610.

ADDITIONAL SOURCES

Borge, Caroline. "Basic Instincts: The Science of Evil." ABC, 2007.

Brown, Derren. *The Heist*. Channel 4, 2008.

Cherry, Frances. *The "Stubborn Particulars" of Social Psychology: Essays on the Research Process*. London: Routledge, 1995.

Dubin, Charles, dir. *The Tenth Level*. CBS, 1976.

Fox, Dennis, and Isaac Prilleltensky, eds. *Critical Psychology: An Introduction*. London: Sage, 1997.

Fratangelo, Dawn. Untitled segment. *Dateline*, NBC, 1997.

Lunt, Peter. *Stanley Milgram: Understanding Obedience and Its Implications*. New York: Palgrave Macmillan, 2009.

Milgram, Stanley. *Obedience*. 1965.

Safer, Morley. "I Was Only Following Orders." *60 Minutes*. CBS, 1974.

Schellenberg, James A. *Masters of Social Psychology: Freud, Mead, Lewin, and Skinner*. New York: Oxford University Press, 1978.

Yuncker, Barbara. "Where Conscience Fails." *New York Post*, February 23, 1964.